UNIVERSITIES AND LIFELONG LEARNING

Higher education in a globalising world

MANCHESTER
1824

Manchester University Press

UNIVERSITIES AND LIFELONG LEARNING

Series editor:
Professor Michael Osborne (University of Glasgow)

Universities and lifelong learning analyses the external engagement activities of universities and third-level institutions and is concerned with the range of activity that lies beyond the traditional mission of teaching and research. This is an area that until now has seldom been explored in depth and has rarely if ever been treated in a holistic manner.

Lifelong learning, the arts and community cultural engagement in the contemporary university: International perspectives
Edited by Darlene Clover and Kathy Sanford

Knowledge, democracy and action: Community-university research partnerships in global perspectives Edited by Budd Hall, Edward Jackson, Rajesh Tandon, Jean-Marc Fontan and Nirmala Lall

University engagement and environmental sustainability
Edited by Patricia Inman and Diana L. Robinson

A new imperative: Regions and higher education in difficult times
Michael Osborne, Chris Duke and Bruce Wilson

Higher education in a globalising world

Community engagement and lifelong learning

Peter Mayo

Manchester University Press

The right of Peter Mayo to be identified as the author of this work has been asserted by him in accordance with the Copyright, Designs and Patents Act 1988.

Published by Manchester University Press
Oxford Road, Manchester M13 9PL
www.manchesteruniversitypress.co.uk

British Library Cataloguing-in-Publication Data
A catalogue record for this book is available from the British Library

ISBN 978 1 5261 4092 0 hardback
ISBN 978 1 5261 6059 1 paperback

First published 2019
Paperback published 2021

The publisher has no responsibility for the persistence or accuracy of URLs for any external or third-party internet websites referred to in this book, and does not guarantee that any content on such websites is, or will remain, accurate or appropriate.

Typeset by Newgen Publishing UK

Praise for *Higher Education in a Globalising World*:

Neoliberalism presents the university with a dilemma: either the university adjusts to the demands of neoliberalism, and is thus disfigured beyond recognition, or it offers resistance and carries out its democratic and community-oriented mission as a counter-current. Mayo shows courage in providing a well-argued book that constitutes a powerful appeal for the university to pursue the second route. The book provides concrete 'on the ground' examples of how this can be done.

Boaventura de Sousa Santos, University of Coimbra,
author of, among others, *Decolonizing the University,*
the Challenge of Deep Cognitive Justice, (2017)

Mayo's book sheds a light on the curious paradox of higher education: its inability to grapple deeply with the issues of lifelong learning and adult education. From their privileged positions as bastions of learning and knowledge, higher education institutions need to do much more with responding to adult learner needs not only in the classroom, but in marginalised communities and local settings. Mayo reminds us that, rather than subscribing solely to the neoliberal agenda of training workers for the state and industry, higher education would do well to educate citizens for the full and abundant life.

Leona M. English, Professor of Adult Education,
St Francis Xavier University, Canada

It is impossible to discuss higher education outside the context of globalisation. Peter Mayo's *Higher Education in a Globalising World* may be the best book we have on the subject. Not only does Mayo offer a stunning detailed analysis of the globalising forces shaping higher education within a dialectic of oppression and resistance, but he does so with a style that is as rigorous as it is accessible and poetic. This book is a must read for any one concerned with how the political landscape of higher education has changed under the impending and powerful forces of globalisation. This book is at once a theoretical and political tool box for rethinking the relationship between power and politics, on the one hand, and higher education and the complex forces of globalisation on the other. If you want to understand how power and resistance mutually engage each other in the 21st century in the struggle over higher education, read this book and then give to your friends.

Henry Giroux, McMaster University Professor
for Scholarship in the Public Interest; The Paulo Freire
Distinguished Scholar in Critical Pedagogy; Author of,
among others, *The University in Chains. Confronting the*
Military-Industrial-Academic Complex (2007), *Neoliberalism's*
War on Higher Education (2014), co-author of *Take Back*
Higher Education. Race, Youth, and the Crisis of
Democracy in the Post-Civil Rights Era (2004)

This lucid and expansive book calls for critical university engagement with local communities to support a 'globalisation from below'. Mayo deftly presents a portrait of lifelong learning that weaves together tropes from social justice movements, feminism, gender studies, climate change, Catholic ritual, class struggles, and intergenerational learning. The examples span the globe, but a prominent place is given to traditions of lifelong learning in Europe and Mediterranean societies, including Southern, Eastern and Arab Mediterranean with their rich social and institutional histories. Drawing on the critical lexicon of the likes of Paulo Freire, Lorenzo Milani, Ivan Illich and Antonio Gramsci, Mayo calls on educators to practice an ethical, engaged pedagogy that ignites 'the popular creative spirit'. This book should be a staple in the critical studies of higher education and lifelong learning.

Linda Herrera, Professor, University of Illinois
at Urbana-Champaign

Peter Mayo presents a comprehensive examination of University Lifelong Learning in the EU, Euro-Mediterranean zones, and the Global South. He aptly presents a critical reflection on the development of University Lifelong Learning and the role it has played in the evolution of higher education. Most importantly, in that the book focuses on all Higher Educational institutions, including universities, academies, and vocational colleges that award degrees, diplomas, and provide certification of professional attainment, Peter Mayo makes a compelling and inspiring case for the re-conceptualisation of the university as an alternative to the existing hegemonic one. The equal inclusion of all tertiary institutions is a hallmark of this book.

Rosalind Latiner Raby, Director, California
Colleges for International Education, Editor-in-Chief,
Journal of International and Comparative Higher Education

Contents

Acknowledgements

I would like to acknowledge the support of a number of friends and colleagues with regard to the development of this book. My deepest gratitude goes to my wife Josephine and daughters Annemarie and Cecilia for their constant support.

My colleague and friend Mary Darmanin deserves great thanks for having persuaded me to embark on research on higher education in Europe for a joint presentation with her at a 2008 International Sociology of Education conference in London. This led me to write a paper around the topic for the journal connected with this conference. Michael Grech, Budd L. Hall, Carlos Alberto Torres and Eugenio-Enrique Cortés-Ramírez provided me with feedback and insights for specific chapters. Great thanks go to them. I am also indebted in various ways (sharing ideas, relevant collaboration, provision of relevant travel opportunities, sharing of material, providing inspiration) to the following: Hasan Aksoy, Paula Allman (late), Pep Aparicio Guadas, Godfrey Baldacchino, Federico Batini, Susan Belcher El-Nahhas (late), Carmel Borg, Joseph A. Buttigieg, Donna Chovanec (late), Paul Clough, Josann Cutajar, Antonia Darder, Leona English, Andy Green, Marvin Formosa, Henry J. Frendo, Henry Giroux, Gordon L. Hay (late), Linda Herrera, Paul Heywood, Anne Hickling-Hudson, Kemal Inal, Antonia Kupfer, D.W. Livingstone, Emilio Lucio-Villegas, Nur Masalha, Andre Elias Mazawi, Maria Mendel, Francois Mifsud, Mike Neary, Maria Nikolakaki, Mike Osborne, Maria Pisani, Milosh Raykov, Najwa Silwadi, Bonnie Slade, Ronald G. Sultana, Alessio Surian, Tomasz Szkudlarek, Paul Spiteri (late), Nicos Trimikliniotis, Hubertus von Amelunxen and Kenneth Wain. The usual disclaimers apply.

Abbreviations

4th IR	Fourth Industrial Revolution
AUM	American University of Malta
CAC	Community Action Centre (Al-Quds University, Al-Quds/Jerusalem)
CACE	Centre for Adult Continuing Education (American University in Cairo)
CAW	Canadian Automobile Workers
CEC	Commission of the European Communities
CEDEFOP	European Centre for the Development of Vocational Training
CINDOC	Centre for Scientific Information and Documentation
CITS	Cooperative Institute for Transnational Studies
CPD	continuing professional development
CPE	continuing professional education
CRC	Cottonera Resource Centre
CREA	Centre for Social and Educational Research (University of Barcelona)
DG	Directorate General (EU Brussels)
EC	European Commission
ECM	Alma Mater Europaea
EGS	European Graduate School
ENFF	Escola Nacional Florestan Fernandez
ESIB (now ESU)	National Unions of Students in Europe (Now European Students Union)
ESL	English as a Second Language
ETF	European Training Foundation
EU	European Union
EUCEN	European Universities Continuing Education Network
GATS	General Agreement of Trade in Services
GCAS	Global Centre for Advanced Studies
GDP	gross domestic product
GSMs	global social movements
HE	higher education

HRD	human resource development
ICT	information communication technology
IEMed Obs	Observatory of the Euro-Mediterranean Policies (Barcelona)
ILO	International Labour Organization
IMF	International Monetary Fund
ISH	Institutum Studiorum Humanitatis
LERU	League of European Research Universities
LGBTQ	lesbian, gay, bisexual, transgender, queer or questioning
LLE	lifelong education
LLL	lifelong learning
MAI	Multilateral Agreement on Investment
MENA	Middle East and North Africa
METU	Middle Eastern Technical University
MIUR	Ministero dell'Istruzione dell'Università e della Ricerca/ Ministry of Education, Universities and Research (Italy)
MOOCs	Massive Open Online Courses
MST	Movimento Trabalhadores Rurais sem Terra/Movement of Landless Peasants
NALL	New Approaches to Lifelong Learning (Toronto)
NCLCs	National Council for Labour Colleges
NGOs	non-governmental organisations
NSMs	new social movements
OECD	Organisation for Economic Co-operation and Development
PASCAL	Place and Social Capital and Learning
PEN	Popular Education Network
PLAR	Prior Learning Assessment and Recognition
PT	Partido dos Trabalhadores Workers' Party (Brazil)
R&D	research and development
RA	research assistant
RAE	Research Assessment Exercise (UK)
REF	Research Excellence Framework (UK)
SAPs	structural adjustment programmes
SDGs	Sustainable Development Goals
SSMs	Southern Social Movements
STEM	science, technology, engineering and mathematics
TA	teaching assistant
TTIP	Transatlantic Trade and Investment Partnership
TUC	Trade Union Congress (UK)
U3A	University of the Third Age
UCE	university continuing education
UfM	Union for the Mediterranean
UILL	UNESCO Institute for Lifelong Learning

UNESCO	United Nations Education, Scientific and Cultural Organization
UNISA	University of South Africa
UNITIERRA	Universidad de la Tierra
UPMS	Universidade Popular dos Movimentos Sociais/Popular University of Social Movements
VET	vocational education and training
WALL	work and lifelong learning
WTO	World Trade Organization

Preface

Budd L. Hall

We welcome Peter Mayo's contributions to the growing literature of both critical university studies and community university engagement. His towering contributions to adult and lifelong education founded on his seminal work on Freire and Gramsci (Mayo, 1999) have been added to year after year by major contributions to critical pedagogy, socialist thought, anti-racist and anti-oppressive studies and Mediterranean Studies. In this book, Mayo draws together many of his discursive powers to cast a light on higher education in Europe and beyond within the context of globalisation. His focus is mostly on universities within the legislative and policy framework of Europe of the past decades. Importantly this work interrogates higher education from two linked streams of globalisation, what he refers to as 'hegemonic' globalisation, the triumph of the neoliberal regime, and 'globalisation from below', the growing movement of decolonisation, resistance and resilience. A very important contribution of this book, which other recent books on higher education and globalisation do not make, is the author's attention to lifelong learning and adult education within European higher education. The role of continuing education and online distance learning are explored both as handmaidens to the neoliberal agenda and as spaces for alternative imaginings. Mayo's book might well be seen as a European analysis that complements and extends another recent critical higher education study, that by Spooner and McNinch, *Dissident Knowledge in Higher Education* (2018).

I very much appreciate Mayo's drawing our attention to the links between adult education, lifelong learning and contemporary issues in European higher education. He reminds us of the nineteenth-century movement of 'extending' the university to the community as illustrated by the creation of the Extension Office of Cambridge University. The university extension model that began in England found counterparts in other parts of Europe. It was 'modernised' in the 1960s and 1970s in most places as Continuing Studies, a more American term, and an emphasis gradually shifted from provision to those left out of formal studies to provision of professional qualifications. But the principles of adult education of respect for the lived experience of adults and the democratic right to learn are very similar to those being either espoused or sought after by the contemporary engagement discourses. It is, however, striking that, with the exception of Mayo in this book, most contemporary discourses on higher education, social responsibility, engagement and innovation ignore both the history of lifelong learning and education and the potential that those principles and institutional innovations might contribute. If we are to see moves towards *Creating a New Public University and Reviving Democracy*, as Levin and Greenwood (2016) suggest, Mayo's book is an essential contribution.

Higher education studies have grown and expanded remarkably over recent years. This interest has been fed on the global side by the explosion of new universities created in both the poorer countries of the Global South and the middle-income countries such as Brazil, India and China (Kumar, 2017). While in the majority of the countries of Europe and other more well-to-do nations, universities are being challenged to demonstrate or renegotiate their relationship with society. Within all of our universities questions about knowledge abound. Some authors speak about a transition beyond the both the concepts of knowledge economy and knowledge society to knowledge democracy (Hall, 2011; Hall and Tandon, 2014). Within the broader concept of knowledge democracy, there are calls for decolonising higher education, decolonising the curriculum and decolonising knowledge itself (Battiste, 2018; Tuck, 2018; Hall, 2018).

The work that Rajesh Tandon and I have been engaged in, under the aegis of our UNESCO Chair in Community Based Research and Social Responsibility in Higher Education, in collaboration with the Global University Network for Innovation and others, has focused on building capacity in the theory and practice of community-based participatory research (www.unescochair-cbrsr.org). Our work is part of the contemporary interrogation of knowledge and epistemology informed by scholars such as de Sousa Santos, to whom Mayo refers in this volume, Visvanathan (2017) and others. Our work would be a contribution to what Mayo refers to as 'globalisation from below' and is based on the critical respect of knowledge created in social movements and community action settings, the value of academics and community intellectuals co-creating knowledge and on the social responsibility of higher education institutions to those communities where they are located (Hall and Tandon, 2017).

In summing Mayo's contribution to finding a way forward for a progressive social-justice oriented higher education, let me draw attention to two of his calls to action. First he says that 'universities can engage in a meaningful process... by re-conceiving of their role as not simply being there to boost the economy,... but also to contribute to a regeneration of democracy and the public sphere'. Second, he tells us that an agenda for the future, 'would therefore be decolonizing and hence a genuinely democratic process. It is... where different voices reflecting and expressing different cultures and knowledge traditions make their presence felt.'

Mayo's book is an invitation to all of us to enter into a crucial discussion of what globalisation means for higher education and how we can take action to keep a focus on the issues of justice, sustainability and peace.

Budd L. Hall, PhD
Professor of Community Development and
UNESCO Co-Chair in Community Based Research and
Social Responsibility in Higher Education
University of Victoria
Canada

References

Battiste, M. (2018). Reconciling indigenous knowledge in education: promises, possibilities and imperatives. In Spooner, M., and McNinch, J. (eds.), *Dissident Knowledge in Higher Education*. Regina: University of Regina Press.

Hall, B. L. (2011). Towards a knowledge democracy movement: contemporary trends in community-university research partnerships. *Rhizome Freirean* 9. www.rizoma-freireano.org/index.

Hall, B. L. (2018). Beyond epistemicide: knowledge, democracy and higher education. In Spooner, M., and McNinch, J. (eds.), *Dissident Knowledge in Higher Education*. Regina: University of Regina Press.

Hall, B. L., and Tandon, R. (2014). *5th World Report on Higher Education: Knowledge, Engagement and Higher Education Contributing to Social Change*. Barcelona GUNI and London: Palgrave Macmillan.

Hall, B. L., and Tandon, R. (2017). Participatory research: 'where have we been, where are we going?' A dialogue. *Research for All* 1(2), pp. 365–374.

Kumar, R. C. (ed.) (2017). *The Future of Indian Universities: Comparative and International Perspectives*. Oxford: Oxford University Press.

Levin, M., and Greenwood, D. (2016). *Creating a New Public University and Reviving Democracy: Action Research in Higher Education*. Oxford: Berghahn Books.

Mayo, P. (1999). *Gramsci, Freire and Adult Education: Possibilities for Transformative Action*. London and New York: Zed Books.

Spooner, M., and McNinch, J. (eds.) (2018). *Dissident Knowledge in Higher Education*. Regina: University of Regina Press.

Tuck, E. (2018). Biting the university that feeds us. In Spooner, M., and McNinch, J. (eds.), *Dissident Knowledge in Higher Education*. Regina: University of Regina Press.

Visvanathan, S. (2017). An introduction to a thought experiment: quality, diversity and the epistemics of university. In Kumar, R. C. (ed.), *The Future of Indian Universities: Comparative and International Perspectives*. Oxford: Oxford University Press.

1

Introduction: globalisation and the HE market

Higher education (HE) is believed to play a pivotal part in the process of globalisation and, as a consequence, it is being transformed, mainly within the context of a supranational union (the European Union, henceforth EU), which set itself the ambitious and unlikely target of becoming the most powerful and competitive 'knowledge economy' in the world by the year 2010 (EC, 2000). By higher education I mean all those institutions and organised forms of learning that occur at tertiary level, that is to say those institutions whose provision extends beyond secondary education and high school. These include universities, academies and vocational colleges that award degrees, diplomas and provide certification of professional attainment. Globalisation is conceived of as an all-embracing concept, incorporating both its economic and cultural dimensions which are often inextricably intertwined, since, as Manuel Castells states:

> We live in a global economy... in which all processes work as a unit on real time throughout the planet; that is, an economy in which capital flows, labor markets, markets, the production process, management, information and technology operate simultaneously at the world level. (Castells, 1999, p. 54)

Nevertheless, as indicated in a study, published by the OECD Directorate for Education:

> Globalisation is not a single or universal phenomenon. It is nuanced according to locality (local area, nation, world region), language(s) of use, and academic cultures; and it plays out very differently according to the type of institution. (Marginson and van der Wende, 2007, p. 5)

Furthermore as Roger Dale (1999) indicates, while 'globalisation does represent a new set of rules, there is no reason to expect all countries to interpret those rules in identical ways, or expect them all to play to the rules in identical ways' (p. 65).

Hegemonic globalisation

There are different kinds of globalisation. According to Carlos Alberto Torres (2005; Rhoads and Torres, 2005a, pp. 8–9) there are: (1) hegemonic globalisation; (2) globalisation from below; (3) globalisation of exchange of people and ideas,

1

and influence on culture;[1] (4) globalisation of the war on terror;[2] and (5) globalisation of human rights.[3] The most relevant forms of globalisation for discussions around HE are the first two and I will give them ample treatment in this volume. I would argue that the other three forms of globalisation are also relevant. The globalisation of exchange of people and ideas is obviously connected with HE, in terms of change in demographics and ethnic composition of staff and students and also international student mobility. This will hopefully have an effect on the nature of knowledge and learning taking place over a period of time. In my view, Torres' fourth type of globalisation, globalisation of the war on terror, is also relevant, especially if, following Giroux (2007), we need to take into consideration the existence, in a number of powerful countries, such as the USA, of the academic-industrial-military complex. The word 'academic' is said to have been included in Dwight Eisenhower's draft before his enunciation of the industrial-military complex.[4] Then there is the globalisation of human rights that becomes relevant for HE in the sense that students and other people have been gathering on streets and in squares over the years, demanding that access to HE be recognised as a human right. They have been arguing that HE should not be governed by the ideology of the market. We have seen this in recent years in Chile and Greece, in particular, and it has also featured in the student protests in England, especially London, with regard to the hikes in university fees, and in Quebec (Giroux, 2014b).

While stressing links between the last three types of globalisation and HE, as mentioned by Rhoads and Torres (2005a), I will explain in greater detail the two major forms of globalisation that will be at the heart of my discussion in the book. I shall start with hegemonic globalisation predicated, for the most part, on the ideology of neoliberalism.

The well-known Portuguese sociologist Boaventura de Sousa Santos, when interviewed by Roger Dale and Susan Robertson, discussed hegemonic globalisation stating that: 'Neoliberalism is the political form of globalization resulting from a US type of capitalism, a type that bases competitiveness on technological innovation coupled with low levels of social protection' (in Dale and Robertson, 2004, p. 151). He goes on to state that

> the aggressive imposition of this model by the international financial institutions worldwide not only forces abrupt changes in the role of the state and in the rules of the game between the exploiter and the exploited... but also changes the rules of the game among the other kinds of developed capitalism. (de Sousa Santos, in Dale and Robertson, 2004, p. 151)

Neoliberalism sought its trial run in the 'First September 11th' – the CIA and multinational backed military coup in Chile on 11 September 1973. This bloody coup against the nationalising socialist experiment of the government led by Salvador Allende paved the way for the policies and blueprints developed by the 'Chicago Boys' who had learnt the neoliberal free market economic model from Milton Freidman and his associates, including Arnold Harberger. It is by now common knowledge that neoliberalism became a global ideology through Thatcherism (the term coined by Stuart Hall) and Reaganomics. It entailed privatisation, deindustrialisation in the UK, an economy financially driven from the 'City' (hence introducing finance-driven reforms), and 'rolling back the frontiers' of the state. It entailed turning public goods into objects of consumption and structural adjustment programmes (SAPs) introduced by the World Bank and International Monetary Fund (IMF) for 'developing' countries, often serving to cut down on social programmes, free health and educational provision – sapping the social life and support out of communities. It comprises the WTO's polices that would also affect educational 'services', the blurring of public and private, and public financing of private needs. The focus is, among other features, on market competitivity, accountability, standardisation and quality assurance, 'trickling down' of wealth, responsibilisation, individualism and cost recovery measures. In the words of Greek sociologist, Panagiotis Sotiris:

> One should never forget that Neoliberalism is not just an economic policy. It is also the attempt towards production of a particular subjectivity centred upon economic self-interest and competition, in sharp opposition to other, more critical forms of subjectivity, such as that of the active citizen or the conscious worker. (Sotiris, 2014, p. 319)

This is the type of globalisation that several social and political actors in the present time, irrespective of their feelings towards it, have to come to terms with. It is the sort of situation that brings politicians who were elected into positions of power on a socialist ticket into contradictory situations, at least in the eyes of those who shared their politics at one stage. Typical of these perceptions is the following excerpt from a published interview with Sergio Baierle of Cidade and a key figure in the Participatory Budget movement in Brazil. It concerns the then Partido dos Trabalhadores (PT) leader, Luiz Inácio Lula da Silva (Lula) and his first term in office as president of Brazil.[5] Asked about policies regarding democratisation in education, Baierle responds:

> So far there is nothing to be lauded within this context... The reform of public universities is also under discussion, which in essence is not different from the essence of traditional World Bank proposals and other international agencies. The fact that a space has been granted to discuss proposals does not alter the limits within which the government has operated. (Baierle, in Borg and Mayo, 2007, pp. 147–148)

Globalisation from below

Then there is 'globalisation from below' or 'counter-hegemonic globalisation', the latter term used by de Sousa Santos which I, however, try to avoid as it sets up hegemony as a sort of binary when it is said to contain within its own interstices the means of its changing nature – probably the reason why Gramsci never used this term. Forces within hegemony interrelate in a dialectical manner. Globalisation from below 'consists of resistance against hegemonic globalization organised (through local/global linkages) by movements, initiatives and NGOs, on behalf of classes, social groups and regions victimised by the unequal exchanges produced on a global scale by neoliberal globalization' (de Sousa Santos in Dale and Robertson, 2004, p. 150). They include social movements from the South and North playing a major role in a variety of fields, notably migrant support, fair trade, women's issues, LGBTQ issues, sustainable development, the fight against poverty, land reform, organic farming, anti-war and nuclear disarmament, anti-racism, participatory budgets and so forth. Many of these are based in the West. There are those, however, which Dip Kapoor (2009) refers to as 'subaltern southern social movements', whose issues and positions might be in contradiction to those of Western movements.[6] This book will not dwell on their involvement, if any with university lifelong learning (LLL), save for those in Brazil or Palestine, but will shed light on their issues and the cultures involved as people continue to migrate from these areas to countries such as the one in which I live and work, helping their cultures to migrate with them. We can speak of portability of cultures and knowledge traditions in this context. This has implications for universities located in the West when engaging with communities that are increasingly becoming multiethnic.

'Globalisation from below' comprises different movements, previously identified with a rather fragmentary identity politics highlighting specific issues, coming together 'on a scale previously unknown' (Rikowski, 2002, p. 16) to target global capitalism. They met in the different venues where the World Social Forums take place and coalesced into struggles targeting the Breton Woods institutions such as the IMF, World Bank and the World Trade Organization (WTO), thus invoking 'an anti-capitalism of real substance and significant scale' (Rikowski, 2002, p. 16). They come together around the idea of capitalism as a structuring force, shaping many of the issues involved.

This type of globalisation is characterised by international networking involving the use of technology for progressive ends. We saw this in the various uprisings around 2011 and 2014 including mobilisations to take to the squares and streets in Greece, Spain, various Arab countries and also places such as Zuccotti Park in New York City or Gezi Park in Istanbul. It often entails the bringing together of people for struggles to change the current state of affairs that have all the marks of the neoliberal hegemonic global system, for instance, as in Istanbul, protecting public space from its takeover by private interests, the interests of a construction magnate well-connected to government – a new kind of enclosure of the commons. It means a country-wide and a continent-wide series of connections to organise against hegemonic capitalism on a global front, seeking therefore to alter the current relations of hegemony.

This book

In this book, I take a critical look at higher education within the context of globalisation as it impinges on several parts of Europe. This chapter is meant as a general introduction to the text, indicating issues faced by HE institutions, especially universities, within the context of different forms of globalisation: hegemonic globalisation and globalisation from below – the two exist not in binary opposition but in a dialectical relationship. Importance is attached to lifelong higher education, specifically via university continuing education (UCE) provision, in the context of the state and its different functions at present. The values that guide my conception of higher education and universities will be exposed as they will govern the critique of much of the present discourse around the area.

The discursive contexts (see Fairclough and Wodak, 2008) in which European higher education policies are formulated, such as the Lisbon Objectives (CEC, 2000) and the Bologna Process (Confederation of EU Rectors' Conferences and Association of European Universities, 2000),[7] provide both constraints and opportunities for actors, institutions, markets and states in this particular sector. For this reason, this book has an international resonance and will contain material regarding both the EU and Euro-Mediterranean zones, as well as references to insights from the Global South.

Globalisation and higher education

Hegemonic globalisation is having a strong impact on higher education as documented in a whole body of literature (see Jessop et al., 2008; Ennew and Greenaway, 2008; Torres, 2009; King et al., 2011; Bhaskaran Nair and Panikka, 2011; Kupfer, 2011; Killick, 2015; Dobbins and Knill, 2014; Zajda and Rust, 2016b; Barrett, 2017; de Sousa Santos, 2017; Westover, 2017; Proctor and Rumbley, 2018; Gleason, 2018; Maniglio, 2018). Hegemonic globalisation is for the most part predicated on the neoliberal ideology, explained earlier. Neoliberalism is the socio-economic model that is all-pervasive in the current discourse and the *modus operandi* of HE institutions worldwide. It is so well documented in the literature (see Callinicos, 2006; Giroux, 2014b; Rhoads and Torres, 2005b) that its main features need not be rehearsed in great detail here save for a few salient points. A key feature is that of HE serving as a consumption rather than a public good. Students and academics are seen primarily as 'clients' and 'service providers' respectively, rather than members of a community of scholarly learners/educators engaging in epistemological co-investigation of objects of inquiry. Furthermore, to get to the heart of the matter at this preliminary stage, or rather to anticipate the main thread of criticism throughout this book, HE for adults features strongly as a consumption good, a liberating consumer delight as the state, in its neoliberal and competition garbs (see Ball, 2007), helps create and sustain a privatised HE market while often reducing funding allocated to the public HE sector (see Giroux, 2014b).

HE LLL, in the form of distance learning or evening diploma and degree courses, often offered through institutions serving as franchise agencies for British and other universities (English and Mayo, 2012, p. 33), plays an important role here. Succinctly, I would argue that hegemonic globalisation, with its underlying neoliberal tenets, has traditionally been characterised by the following, each of which has ramifications for the HE sector, although not to the same degree in all countries:

- a strong private sector bias – reduced growth of public spending on public education and the pursuit of other sources of funding;

- the transition of education and other formerly public goods to a consumption service (Hill et al., 2005), with the blurring of public and private divisions – including the blurring of private and public in HE;
- an obsession with developing the country's 'human resources', a euphemism for the term 'human capital' (OECD, 2007), which is often unabashedly used in HE policy discourse (EC, 2006a, p. 23; CEC, 2006a, p. 10), as part of re-mantling the state (Pannu, 1996) into a neoliberal or, possibly, as envisaged in certain contexts through a 'Third Way' politics, a Workfare state (Ball, 2007), to create the right infrastructure for investment and mobility;
- vocationalising many sectors of lifelong learning, including education for older adults (non-sustainability of pension schemes) (Borg and Mayo, 2008);
- public financing of private needs (Gentili, 2001; Borg and Mayo, 2006) through, in certain cases, partly financing, directly or indirectly, a competitor HE market (Gentili, 2005, p. 143) or facilitating the presence of a business agenda in public universities;
- international quality comparisons – standardisation, league tables, equivalences, harmonisation and specific emphasis on ICT and maths and science. The EU, the OECD and even UNESCO have provided quality indicators in this regard, although each with different emphases (see Surian, 2006). Some have gone so far as to argue that what we have, in this context, is an 'evaluator/ive state' (Gentili, 2005, p. 141; Neave, 2006; Zajda and Rust, 2016b);
- state intervention in specific sectors as manifest in recent months owing to the credit crunch and other economic setbacks.

How do the above features affect dominant policy discourse in the area?

Markets

The intensification of globalisation, occurring through massive breakthroughs in information and communication technologies, has led to an opening of borders and a liberalisation of services. The fiercely contested General Agreement of Trade in Services (GATS), having been debated in the context of the WTO, would, had its hitherto disrupted negotiations been finalised, have had a bearing on all services within the context of education (de Siqueira, 2005; Hill et al., 2005, pp. 21–24; Verger and Bonal, 2006) and would include higher education. Much of what would pass for higher education, especially university commercial extension wings and private institutions that offer continuing education courses against payment governed by the market and therefore run on commercial lines, would be seen as a service and would therefore be subject to GATS.

Already without the GATS provision, public HE institutions in various countries face stiff competition from foreign agencies operating in the field, many of which benefit from greater economies of scale. They even enter areas that have hitherto not been catered for by the local agencies. Open and other universities,[8] have been very visible internationally in this area. The tremendous revolution in information technology that has led to, and characterises, the intensification of globalisation has ushered in important multiple forms of HE delivery. Platforms are varied with impressive and effective forms of visual and auditory interaction. The global HE centre can reach learners anywhere and across time zones (Borg and Mayo, 2008).

The opening of borders and multiple regional markets has facilitated mobility of capital (fast-paced economic and financial exchange) and labour, although certainly not on a level playing field. This has led to the need for flexible workers and therefore the constant retooling of labour. Retooling is a key operative word in the context of lifelong learning, especially in the widely circulated discourse regarding the need to learn and relearn to keep up with the fast rate of techno-logical change – one of the most common platitudes bandied about by politicians, heads of training units and education policymakers. In short, we must continue re-educating ourselves or re-learning to dance to an ever-changing or evolving tune in classic 'structural functionalist' sociological fashion. It is our fault if we do not do so, or the fault of the company for not investing in training for this purpose, never mind the fact that small firms do not enjoy the economies of scale to render in-house training a viable proposition, facing the danger of poaching to boot. Blame is also apportioned to universities and other HE institutions for not being in tune with industry's ever-changing needs – never mind the fact that formal educational institutions, encumbered by administrative setups, and increasingly bureaucratic ones at that, are the least likely to be flexible enough to adapt to the constant fluctuations of the economy and the labour market – once a standard criticism of Human Capital Theory in education (Sultana, 1992, p. 298).

LLL, initially promoted by UNESCO as lifelong education (LLE), but subse-quently carried forward more forcefully with regard to potential policy impact by the OECD (1996, 2007) and the EU (CEC, 2000, 2001a), has become an important concept within the global HE discourse, and certainly the EU discourse. This will be the subject of the next chapter.

The need to have flexible workers places the emphasis on learning and skills, upgrading being not a time-conditioned process but ongoing throughout life, given, and here goes the cliché once again, the rapidity with which changes in the labour market are said to take place. Hence pressures are exerted on univer-sities to provide continuing education programmes in the context of LLL. Martin Carnoy (1999) argues that globalisation has brought with it a perceived growth in demand for products with high level of skill, thus underlining the importance of skills upgrading (p. 15). This has obvious implications for the HE sector with respect to not only graduate employability but also its various extension and con-tinuing education services.[9]

This forces countries to engage in spending on education for a more educated flexible and mobile workforce, in order to attract and maintain investment as well as remain 'competitive' more generally in the global economy. There has been an expansion of higher education. Governments are often held to ransom by poten-tial investors in terms of the conditions they expect and demand, including the provision of the labour force they require according to present needs and perhaps future projections. There were also attempts to create measures to take a government to court for not maintaining the conditions under which the decision to invest there was taken. MAI and TTIP are examples of these attempts, examples enough to scare anyone with social justice at heart. LLL, including HE LLL, of a specific and reductionist type and not in its broadest contexts, can feature in such agreements.

In countries not having the right infrastructure to cater for such an increase, including those that only recently established a public university, this can mean buying education services from outside. Distance learning, a key form of university and other HE LLL, plays a major role here. So do franchise agencies or hastily set up institutions buying programmes from foreign bodies without any concern for the contexts in which the learning takes place. It offers opportunities to all kinds of providers, including businesses in non-academic fields, jumping on the international HE market bandwagon seizing lucrative opportunities and offering quick-fix solutions to a country's perceived HE shortages.

These occurrences are of great relevance to globalisation's impact on HE, especially with respect to established and recognised institutions where the 'concern for standards', and the workload of a limited, suitably qualified academic staff, precludes them from offering degree courses in a variety of areas and through alternative routes (Borg and Mayo, 2008). The monopoly of one public institution, once very much a characteristic of such small EU member states as Luxembourg, Malta and Cyprus or the small UK overseas territory in Europe, Gibraltar (having established its own university through a university act in 2015),[10] is thus challenged (Mayo et al., 2008). In the cases of small states, they are also challenged not only through online learning sources or foreign universities reaching out to distant terrains but also by new locally based institutions reaching out to and catering for an international student market – in short, enlarging what would otherwise be a small local market. Cyprus is a case in point. Until 1992, Cyprus (save for the part under Turkish control)[11] did not have a university, for reasons that lie beyond the scope of this discussion. Then a public university (now ranked in the top 500 in the Times World University Rankings – a meteoric rise in such a short time) opened its doors, primarily for a selected local market. Now the number of Cypriot universities has increased, catering primarily for an international student market. The two universities offering adult education through departmental structures are obviously the public Open University of Cyprus which, at present, offers degrees mainly at graduate level, with 5,200 students and 25 programmes of study for the 2017–2018 academic year,[12] and the private Frederick University which has distance education programmes[13] including a Master's in Adult Education.

Challenging one institution's monopoly through the creation of an HE market comprising public and private institutions (although the distinctions increasingly become blurred) is often encouraged by governments seeking to boost the country's graduate numbers to enable them to reach 'international levels' in accordance with the Lisbon agenda. Satisfying the Lisbon criteria is a priority in such countries. These private institutions, often acting as mediators for recognised foreign bodies or, as in the case of Cyprus (e.g., Intercollege now the University of

Nicosia or Fredrick College becoming Frederick University), being upgraded to the status of recognised universities, alleviate the government's burden of having to finance the increase in public higher education, in addition to partaking fully of a globalised international, especially non-EU, HE student market. Market-driven HE, including market-driven UCE, is therefore seen to perform useful roles with respect to earning foreign exchange (see Vossensteyn and Dobson, 1999) and enhancing graduate numbers.

Role of the state

A major point to be analysed in this context is the role of the state. One of the greatest myths being bandied about in this contemporary neoliberal scenario is that the nation-state is no longer powerful in this period characterised by the intensification of globalisation. Deregulation was brought in to expedite the process where various forms of provision, private and formerly public, were left to the market. Yet, as Andy Green (1990, 2013, pp. 316–318) argues and shows historically, all the now rich countries have built their economies around a strong state presence with the adoption of all sorts of measures such as import substitution and import tariffs to support the 'infant industry'. And yet the main international agencies regulating the world economy, acting in the interests of some of these nations, notably the USA, advocate a free market economy for emerging nations, based on the myth that today's rich countries prospered 'through liberal economic policies' (Green, 1990, 2013, p. 317).

Furthermore, the credit crunch starkly laid bare the folly of this conviction as new forms of regulation are being put in place with the state, meaning the national state, intervening to bail out banks and other institutions in this situation. As the Brazilian educator, Paulo Freire put it so clearly years before the recent credit crunch (he died in 1997), thus showing remarkable prescience:

> Fatalism is only understood by power and by the dominant classes when it interests them. If there is hunger, unemployment, lack of housing, health and schools, they proclaim that this is a universal trend and so be it! But when the stock market falls in a country far away and we have to tighten up our belts, or if a private national bank has internal problems due to the inability of its directors or owners, the State immediately intervenes to 'save them'. In this case, the 'natural', 'inexorable', is simply put aside. (Freire, in Borg and Mayo, 2007, p. 3)

Furthermore, policies regarding asylum-seeking are left in the hands of national EU member states. There is no common EU policy in this regard. Even access to EU citizenship occurs via the single nation-states, each one of which has its own particular regulations and processes.

The state and its agencies are nowadays said to work not alone but within a loose network of agencies – governance rather than government in what is presented as a 'heterarchy' of relations (Ball, 2010). Despite appearing *prima facie* to be heterarchical, such relations under capitalism can, in actual fact, be hierarchical and less democratic than they might appear to be. This certainly applies to relations between states and non-governmental organisations (NGOs) or labour unions, both important providers of adult education and possible complementary partners in a process of university extension. The relations are characterised by the ever-present threat of co-optation, often within a corporatist framework (see Offe, 1985, on this in terms of disorganised capitalism; Panitch, 1976).[14] Structured partnerships between state and business, reflected in market-oriented 'employability' continuing education programmes, as well as between 'public' and 'private', tend to emphasise the link between the state and the imperatives of capital accumulation.

For Antonio Gramsci, for instance, the agencies constituting bourgeois civil society (*bürgerliche gesellschaft*) buttressed the state. Gramsci focused primarily on the ideological institutions in this network. One must however also mention the point made by Nicos Poulantzas when underlining that the state also engages in economic activities that are not left totally in the hands of private industry. University continuing education that is market oriented constitutes one important economic activity of this kind. Poulantzas stated that, under monopoly capitalism, the difference between politics, ideology and the economy is not clear. It is blurred. The state enters directly into the sphere of production as a result of the crises of capitalist production itself (Carnoy, 1982, p. 97). One might argue that this point has relevance to the situation today. In the first place, industry often collaborates in policy formulation in tandem or in a loose network with the state, just like NGOs or labour unions do.

Nowhere is the role of the state as economic player more evident than in higher education (see Giroux and Searls Giroux, 2004; Giroux, 2014b), an area that, although traditionally vaunting relative autonomy, as most education institutions do, constitutes an important domain of hegemonic struggle. The division between public and private in this sector is increasingly blurred. So-called 'public univer-sities' are exhorted to provide services governed by the market and which have a strong commercial basis. Furthermore the state engages actively through direct and indirect means, and, in certain places, through a series of incentives or 'goal cushions', to create a higher education competitive market as part of the 'competi-tion' state (Jessop, 2002). The state regulates these agencies by working in tandem with them. It is certainly no neutral arbiter of different interests, even though it appears to be so, as it also engages in structured partnerships with industry to secure the right basis for the accumulation of global capital. In this regard, one can argue that the state is propped up not only by the ideological institutions of what Gramsci calls 'civil society'[15] but by industry itself (it is part of industry), while it sustains both (it props up both these 'civil society' institutions and industry) in a reciprocal manner to ensure the right conditions for the accumulation of cap-ital. HE is part of this complex of civil society, often interacting with the political (army, police etc.), the separation between civil and political society being heur-istic. HE's being part of the interaction between political society becomes all the more pronounced if we are to give credence to the notion of 'industrial-academic-military complex' mentioned by Giroux (2007).

All this goes to show that the state, the nation-state, is an active player and has not receded into the background within the context of hegemonic globalisation.

On the contrary, in its repressive, ideological and commercial forms, the state remains central to the neoliberal project.

What kind of university?

What we are witnessing is a re-conceptualisation of the university. Authors like Giroux (2007, 2014b) and Giroux and Searls Giroux (2004) have forcefully argued that the idea of the university as a public good is being eroded in the public discourse. In a number of countries, not least the United States, we have been witnessing the emergence of the 'corporatised' university. There are those who would argue that universities need to change in tune with the times. The old 'elitist' ideals, or rather individualising myths, of *Bildung* and the Humboldtian academy (Fuhr, 2017), if ever they took root in universities throughout Europe, have been called into question.

This could be an exciting time for universities and higher education, as new challenges are being faced and new frontiers explored. For the time being, however, the general staple is that of what Lyotard called 'performativity' and the forging of a closer nexus between productive science, ICT, research and development and business. Divisions between technical or indeed polytechnic universities and 'other' universities are being drawn. In many universities and institutions of higher learning, knowledge is packaged and modularised and its delivery is being constrained by the contours of 'corporate time' as opposed to 'public time'.[16] Hence corporate business interests take precedence over public interests at all levels including that of continuing education increasingly being conceived of as a consumer rather than a public good and as a means of providing those who can pay for it with forms of credentialing that serve as positional goods. No wonder that extension, online or evening programmes in business administration, project management and ICT are the most visible courses on offer.

A certain discourse of rationalisation is creeping into the systems of certain countries, most notably those of Italy, whose universities might well have exaggerated on the number of courses and specialisations provided. This, in 2008, led the then-Berlusconi government to embark on a cutting-down exercise with regard to course provision and which undermines the concept of 'massification', said to be a product of the 1968 protests and until recently a feature of the Italian and other university/HE systems (Todeschini, 1999, p. 190).

Funding for most of the arts, with the exception of history and languages, was considerably cut down if not withdrawn in, for example, UK universities, where the focus of government spending is science and technology. Meanwhile, research universities that can count on endowments will continue to exist – the Oxfords and Cambridges of this world – but primarily on a mainstream, full-time basis. However, we could well have a stratification in terms of research, teaching and regional universities.

This having been said, specifically by a former EU commissioner for education and culture, let us not forget the list of positive principles found in the Bologna Process, the analyses of which have varied from content analyses to discourse analyses (see Fairclough and Wodak, 2008). These aspects have been outlined by Boaventura de Sousa Santos (2015). For example, contrary to the kind of classification mentioned, de Sousa Santos imagined a scenario where the process

> managed to strengthen the relationship between teaching and research, and, while rewarding excellence, it made sure that the community of university teachers would not be divided between two stratified segments: a small group of first class university citizens with abundant money, light teaching loads and other good conditions to carry out research, on the one hand, and, on the other, a large group of second class university citizens enslaved by long hours of teaching and tutoring with little access to research funds only because they were employed by the wrong universities or were interested in supposedly wrong topics. (de Sousa Santos, 2015, pp. 301–302)[17]

De Sousa Santos went on to mention seven other important 'positive' aspects in an imagined university learning and research community, including the following: 'abandoning the once fashionable concept of human capital after concluding that the universities should form full human beings and full citizens and not just human capital subjected to market fluctuations like any other capital'. This would have 'a decisive impact on the curricula and on the evaluation of performances'. Furthermore, he imagines a non-neoliberal scenario where 'the European Union and the European states' are convinced

> that they should be financially more generous with the public universities not because of corporatist pressures but rather because the investment in an excellent public university system is probably the best way of investing in the future of a Europe of ideas, the only way for Europe to remain truly European. (de Sousa Santos, 2015, p. 302)

Such an investment would include making broad swathes of educational areas accessible to ordinary citizens in terms of online accessibility and outreach programmes against a nominal and highly affordable fee, which can also be covered by tax rebates.

Is this wishful thinking? This is very much the case at present. What Boaventura de Sousa Santos is auguring strikes me as being the exact opposite of what appears to be occurring on the ground – its antithesis, if you will. Let us say, however, that hope springs eternal. Sousa's tongue-in-cheek comments might suggest that even Bologna and the kind of university it can develop can allow scope for alternative ways of conceiving of universities/HE. This would contradict the former commissioner for education and culture's dictum 'Bologna cannot be implemented à la carte' (Viviane Reding, in Tomusk, 2004, p. 75).

Voldemar Tomusk goes so far as to argue that there are conflicting agendas involved that could have led to Bologna's dissolution (Tomusk, 2004, p. 93). De Sousa Santos, for his part, presents us with two visions of a university currently 'at a crossroads'. The excerpt just quoted forms part of the second vision, which stands as an alternative to the hegemonic one. He urges us to make sure it is the second vision, the more holistic one, that is realised, one that, I argue, would allow for a more holistic UCE or lifelong education provision, in contradistinction to the narrowly oriented market-driven one. This highlights the role of human agency within the emerging structures of university reform. It also prompts us to avail ourselves of current concerns about the future of the university to search for the liminal spaces available to us, often present in the interstices of the same universities themselves, for instance in occasional staff and public seminars, to foreground heterotopias concerning HE – in short, to avail ourselves of this time of rethinking and questioning to explore alternative models and futures than the one being drummed into us time and time again. For instance, I would argue the following: all those who have the university and public continuing/lifelong education at heart are called on to effectively serve as human agents in the struggle for preserving and opening up democratic HE spaces motivated by the principles of and commitment to social justice. I have written this book with this purpose in mind. It is the *leitmotif* of the entire book and therefore informs my analysis throughout.

I then go on to examine the different conceptions of lifelong education, from the heady days of UNESCO with its broad humanistic interpretation of the concept that, alas, had little impact on policies, to the more apparently reductionist industry-oriented interpretation prevalent today. The views expressed in this chapter frame the context for my analysis of the HE discourse and UCE provision in the chapters that follow. I will then show how issues raised in the first two chapters affect dominant policy discourse in higher education. It is to a more in-depth analysis of this discourse, as provided primarily by the EU, that the book turns in Chapter 3. Drawing on numerous communications from the EU and other organisations, including the OECD, I analyse the discourse and the portability of policies that occurs across European nations in this regard. I then extend the discussion into what has been conceived of as a 'Euro-Mediterranean higher education research area', although, it must be said, with hitherto little tangible results. I underline the pitfalls that need to be avoided unless, in their over-zealousness, the 'Bologna missionaries' can be perceived as seeking to exploit another neo-colonial market.

The chapter that follows critically explores university lifelong learning throughout Europe and beyond. I discuss the development of the concept of university lifelong learning, the diversity in university lifelong learning provision, the institutional changes that have taken place in a number of HE institutions to accommodate the EU vision and the limits imposed by institutions in the process of implementing this vision.

This leads to a discussion, in the same chapter, concerning issues involved in developing an alternative LLL vision for universities and HE institutes moving back and forth in time to tease out some of the ongoing questions concerning marginalisation, imaginative uses of marginal spaces and innovative pedagogical and cross disciplinary areas that have emerged and can potentially emerge from these exercises. This chapter is international in scope as were the preceding two chapters, underlining examples of a counter-discourse or hybrid discourse in university and HE LLL with social justice as the goal.

The subsequent chapter carries forward the social justice agenda, drawing primarily on Paulo Freire and other writers/educators to highlight issues concerning university or HE LLL and community involvement. Some of the themes broached in the earlier chapters will be revisited in the context of LLL, universities/HE and the community, especially the recurring theme of *praxis* entailing researching the community to derive the basis on which education in the area can be developed. The issue of migration and the different knowledges and knowledge traditions migrants bring with them into the community is given tremendous importance, as the anticipated increase in migration from South to North is also discussed in the context of LLL for sustainable development. This chapter is followed by a grounded chapter where I reflect on a project of community engagement involving the university where I teach, discussing the object of investigation – Holy Week/*La Semana Santa* – in the project from both a global and local perspective, i.e., with reference to Malta and Spain, drawing on traditions and related artistic representations from England, Italy and Latin America.

The short concluding chapter provides a recapitulation of the main themes and a look to the future with special attention attached to the role of educators as transformative intellectuals in this process. The chapter synthesises some of the main points addressed in the previous chapters and maps out a road for university continuing education that is conceived of as expansive as opposed to reductionist, the latter in the sense of being confined to the labour market. I take my cue here from the use of the concept of LLL in the UN's Sustainable Development Goals. The chapter looks at some of the resistances documented in various parts of Europe and in the literature, as well as alternative forms of university activities. In keeping with my values, they promote the notion of higher education and learning as a form of continuing education, as a public good, an essential ingredient of a genuine grassroots democracy. I argue for an attempt to 'take back' (Giroux and Searls Giroux, 2004; Giroux, 2014b) many of the humanities and social sciences, as well as interdisciplinary studies (e.g., cultural studies), the major casualties of the neoliberal onslaught, to their places of origin – adult education. I argue, however, that this should be a struggle on two fronts, the university campus and the community.

Notes

1 'A third form of globalization is represented by the movement and exchange of people and ideas and the subsequent influence on culture' (Rhoads and Torres, 2005a, p. 8).

2 'The fourth manifestation of globalization concerns the international war against terrorism, largely prompted by the 9/11 attack in New York. The response has been militaristic but the emphasis has also been on security and control of borders, people, capital, and commodities. It is (ironically) the reverse of the open markets of neoliberalism. The theme of this form of globalization is security as a precondition of freedom' (Torres, 2005, p. 205).

3 'With the growing ideology of human rights taking hold in international law, many traditional practices endemic to the fabric of particular societies or cultures (from traditional to esoteric practices) are now questioned, challenged, forbidden, or outlawed' (Torres, 2005, p. 205).

4 Dwight Eisenhower referred to the situation in the USA when coining the phrase 'military-industrial complex'. It has been reported that he used the phrase in what was a modified famous speech of his. In the draft, he is believed to have referred to the 'military-academic-industrial complex' an expression that was later also used by Senator William Fulbright (Giroux, 2007, pp. 14–15).

5 The PT has, since its inception, professed a socialist politics manifested in a variety of policies at state and municipal level. Paulo Freire's ideas about educational reform in São Paulo, when Education Secretary there, have to be seen in the context of these policies which even gave rise to the Participatory Budget in Porto Alegre in Rio Grande do Sul. Much, perhaps too much, was therefore expected of the Lula government, in its initial period of power at the Federal level, in terms of stemming the Neoliberal tide. I often heard the statement 'We have won the government but not the state' by PT supporters.

6 Kapoor writes: 'Often ecological NSMs [new social movements] and GSMs [global social movements] contradict SSM politics, as the former speak from the relative security of their remote urban locations (consuming resources "here" while aiming to "protect nature over there," while disregarding the contradictory plight of subalterns "in nature over there")' (Kapoor, 2009, p. 80).

7 'The series of steps coordinated by Ministers of Education to bring about harmoniza-tion of the structure of higher education cycles inside the European Union and other signatories to the process' (Jessop et al., 2008, p. 3).

8 See Macedo et al. (2003), on the importance of this language in a globalised context and Deem et al. (2008) for its importance in the emergence of so-called 'word class institutions' according to international rankings.

9 See the various contributions to Osborne and Thomas (2003) regarding UCE in Europe.

10 www.unigib.edu.gi/.

11 Universities were set up partly as a means of populating Northern Cyprus with Turkish and other students. There is an external campus of the prestigious Middle Eastern Technical University (METU) with its main campus in Ankara, and of Istanbul Technical University. There is also a campus of the University of the West of Scotland whose main campus is at Paisley, Scotland, and at least two other degree-granting colleges. In short there are 24 universities in this part of Cyprus. This is an astonishing number for such a small area. The Republic of Northern Cyprus is recognised only by Turkey. www.cypnet.com/north_cyprus_education_universities.php.

12 www.ouc.ac.cy/web/guest/university.

13 www.frederick.ac.cy/programs-of-study/distance-learning.

14 These organisations establish formal and informal links, parliamentary and extra-parliamentary, with key agents of the state in return for the advancement of their cor-porate interests. (See Held, 2006 p. 172).

15 Gramsci does not view 'civil society' (*bürgerliche gesellschaft* – bourgeois civil society), the way it is conventionally regarded nowadays, as the third sector between the state and industry. For Gramsci, civil society, which has a long history with various interpret-ations, is the entire complex of cultural, knowledge, spiritual and social institutions and other agencies, a broad spectrum comprising agencies ranging from schools, churches, the press and cultural centres to, for example, the Red Cross, Oxfam, Caritas and social clubs. These co-exist (some even interacting) with the repressive forces (army, police, etc.) of political society. Together they sustain the state, which needs to be looked at integrally – hence the division between civil and political society existing mainly for heuristic purposes (Mayo, 2015, pp. 36–37).

16 'Public time' refers to the slowing down of time 'in order to question what Jacques Derrida calls the powers that limit "a democracy to come", as opposed to 'corporate time', 'accelerated time in which the principle of self-interest replaces politics and consumerism replaces a broader notion of social agency' (Giroux and Searls Giroux, 2004, p. 227).

17 Keynote address delivered at the meeting on the occasion of the 'XXII Anniversary of the Magna Charta Universitatum', held at the University of Bologna, on 16 September 2010.

2

Changing conceptions of lifelong education/learning

Introduction

This chapter will focus on the development (Wain, 2004, pp. 1–90) of lifelong education (LLE)/learning (LLL). This constitutes the key aspect of contemporary European universities' work being analysed in this book. The chapter will discuss the development of the concept from its promotion by UNESCO and later formulations and emphases, most of which reflect OECD and EU agendas. The implications of the discursive shift from LLE to LLL will be considered, as will the relationship between several features of the current adoption of the concept and the neoliberal tenets of hegemonic globalisation.

Dominant concept in education

It would not be amiss to state that LLL constitutes one of the dominant *doxa* in education policymaking worldwide, particularly in the Western world. At face value, it seems a relatively neutral concept, although very few concepts, if any, are really neutral in policymaking. A closer look at its basic tenets and the way the discourse evolved from its promotion by UNESCO and the so-called Faure Report, *Learning To Be* (Faure et al., 1972), to contemporary times indicates that it gradually began to encapsulate all the basic aspects of modern, market-oriented conceptions of education.

The expansive UNESCO conception

The UNESCO version of LLE, which attached great importance to adult education and non-formal education, was promoted through a body of literature comprising books and papers by a variegated group of writers (ranging from liberal to Marxist) with a strong humanistic base. The names of Paul Lengrand (1970), Ettore Gelpi (1985), Ravindah Dave (1976), Bogdan Suchodolski (1976) and Arthur J. Cropley (1980) come to mind, together with the authors of the Faure Report (Faure et al., 1972) mentioned earlier. Some of these writings had their basis in scientific humanism (Wain, 2004, pp. 16–19), a philosophical outlook that foregrounds human rather than religious values. UNESCO's first director-general,

Julian Huxley was associated with scientific humanism (see Finger and Asún, 2001, p. 22).

At the risk of generalising from among the work of a diverse group of writers, one can say that this movement provided an expansive and humanistic view of the entire process of human learning 'from the cradle to the grave'. They promoted what was therefore an all-embracing concept covering education throughout the whole lifespan and comprising the various sources of learning to which a person can be exposed. And yet, despite this basic underlying tenet, the concept is often used interchangeably with adult education. This tends to confuse the issue. One can speak of inconsistencies in the various uses of the concept, and the same would apply to LLL. This loose usage becomes more frequent these days as the term LLL tends to be more attractive for funding purposes than 'adult education'. Funding mechanisms are perfect vehicles for the further inculcation of any ideology that resides in language. On the other hand, adult education would, in my view, be a crucial component of any LLE or LLL strategy. And yet what compounds the issue is that the EU uses LLL primarily in relation to persons in the 25–64 age bracket (Eurostat, 2016), very much the (paid) working age bracket.

With regard to LLE, Wain (2004, pp. 19–21) refers to two waves of writing in the area, namely the more evolutionary utopian wave and the alternative prag-matist approach. Wain had argued that the utopian wave can be easily criticised on the grounds that it provides a very optimistic view of a 'common humanity'. Difference is here subsumed under a single model, according to which a common destiny beckons (Wain, 1987, p. 230) – still in the realm of utopia rather than heterotopia. Wain refers to an alternative model of the 'learning society', the par-ticular social conception that necessitates LLE, proposed by those members of the second wave of 'pragmatist' writers who 'are ready to reverse all these tendencies, to take different societies as they are' and who

> are thus ready to argue that there is not any one model of such a society that can be universally imposed, and that the shape any 'learning society' will take depends upon an ongoing dialectical relationship between the ideological, economic, cultural, edu-cational features *that it already has.* (Wain, 1987, p. 230, emphasis in original)

Wain includes Gelpi among those who favour a pragmatist approach to LLE and the idea of a learning society: a historical and a comparative approach with the emphasis being placed less on the concept's future possibilities and more on the actual present day reality (Wain, 2004, p. 19). Gelpi once wrote:

> My thinking is that lifelong education, fundamentally, belongs to the history of edu-cation of all countries; it is not therefore a new idea. It lies in the Chinese tradition, in Indian Buddhism; it lies within Greek philosophy and within the spirit of the European Renaissance. The real revolution today lies in the *popular demand* for life-long education, not in the idea itself. (Gelpi, 1985, p. 18, emphasis in original)

In short, it is not a question of simply moving towards a process or system of LLE but more a question of examining what form LLL takes at a particular time and in a specific context. The same applies to the related concept of the 'learning society' – a society composed of people engaging in different forms of LLE. While those who share the utopian and evolutionary first-wave view would use slogans such as 'towards a learning society', those who subscribe to the second-wave view would be more interested in the shape learning societies take or took in different contexts and at different times in history. Comparative empirical research would be of prime interest to the latter.

This position made sense when viewed in the context of UNESCO's all-embracing educational policy, which had to recognise the fact that, in continents such as Africa and regions such as Latin America, education for everyone would not necessarily have resulted in the creation of new and expensive formal structures of learning. To the contrary, it would have had to entail appreciation and recognition of the many 'learning webs', to adopt Ivan Illich's terminology, and non-formal-education experiences and traditions that abound in these places. Latin American popular education, spearheaded by the towering figure of Paulo Freire, comes to mind. This point also recalls accounts of tribal intergenerational 'knowledge transfer' involving community elders and other forms of indigenous knowledge.

These were given short-shrift by promoters of Western colonial education as part of their so-called 'civilising mission', and yet they were preserved, revitalised and survived colonial repression. We immediately think here of African countries and First Nations communities in the Americas. We also think of other indigenous populations such as the Aborigines, Māori, Inuit and Adivasi.

The foregoing enhances the expansive nature of the concept as developed within the UNESCO framework. It encompassed a wide range of education modes, settings and 'learning societies'. The writings captured the imagination of many operating in the education and social research fields. In its more pragmatist form, LLE must have appealed to sociologists dealing with issues such as hegemony in its Gramscian sense[1] and the implicit notion of a 'learning society' embedded in Gramsci's affirmation that every relationship of hegemony is an educational relationship. Others, inspired by Habermas, found much purchase in connecting the 'learning society' to the idea of a democratic public sphere in which education plays its part, very much tied to the concept of an 'educated public'. Alas, however, the older concept of LLE, although bandied about by educationists and politicians as part of the then-trendy education discourse, did not have a direct effect on education policy itself. There were those who intimated that the concept was already being diluted in Latin America (La Belle, 1986), where it was frequently accorded a 'secondary labour market' economic-oriented twist in projects promoted through foreign 'dependency' aid.[2] These were early examples, in 'informally Western colonised' territories, of how UNESCO's expansive philosophy on paper (a different UNESCO then to the one that has existed following the Soviet Bloc's demise) can be distorted. It anticipated what was to transpire on a global scale. This is hardly surprising given that neoliberalism, which would embrace and change the concept ideologically, had its violently repressive 'trial run' in one of these territories.[3] It can be argued that the birth pangs of this ideology were extremely sanguinary.

The LLE movement gravitating around UNESCO faded away in the late 1980s, while the concept of LLL had by then already been used by the OECD. The OECD, for its part, placed the emphasis on 'learning' rather than 'education' in what seems to have been a far from innocent discursive shift (Tuijnman and Boström, 2002). The emphasis began to be placed less on structures of educational provision and more on individuals taking charge of their own learning (Tuijnman and Boström, 2002, pp. 102–110). The 'self-directed' learning concept was borrowed from the old discourse. This old term, however, facilitated a liberal 'individualistic' appropriation of the concept. This ignores instances, in the UNESCO literature – Dave (1976) and Suchodolski (1976) being fine examples – where explicit reference to the collective dimension of people 'taking charge' of their own learning together is made – this despite the frequent invocation of Paulo Freire's work and the fact that the idea of a 'learning society' or 'education-centred society' (Suchodolski, 1976) presupposes this.[4] The concept of collectively directed learning is a recurring one in the rest of this book.

One can argue that the emphasis in this new appropriated discourse is centred on the learner rather than on learning structures. The flip side to this, however, is that it places the onus squarely on the individual. This is a key underlining feature of the shift in the discourse. Education and learning become an individual rather than a social responsibility. *Responsibilisation* is the term used in critical sociological quarters to describe this situation.

LLL thus conceived becomes part and parcel of the neoliberal turn in education which renders the whole process a consumption rather than a public good. It places emphasis less on structures and entitlement and more on the individuals taking charge of their own learning, often at considerable expense. It minimises the role of the state and leaves everything to the market.

Blame for failure is to be apportioned on to the individual rather than the state's inability to provide the right structures for effective learning to take place at different stages of a person's life. Many aspects of LLL are marketed as consumption goods, especially university extension study units recognised within the European credit transfer system (ECTS). Several learning opportunities are therefore provided at a price through the establishment of an education market.

The discourse also made its way into the EU's adoption of LLL. The economic imperatives of this discourse were reflected in the EU Memorandum on LLL's definition of the concept: 'all purposeful learning activity, undertaken on an ongoing basis with the aim of improving knowledge, skills and competence' (CEC, 2000, p. 3). This definition was formulated within the context of the European Employment Strategy launched at the Heads of State European Council, Luxemburg, 1997 (CEC, 2000, p. 3). It can be said, therefore, that the EU was initially pushed to adopt this discourse by not educationists, philosophers or social scientists, as had been the case with UNESCO, but the European Roundtable of Industrialists. There can be no mistaking the original motivation for the adoption of the concept.

The declared goal was to render the EU the strongest and 'most competitive knowledge economy in the world' by 2010, a target that, as with many EU targets (see the 2020 poverty decrease target[5]), was not reached. It did, however, leave few in doubt regarding the emphasis in the discourse. The definition of LLL was criticised during the relevant Memorandum consultation process, where a number of educators and education policymakers had their say as members of certain EU epistemological communities (e.g., the Grundtvig working group). It was argued that it placed too much emphasis on the employment and labour market aspects of learning (CEC, 2001a, p. 9) to the detriment of a more holistic and socially oriented approach. It was subsequently tweaked to read 'all learning activity undertaken throughout life, with the aim of improving knowledge, skills and competences within a personal, civic, social and or/employment-related perspective' (CEC, 2001a, p. 9). This change offered hope in that it showed that institutions are not monolithic and contain spaces, within their interstices, where struggles for renegotiation and change can occur. This notwithstanding, the general view concerning LLL remained neoliberal, for the most part, albeit laced with some sanitising humanist and social democratic trappings. There are those, including me, who entertained the prospect that ten years of consultation would yield a more balanced view of the LLL/LLE policy discourse, more expansive in scope than the reductionist one hitherto promoted. Like me, they must have been left bitterly disappointed. A much anticipated and promised 'Ten Years After' LLL document never saw the light. Instead what emerged was a rather skimpy 'EU Agenda for Adult Learning' document that smacked of a desperate, possibly 'last-ditch' attempt to maintain adult learning on the EU agenda. Despite its failure to deliver on a global scale, the neoliberal agenda was to be carried forward. It would seem that those who wield the greatest political influence in the EU would brook no attempt to significantly modify the Union's accepted LLL tenets, despite ten years of contestations, clarifications and attempts at renegotiation and reformulation.

Education, therefore, according to these tenets, remains something that one acquires as a 'positional good' and at an expense. People are exhorted to organise their budgetary spending, through financial literacy promotion campaigns, in such a way that they invest in their continuing education on which their employability chances depend.[6] Employ*ability*, however, does not, as Ettore Gelpi (2002) astutely remarked in his last book, necessarily mean employ*ment* in a context where lack of jobs is often part and parcel of the crisis of the capitalist system itself and has often little to do with people's lack of investment in their own learning (echoes of Ivar Berg, 1974). The more recent, largely economic-oriented discourse on education has made the LLL concept a panacea for existing social ills. These include the capitalist system's inability to provide jobs with a measure of security, with the resultant emergence of a *précarieté* situation, in a world characterised by 'liquidity' (Bauman, 2005, 2013), 'risk' (Beck, 1992) and 'obsolescence' (O'Sullivan, 1999). A strictly reductionist LLL notion suits this scenario perfectly as it serves as the means to present a 'jobs crisis' as a 'skills crisis' (Marshall, 1997). Rather than focus on a system that cannot create jobs and jobs related to different levels of educational attainment, there is a focus on blaming people for not learning the skills demanded by industry.

The truth is that, in many parts of Europe, youngsters are gaining greater qualifications than their parents ever dreamed of obtaining and yet cannot enjoy their standard of living, a point to which I return in the chapter that follows. This has been a recurring battle cry of the many *indignados* occupying various parts of the diminishing public spaces in Europe and across the Atlantic. The whole idea of LLL, as currently promoted, gravitates around the notion of a 'knowledge economy' (Maniglio, 2018, p. 41), which might not lead to the level of employment and financial rewards being anticipated, given the global competition for the few high-paying, middle-class jobs available (Brown et al., 2010), a point to be elaborated on in the discussion on credentialism in the next chapter.

Furthermore, the LLL discourse is being promoted with great vigour and vehemence in industrially developing countries. There seems to be little recognition of the fact that an increase in investment in LLL, with economic returns in mind, without a corresponding reciprocal investment in the economic sector, perpetuates, and probably exacerbates, the situation of 'education for export' that has been a characteristic of colonial and neo-colonial policies to date. Put simply, countries are urged to invest in LLL, especially (but not only) science, for economic purposes, and yet there is little investment in the corresponding economic sector that would otherwise provide the recipients of these educational investments with jobs in that specific country. The recipients of this education have no alternative but to leave the country in search of adequate employment relevant to their further studies. They would often try to settle in the richer countries. What they are effectively provided with is an 'education for export'.

The LLL discourse occasionally ventures beyond the strictly economic-oriented to encompass 'wellbeing', with its great market pull. Wellbeing as a term has made its presence felt within the contemporary fabric of universities with at least one case of an entire faculty named that way.

This provides people (those who can afford the relevant programmes, including university-sponsored extension programmes) with opportunities for learning to cope with emotional stress said to emerge from the brain's chemical imbalances (certainly not to be discounted). What is not said, however, is that for all the talk of 'get on your bike', 'pull up your bootstraps' or, I would add, 'invest in LLL', much anxiety is caused by the dysfunctional structuring capitalist forces that are shaping people's lives. They generate a sense of insecurity and despair deriving from the current situation of austerity, precarious living and inability to plan for the long term (Cooper and Hardy, 2012, pp. 60–61).

This is all part of what Mark Fisher calls 'Capitalist Realism' (2009, p. 19), based on the notion that people can see through the fact that capitalism and neoliberal policies have not delivered 'big time' but, at the same time, cannot come up with any alternatives. Many have constantly been remarking that the Left itself has gone 'bankrupt' (Giroux, 2014a) – no pun intended given the bank-induced financial meltdown at the heart of the current crises. The radical call is for forms of adult learning that do not treat the symptoms but provide an identification and critical reading of the causes that lie within the structuring capitalist forces at play (Mayo, 2017a).

Echoing Freire, we require a dose of critical literacy that enables us to unveil the contradictions that exist in society. In short, we require learning for social change and not simply for individual adjustment and accommodation: the 'ideology of accommodation'. Alas, 'social wellbeing' is becoming part of the widespread *doxa* to such an extent that it can insidiously pervade the adult education field, rendering the kind of provision of which it will form part of 'learning for domestication', to adopt another Freire phrase.

It is against this global scenario and underlying tenets of international policy documents that any university LLL initiatives can be viewed. Drawing on Gramsci's elaboration of hegemony, I cling to the view that institutions, such as the EU, which furnish us with policy guidelines, are not monolithic. Echoing Foucault, one can keep in mind that there is no power without resistance, although this resistance is never external to the power structure itself:

> Where there is power, there is resistance, and yet, or rather consequently, this resistance is never in a position of exteriority in relation to power. Should it be said that one is always 'inside' power, there is no 'escaping' it, there is no absolute outside where it is concerned…? (Foucault, 1990, p. 95)

There can therefore be no illusion that the struggle for renegotiation and change within universities, as with other institutions for that matter, is straightforward, fraught as the struggle is with contradictions. Likewise, Gramsci would argue that hegemonic structures contain within them spaces wherein the very same hegemonic arrangements can be contested, challenged and gradually transformed. The same proviso made as a result of Foucault's insight would apply.

For this very reason, it is important to see how EU universities embrace and reconstruct the dominant LLL policy discourse, possibly *reinventing* it for non-reductionist educational ends, more so given that these HE institutions are increasingly dependent on EU funding.

The overemphasis on work, employability and ICT indicates that the contemporary discourse is far removed from a broad conception of education that takes on board the different multiple subjectivities found in each individual. The discourse still gravitates around the notion of a knowledge economy which, as certain research from Canada shows (Lavoie and Roy, 1998), is not the 'reality' people are made to believe it is. In Europe, this view of LLL is particularly fuelled through ESF funding on which many organisations in adult learning are increasingly becoming dependent. It is a discourse that, as argued in this chapter and the ones to follow, limits human beings to being consumers and producers, the two sides of Marcuse's (1964) one-dimensional man. This stands in contrast to a discourse that expands the conception to embrace a more holistic view of persons who have the skills to engage critically and collectively in the public sphere and not only *in* but also *with* the work process.

This latter type of engagement recalls and perhaps underlines the need to revitalise that longstanding and historically rich tradition of adult education known as workers' education. In my view, this area represents one of the richest dimensions of the field. Connected to university LLE provision, especially through such agencies as the Oxford Delegacy for Extra-Mural Studies, it was rich enough to attract quite a range of leading twentieth-century UK-based intellectuals. These included Raymond Williams, Richard Hoggart and Edward P. Thompson. They engaged in and wrote about the field. They wrote not of 'employability' but of employee empowerment and access to various types of knowledge that allows them to develop beyond being simply producers and consumers, these days, to becoming social actors, fully capable of contributing, individually and most likely collectively, to changing the world around them (Martin, 2001).

Really and critical active citizenship

This would entail a notion of citizenship that can be called 'really and critical active citizenship', embracing the 'collective' (in the sense of people working and acting together, complementing each other). This stands in contrast to the notion of the atomised individual citizen that is often promoted by the dominant discourses surrounding citizenship. As I shall show, this notion is prominent in the policy discourse concerning university LLL. The hegemonic view of atomised individuals and citizens is evident, for example, in the competitive nature of grading, ranking and final certification and in the notion of student performance as individualistic. I am here referring to the idea of atomised individuals who facilitate *governmentality*, in Foucault's sense of the term. 'Governmentality' refers to the state's production of citizen behaviour according to its policies, fostering mindsets and practices that allow subjects to be governed 'at a distance' (English and Mayo, 2012, p. 28).

Many of the issues being faced throughout society call for coordinated collective actions involving both ICT and the streets and squares, as the numerous demonstrations in Greece and other parts of Europe, as well as many parts of the Arab world, have shown, albeit not necessarily attaining the desired outcomes (the struggle remains an ongoing one). They are also public, and not simply individual, issues that entail social responsibilities and coordinated social action.

As the literature on this kind of action has shown time and time again, this ongoing social engagement entails constant learning and relearning – a notion of LLL that constitutes a refreshing alternative to the one that prevails in the dominant discourse (Wain, 2004; Williamson, 1998; Livingstone, 2013; Mayo, 2017a). It is a type of LLL that has been occurring for years but which has not always been recognised as such. It is one that is inextricably intertwined with ongoing popular struggles for the creation, safeguarding and enhancing of genuinely democratic spaces. Some of the more exciting projects of university involvement, mainly through socially committed academics or clusters of academics, outside the institution's hallowed walls and within communities (e.g., initiatives by University of Seville academics in the preparatory work among citizens for a participatory budget), were carried out with this goal in mind.

The UN conceptualisation: a more holistic approach

In short, a more holistic notion of LLL is being called for. This is very much in synch with the UN's Sustainable Development Goals (SDGs). It is heartening to note that LLL features among these goals (UN, 2015) where emphasis is placed on a holistic and bio-centric approach to learning in diverse settings – formal, non-formal and informal. For LLL to be relevant to sustainable development, therefore, it needs to be stripped of its 'mid-1990s +' strictly economic-oriented baggage to resume the kind of broader conceptualisation provided by UNESCO in the 1970s. This is also in need of revitalisation as times have changed since then. For instance, there is the need to move away from a strictly *anthropocentric* worldview. This view is characteristic of the age of modernity, in which a number of LLE writers, gravitating round UNESCO, were steeped. The call, in keeping with the UN SDGs, is to embrace a *bio-centric* worldview. This view would prevent people, shaped by modern science, from conceiving of the world as a machine, and therefore from being inclined to manipulate nature in any way they wished without regard for the non-human world (O'Sullivan, 1999). The alternative worldview is one whereby people learn to develop as ecological selves engaged in not only social relations but also human–earth relations (Hart, 1992). This is the kind of ecologically and community-oriented LLL being called for through not only the UN SDGs but also such earlier declarations of fundamental values as the Earth Charter, in the context of which Freire-inspired 'eco-pedagogy' projects have been developed (see Gadotti, 2010; Kahn, 2010).

The UN's conceptualisation of LLL thus spurs on important providers, such as universities, to not simply satisfy economic 'employability' requirements but also, and more importantly, to address broader democratic and inclusive bio-centric concerns. This continues to justify the struggle to conceive of the university as a seat of holistic LLL (in the old sense of learning at different stages of one's life) which contributes to both the economic and democratic needs of society within the context of sustainable development.

In the next chapter, we shall see that a broader notion of LLL is returning to the agenda for education with respect to what is being heralded as the Fourth Industrial Revolution (4th IR) but with undertones still connected with employability, given the anticipated joblessness that this revolution is likely to bring about. We are told that LLL must, in this context, be linked with creativity, contain a good dose of liberal arts to render people critical thinkers and so forth. Employability remains the recurring purpose of LLL, in keeping with the dominant discourse, although the propagators of the 4th IR are calling for a broad holistic notion of LLL, although one still meant to serve the interests of capital.

Notes

1 As I write in my recent book on *Hegemony and Education under Neoliberalism*, with specific reference to Gramsci's thought (Mayo, 2015), I would interpret this concept as referring to a situation in which most arrangements, constituting a particular social reality, are *conditioned* by and tend to support the interests of a particular class or social grouping. Hegemony incorporates not only processes of ideological influence and contestation but, as Raymond Williams (1976, p. 205; 1977, p. 110) argues, a 'whole body of practices and expectations'. Note that I use the word *conditioned* instead of *determined* to allow for that sense of agency necessary for change to occur within the interstices of the hegemonic structure itself. This applies to university and other educational institutions, none of which are monolithic. One can work 'in and against' them, tactically inside

but strategically outside. This is based on the recognition, highlighted by Gramsci and others, that hegemony is never complete, the ensemble of relations it contains are open to negotiation and renegotiation, hence my choice of *conditioned* to avoid giving hegemony an over-deterministic weight.

2 There are those such as Rosa Maria Torres (2013) who have presented LLE/LLL as a Western concept detrimental to the concerns of Latin American adult and youth education.

3 The reference here is to the 1973 coup in Chile.

4 Freire emphasised the collective dimension of learning based on the notion, well explained in *Pedagogy of the Oppressed* (Freire, 1970, 2000), that one does not really liberate oneself on one's own; genuine liberation can only take place in concert with others, hence his emphasis on the collective dimension of learning. My modifications of earlier writings of mine with regard to the old UNESCO discourse on LLE and the collective were inspired by a conversation I had with my colleague, friend and former teacher, Kenneth Wain.

5 Outgoing president of the European Commission José Manuel Durão Barroso stated, in an October 2014 address to an EU conference on poverty, that, rather than decrease, the poverty (relative and absolute) figure in the EU, then standing at 80 million, is likely to reach 100 million by 2020.

6 This 'financial literacy' drive is also increasingly viewed with suspicion for its 'blaming the victim' connotations (see English and Mayo, 2012, p. 33).

3

The EU's HE discourse and the challenges of globalisation[1]

Introduction

In this chapter, I shall focus on particular aspects of the discourse and its implications for HE settings as promoted by one of the supranational organisations (the EU), which, again in the words of Roger Dale, helps create a 'globally structured agenda for education' (Dale, 2000). The discursive contexts in which higher education policies are formulated include the Lisbon Objectives (EC, 2000; CEC, 2005) and the Bologna Process (Confederation of EU Rectors' Conferences and Association of European Universities 2000), as well as a series of communications by the Commission of the European Communities (CEC) and the European Council (EC). Some implications of this discourse for HE and a LLL HE market are drawn out.

Policy discourse

The EU's discourse with regard to HE has been developed and consolidated over a number of years and in a series of communiqués and related documents, primarily those that follow up on the agreement of the European Councils of Lisbon (2000) and Barcelona (2002) to:

- render the EU the most 'competitive' and 'dynamic knowledge-based economy in the world by 2010';
- render the EU's education and training systems 'a world quality reference' by the same date; and
- 'create a European Research and Innovation Area' (EC, 2000).

The documents deal with a variety of interrelated areas, notably lifelong learning (CEC, 2001a), mobility (CEC, 2004), cooperation with third countries (CEC, 2001b), the role of universities in the 'Europe of Knowledge' (CEC, 2003), brain-power mobilisation (CEC, 2005), knowledge society (EC, 2006a), internationalisation (CEC, 2006a),[2] modernisation (CEC, 2006a), quality assurance (EC, 2006c), innovation and creativity (CEC, 2008), governance (Education and Culture DG, 2008) and HE university–business cooperation (EC, 2008), among others.

A number of keywords emerge from these and other related documents, as well as documents by agencies that dwell on the implications of these policy directions, such as the Council for Industry and Higher Education (Brown, 2007) and the League of European Research Universities (LERU, 2006). The keywords include 'knowledge economy', 'competitiveness', 'entrepreneurship', 'lifelong learning', 'access', 'mobility', 'outcomes and performance', 'quality assurance', 'innovation and creativity', 'diversification', 'privatisation', 'internationalisation', 'autonomy' and 'business–HE relationships'.

Once again, the list is not exhaustive but contains the key terminology on which the EU's HE discourse rests. I shall now unpack a number of these terms before critically analysing their implications for this specific sector of educational provision. The key terms and phrases in the dominant discourse, concerning the changing nature of universities in this day and age, suggest a role markedly different from what had been attributed to the often-invoked 'Humboldt tradition', an 'invented' tradition that has been referred to as a 'myth' (Ash, 2008, p. 41) and which, in its original conception, differs considerably from what certain EU documents present as the tradition as it is being interpreted these days: a university graduate being also a researcher to function adequately in the knowledge economy (see Simons, 2006) or a university student being a client to whom a service is provided rather than being part of a university community of scholars. In fact, a European Commission 2003 document dealing with the role of the universities in the 'Europe of Knowledge' is explicit in this regard, thus contradicting other documents by the same institution referred to by Maarten Simons (2006):

> European universities have for long modelled themselves along the lines of some major models, particularly the ideal model of university envisaged nearly two centuries ago by Wilhelm von Humboldt in his reform of the German university, which sets research at the heart of university activity and indeed makes it the basis of teaching. Today the trend is away from these models, and towards greater differentiation. (CEC 2003, pp. 5–6)

The trend is towards a differentiated model centring on a 'knowledge society', rather than 'knowledges society' (I will take this up later; see de Sousa Santos, 2017, p. 234), and 'knowledge-based economy' (CEC, 2005), the latter a much-used concept, often attributed to Peter Drucker.[3] As I have shown, the concept lies at the heart of the Lisbon Treaty. It is the key concept set to place the continent's education and training systems at the forefront of this bold EU attempt to compete with the rising economic forces in Asia and the USA and those of transnational corporations. And HE institutions are implicated in this process,[4] with their triple helix of education, research and innovation serving as the means for Europe to compete on high 'value-added' terms – technology refinement and take up, cross-border association and the sustainment of complex communities (Marginson and van der Wende, 2007, p. 7). The 'knowledge economy' and its related 'knowledge society' are therefore the central all-embracing concepts in the EU's discourse concerning education, training and culture,[5] and particularly its HE discourse (Dale and Robertson 2002, p. 28). They appear throughout the major EU documents. The following statement sums up the importance of the 'knowledge economy' concept and the particular framework for education in which it is enshrined: 'Investment in human capital though is one of the key factors for strengthening Europe's position in the knowledge economy and to increasing social cohesion in the twenty-first century' (EC, 2006a, p. 26). The economic-oriented discourse[6] regarding education and HE renders *de rigueur* the use of another important concept: that of competitiveness. Universities are meant to compete in the marketplace of knowledge. The constant references to university classifications (Rust and Kim, 2015) such as those coming out of Shanghai or Spain, or through Thomson-Reuters are indicative of one aspect of competitiveness, that which occurs among universities. Reference is here made to the arguable, although consulted, World University Rankings as produced by Jiao Tong University's Institute of Higher Education in Shanghai, the Times Higher Education Supplement rankings or the Webometrics Ranking of World Universities compiled by the Cybermetrics Lab (Centre for Scientific Information and Documentation, CINDOC), which is a unit of the National Research Council of Spain.

There is, however, another side to competitiveness that ties in with the concept of the knowledge economy, namely that of contributing to the creation of a dynamic economy (CEC, 2005). In arguably its major communiqué regarding the way universities should function in this day and age, the European Commission makes 'competitiveness' a key operative word. We are told at the outset that: 'at the informal meeting at Hampton Court in October 2005, Research and Development and universities were acknowledged as foundations of European competitiveness' (CEC 2006a, p. 2), which is indicative of the overall tenor of the communiqué. In fact, the European Students' Union concluded their reaction to the document by stating that there is more to a modern university than the ability to contribute to a competitive global economy (ESIB, 2006, p. 3) to indicate the extent to which the discourse of competitiveness pervaded this and, I would add, other EU documents concerning HE, as well as documents that draw and elaborate on the EU discourse (e.g., Brown, 2007). Competitiveness is advocated across and within universities and among academics and students themselves. Classifications such as Google Scholar rankings within universities and within specific domains might be contributing to this process.

With the focus on competitiveness and knowledge economy, it is hardly surprising that, as stated in the previous chapter, the discourse on lifelong learning, the key term and concept from the EU's lexicon discussed in this book, differs considerably from that originally propounded by UNESCO in the late 1960s. We have seen, earlier, how the concept of lifelong learning, as adopted by the EU, is closely tied to the idea of a knowledge-based economy and is similar to that of the OECD (1996, 2007).

In its *Memorandum on Lifelong Learning* (CEC, 2000) the Commission posits, at the outset, that:

The conclusions of the Lisbon European Council confirm that the move towards lifelong learning must accompany a successful transition to a knowledge-based economy and society. Therefore, Europe's education and training systems are at the heart of the coming changes. They, too, must adapt.[7]

Later in the same document, when outlining the vision for valuing learning specifically within a lifelong and life-wide learning perspective, the Commission states: 'In the knowledge economy, developing and using human resources to the full is a decisive factor in maintaining competitiveness' (p. 15). I have shown, in the previous chapter, that the economic-oriented tenor of this document is highlighted by Bauman (2005, 2013), Wain (in Borg and Mayo, 2004) and Borg and Mayo (2006). Specifically regarding HE, the Commission states that 'development of entrepreneurial, management and innovation skills should become an integral part of graduate education, research training and lifelong learning strategies for university staff' (CEC, 2006a, p. 6).

The overall discussions and references to lifelong learning deal with other issues that are relevant to the EU's discourse regarding HE, including those of access, notably access of school leavers without formal qualifications but who learn through alternative routes (CEC, 2003, p. 9), access of women to science and technology (CEC, 2003, p. 19) and access to HE of people of different ages, including older adults (CEC, 2006a, p. 7).

In addition, the contribution expected of universities to lifelong learning strategies leads them gradually to widen the conditions of access to this area of tuition (in particular to allow access to those not coming through the route of upper secondary education), through better recognition of skills acquired outside university and outside formal education (CEC, 2003, p. 9).

This reflects one aspect of 'social Europe' that contrasts with the apparently neoliberal tenor of some of its other discourses.[8] The concern with breaking barriers to access highlights another aspect of EU policy and its discourse on education, notably that of mobility. Programmes such as Erasmus, Leonardo and Socrates and actions such as Grundtvig, now subsumed under the Lifelong Learning Programme, have allowed and continue to allow the possibility for student and teacher/academic exchanges throughout Europe (CEC, 2004). For this mobility to occur, standards are to be safeguarded and the need for quality assurance is emphasised – this is often defined as outcomes-based (see Education and Culture DG, 2008). Furthermore, a certain degree of harmonisation and a smooth credit transfer system need to be in place. The overall emphasis in the discourse on mobility (CEC, 2004), outcomes and transfer (Confederation of EU Rectors' Conferences and Association of European Universities, 2000) is linked to the notion of 'Europeanisation' – a Europe without barriers – also in the HE field.

'Europeanisation' that entails strategies for a greater network of collaboration, including student and academic exchanges throughout an entire continent is, however, to be distinguished from that other term that forms part of the contemporary EU *doxa* for HE, namely that of 'internationalisation' (Marginson, 2007). According to Simon Marginson (2007), Europeanisation

> has one set of origins in the growth of international mobility of people and ideas; another set of origins in the international cooperation between EU countries in

their economic, social and cultural activities; and a third set of origins in the explicit commitment to a common European higher education zone in order to facilitate such international activities within Europe. At the same time international cooperation in higher education is expected to enhance the global competitiveness of Europe as a whole.

Access and mobility are now to occur beyond European or strictly EU borders as part of the drive towards competitiveness with respect to universities in the USA, as clearly indicated in 2004 by Jan Figel, the then EU commissioner for education, training, culture and multiligualism (Figel, 2006, p. 4). The quest to render European universities visible on the world stage, in keeping with the quest for a much-desired supremacy in the global knowledge economy, led to schemes in which partnerships are established with 'third countries', including those in Latin America through the Alfa programme (CEC, 2001b, p. 6). However, this drive is being intensified to attract more non-EU fee-paying students to European universities (CEC, 2006a, p. 10) and thus compete with the USA, which has hitherto enjoyed the lion's share of foreign student recruitment and whose universities and research institutions surpass those of Europe in attracting 'top level' students and researchers (CEC, 2003, p. 21).

This immediately raises the issue of 'diversification', a key term in the EU discourse on HE. There is talk of diversification of students in terms of age (lifelong learning), EU nationals from different countries (through mobility structures) and students from outside the EU. It is argued that there should be diversification of provision throughout the HE system itself, diversification of universities and other HE institutions. Some institutions are meant to be 'big league' players serving as world-class research institutions, some are meant to be purely teaching institutions while others are meant to have a regional focus; that is to say, to gear their teaching and research to regional development needs. The EC communiqué of 2006 states explicitly that not all institutions need to strike the same balance between education and research (CEC, 2003, p. 18; 2006a, p. 4). Jan Figel was, however, less prudent in the way he made the same point in his then capacity as EU commissioner for higher education:

> In the US, the huge levels of research funding are overwhelming[ly] concentrated on around 100 research intensive universities and fewer than 250 institutions award postgraduate degrees… Europe's universities should be allowed to diversify and specialise: some must be able to play in the major league, but others should concentrate on regional or local needs and perhaps more on teaching. (Figel 2006, p. 7)

The discourse points to a scenario smacking of a hotel star classification system (Borg, 2005, p. 31). The diversification, however, does not end there. The biggest source of diversification is the existence of public and private institutions in an HE market, even though the distinction is rarely clear cut. There is a strong element of hybridisation as funding policies, including those of the national or federal state, often serve to sustain the market. Private universities benefit through state funding policies, with students eligible for scholarships and other funding. So-called private universities like Oxford and Cambridge are said to provide a public good.

Also Scott (2007) argues that although there are private HE institutions in Britain, they are incorporated in what he calls a nationalised system of HE through a series of nationally imposed classifications, methods of evaluation and quality assurance mechanisms. In Italy, for instance, any private university that is approved of by the Ministry of Education, Universities and Research (MIUR) is considered to be and designated as public and receives funding from the state and communal and regional entities. The total funding for private universities by the state amounts to 14.3 per cent when compared to the 73 per cent allocated to state universities.[9] The same applies to certain Catholic universities, such as the biomedical Catholic campus in Rome and the Catholic medical school San Raffaele in Milan. In contexts such as these, the relationship between public and private is complex. The issue of privatisation concerns not only the nature of some of the universities that play their part in the market but also the sources of funding provided to both public/private institutions. A document on governance by the Education and Culture DG (2008) demonstrates the way different funding strategies are being pursued and refers to the promotion of diversification in this regard, with reference to loans, donations and contract research.

The major emphasis that can be seen in the EU's HE discourse is the forging of university–business partnerships. In 2008, the first European Forum on cooperation between higher education and the business community took place (CEC, 2008). The communication on the modernisation of universities and HE institutes underlines the importance of a 'structured partnership with the business community', although this comes with the rider that 'the public mission and overall social and cultural remit of European universities must be preserved' (CEC, 2006a, p. 6).

This partnership is meant to create opportunities for the sharing of research results, intellectual property rights, patents and licences, and allow for placements of students and researchers in business, thus enhancing the career prospects at all stages of the students' career and creating a better match between HE outputs and job requirements. It also can help convey, according to the communication, a stronger sense of 'entrepreneurship' (Maniglio, 2018, p. 146), another key HE term that is intended to enable persons to contribute effectively to the competitive economic environment described earlier (CEC 2006a, 2006b; EC 2006b).[10]

> Entrepreneurship refers to an individual's ability to turn ideas into action. It includes creativity, innovation and risk taking, as well as the ability to plan and manage projects in order to achieve objectives. This supports everyone in day-to-day life at home and in society, makes employees more aware of the context of their work and better able to seize opportunities, and provides a foundation for entrepreneurs establishing a social or commercial activity. (CEC, 2006b, p. 4)

The area of business–HE (including university), partnerships, in which entrepreneurship is exalted as a highly prized virtue, has characterised the HE scenario in the country often identified as the EU's major competitor in the field – the USA – as the writings of Henry Giroux and associates have indicated (Giroux and Searls Giroux, 2004; Giroux, 2007, 2014b). With respect to the USA, Commissioner

Figel points out that Europe lags behind the USA in terms of the GDP percentage spent on HE but points out that the difference 'consists pretty much entirely of private funding' (Figel, 2006, p. 4). In 2014, HE expenditure within the EU member states ranged from one fifth to one third of total educational expenditure.[11] In 2014, the average public expenditure on HE relative to GDP for the EU-28 was 1.3 per cent.[12]

The issues of entrepreneurship and economic success in a global competitive environment place the emphasis, as indicated in the above definition of the former term, on creativity and innovation, two more keywords in the EU discourse with obvious ramifications for HE provision. Creativity is considered by the Commission as a ' "driver" for entrepreneurial and social competences' (CEC, 2008, p. 5). Documents focusing on this aspect of the EU discourse – creativity – were produced in the buildup to 2009, which was designated the year of creativity. The competences involved include 'mathematical competence and basic competences in science and technology', 'digital competence', 'learning to learn', 'social and civic competences', 'sense of initiative and entrepreneurship' and 'cultural awareness and expression' (CEC, 2008, p. 2). The emphasis on maths, science and technology is in keeping with the discourse of the Lisbon objectives (Vella, 2005). The issue of innovation is taken up in a study by the League of European Research Universities (LERU, 2006). This study compares the way research is used in Europe with the way it is made use of in the USA and Asia. It is argued that better use of research is made in the USA and Asia than in Europe. The study underlines the discourse of competitiveness in a global economy, which is the EU's main discourse with regard to HE. All the other concepts in the EU discourse in the area tend to stem from there.

Critical analysis of the EU discourse on higher education

Migration of policies

The discussion thus far has been at a general level. Yet what renders the whole process interesting is the manner in which policies migrate to countries within the EU fold or others that have strong ties to the EU. There is a whole process of lending and borrowing taking place (Sultana, 2008) and adjustments have to be made depending on context. The issue of internationalisation strikes me as being one area where adjustments are made in the policy migration process. And it is here where the hegemony of English (see Macedo et al., 2003; Deem et al., 2008) makes its presence felt. For instance, Finland, like many other EU countries, sought to substantially increase its percentage of foreign students studying in the country. This required Finnish universities and other HE institutions to teach more courses in English. A development plan by the Ministry of Education set this process in motion (Kaiser et al., 2006, p. 16). English is already taken for granted in the neighbouring country of Sweden, which therefore places emphasis on non-English modern languages in its HE admission decisions. Portugal, by contrast, seeks to internationalise by virtue of two policy strategies: universities can offer courses and students can take exams in a language other than Portuguese, while national universities are encouraged to offer joint degrees with foreign universities, something that other EU universities are doing (the University of Malta offers joint Master's degrees with American universities, including degrees in conflict resolution with George Mason University), especially through the Erasmus Mundus joint Master degree programme, another means of internationalisation.

Where the system is very variegated, however, the transfer of policy becomes more complicated. Take the situation in Germany, where a 1994 constitutional change favours the Lander as opposed to the Federal government in certain policies. This renders German HE more diverse and less easy to monitor (Kaiser et al., 2006, p. 28). Meanwhile in France, the Bologna Process brought about a change among universities in terms of offering a three-cycle system of Licentiate, Master's and doctorate. This policy did not transfer, however, to the Grandes Écoles, which have persevered in their own way of doing things and of developing their own curricula (Chevallier and Paul, 2007, p. 162).

The other issue that comes into play when discussing policy migration between EU countries is the weight of tradition or, as Jussi Valimaa (2007) calls it, the traditions and historical layers in the HE system and universities. These are not extinguished easily and have a bearing on the type of interaction between the novel or the recently imported and the old. Valimaa indicates how new policies imported in Finland from the EU and elsewhere will need to be modified in a manner that reconciles these policies with other policies that have a longer history in the country.

Other recent traditions had to give way in view of anomalies caused by the issue of student mobility. The case of Austria and its open admissions policy stands out here. Because German students found it easier to enter Austrian universities than their own German ones, a change had to be brought about, in accordance with the EU Treaty, to the Austrian regulations regarding admission to universities – *Universitätsgesetz*. Additional exams before and during studies are now mandatory for all students irrespective of their origin (Kaiser et al., 2006, p. 13).

The foregoing examples are indicative of the complexity of the policy transfer issue within the EU. Many exogenous and indigenous factors come into play and, in certain contexts, it could well turn out to be a case of old habits die hard, as in the case of the Grandes Écoles.

Neoliberal tenor?

Much of the tenor of the discourse concerning universities in Europe, as captured in many of the keywords in the EU's HE documents, is neoliberal, which constitutes the major ideology underlining hegemonic globalisation. This discourse, admittedly, must also be viewed alongside the official discourse of 'social Europe' as manifest in the concepts of 'active citizenship' and 'social cohesion'. The neoliberal tenor exalts the market and has turned education from being conceived of as simply a public good into also becoming a consumption service. Higher education is no exception. Higher education is being regarded as a terrain increasingly characterised by privatisation, profit-making and competitiveness. It is an ideology that is gradually leading to the 'businessification' (Allen et al., 1999) of HE, although perhaps not yet on the lines already manifest in the USA, where universities are being corporatised and the knowledge they produce and disseminate is being commodified (Giroux and Searls Giroux, 2004), even sold *en bloc* to other universities.[13]

The triple helix

The much-augured forging of links between universities, other HE institutes and business, with a view to providing a better match between degrees and jobs, between research and the imperatives of a 'knowledge-intensive' economy, besides the implication by a former EU commissioner that privatisation can be the one factor that can enable Europe to bridge the gap with the USA in terms of GDP expenditure on HE, suggest that the European HE sector is being driven down the business route. The extent to which a specific EU member state would pursue this route will probably be conditioned by the politics of the government at the helm. Some favouring a 'third way' politics are likely to contribute to the creation of a 'competition state' HE market scenario involving private and public provision or hybridisation with respect to both. Other ideas include those of then Minister Mariastella Gelmini in 2008, when Berlusconi was still premier of Italy. It was suggested that Italian universities consider becoming private foundations (Ballio, 2008; ESIB, 2008), a suggestion that, coupled with the announcement of cutbacks in the Italian elementary school system, led to a reaction on Italian campuses (ESIB, 2008) and in the Italian press regarding the demise of the university 'as we once knew it'.

A shake up?

Whatever the 'take up' in different member states, we are confronted by a discourse that can have the merit of trying to shake up the HE education sector in various parts of Europe to, among other things, enable it to rid itself of some of its traditional shackles.

There have been allegations of nepotism (Calabro, 2008; Viviano, 2008) and 'feudal systems' (Carlucci, 2008) in the university system of certain countries. Ask any young doctoral graduate in Italy seeking to break into the country's university system. The word 'feudale' (feudal) immediately comes up, as many such graduates seek pastures new abroad, jobs in Italian universities being thin on the ground. The European discourse, however, reflects the EU's general position regarding education and the so-called knowledge economy. It is a discourse that continues to be vocational, in which much of what is valued as learning is narrowly competence-based (Batini, 2008; Mayo, 2008; Surian, 2008) and tied to economic interests, reminiscent of Message 4 of the EU's Memorandum on Lifelong

Learning (Bauman, 2005, 2013; Wain, in Borg and Mayo 2004, p. 22; Borg and Mayo, 2006).

HE business partnership

The emphasis on a structured partnership between HE and business tends to undermine the notion of autonomy that is given importance in the EU's discourse concerning HE. It seems as though the concern is with freeing academic autonomy from the shackles of government bureaucracy to allow institutions the flexibility necessary to compete in the global HE marketplace on the basis of knowledge, research and innovation. It seems, however, that what applies to the state does not apply to business. The European Students' Union rightly argues that 'The call for an increase in private funding puts university autonomy under siege' and can lead to a 'situation where the need for private financing imposes a research agenda on the university, directed by the business community' (ESIB, 2006). The students' union sees this as 'more than conflicting with striving to ensure real autonomy'. The conflict has become more evident these days as new layers of administration, comprising people external to the universities, are being imposed, a point to be highlighted further on (Elkjaer, 2017).

Shift in power

For all the talk of safeguarding universities and HE institutions from bureaucratic constraints, recent practice in universities both in North America and Europe has led to a shift in power from the academic sector to the bureaucratic sector, not least because of the requirements among EU member countries of harmonisation processes, the obsession with Lyotard's notion of 'performativity' (everything to be translated into easily measured outcomes) and other modes of conforming to the Bologna Process.

This too impinges on the university's autonomy. For, as Pablo Gentili (2001) points out:

> It has been widely noted that evaluative processes generate funding priorities that – as they reward 'the best' and punish 'the worst' – themselves turn into powerful normative criteria. These become a kind of unofficial curriculum, which regulates and strongly influences the pedagogical decision making of educational institutions. Evaluations, in this case, not only 'evaluate'; they also establish criteria for planning and goals which must be implemented and met in order to avoid punitive measures in the future.

Knowledge economy?

Furthermore, the current emphasis on the need for a 'knowledge economy' has been perceived, in certain quarters, as an attempt by private enterprise and industry to construct a 'skills crisis' in Europe rather than admit to a 'jobs crisis'

(Marshall, 1997, 59). Higher education is therefore expected to respond to this 'skills crisis'. The Canadian sociologist, D. W. Livingstone (2013) provides data from his own country that support the criticism concerning a misplacement of emphasis (substituting a jobs crisis with a skills crisis) and challenges the claims of those celebrating the arrival of the 'knowledge-based economy'. Drawing on a report by Lavoie and Roy (1998), Livingstone writes:

> In spite of fairly rapid growth over this period, knowledge workers still made up less than 10 percent of the labour force in 1996. While details of this occupational classification may be disputed, it is clear that the vast majority of the Canadian labour force continued to be employed in jobs that require fairly routinized transmission of data, processing of goods or provision of personal services. (Livingstone, 2013, p. 39)

He argues that the presence of a learning society is not supported by compelling empirical evidence to convince one of the existence of a knowledge economy. This vision is also not matched by the necessary concomitant economic reforms 'that address basic dimensions of work reform, including the *redistribution of paid work time* to reduce current polarization and the *democratization of paid work* to give more workers' greater opportunities to apply their extensive acquired knowledge' (Livingstone, 2013, p. 50, emphasis in original). In addition to the above strictures, we have the ever-increasing issue of the 'credential society', in Randall Collins' terminology (Collins, 1979). Credentialism, as is well known in educational sociology circles, entails holding qualifications, such as certificates, diplomas and degrees, to be eligible for employment in certain areas. We are, however, facing situations when youngsters are complaining that they hold more qualifications than their parents did but cannot enjoy or even hope to enjoy their standards of living (English and Mayo, 2012, p. 119). Even Brown, Lauder and Ashton (2010) challenge the commonplace view that the acquisition of more education, and therefore credentials, is conducive to greater individual and national prosperity. Drawing on secondary documented sources they highlight 'the global competition for rewarding, middle-class jobs. They write about what constitutes "an auction for cut-priced brainpower" sustained by an explosion of higher education worldwide' (English and Mayo, 2012, p. 80). They make reference to growing economies such as those of China and India. It is argued that these economies are conditioning a world economic labour market 'characterised by the provision of a new global high-skill, low-wage workforce that is leading to a paucity of good, financially rewarding jobs' (English and Mayo, 2012, p. 80).

We are told that '[t]he struggle for these few jobs will leave many highly qualified people disappointed having to make do with underemployment, precarious living conditions and possibly poverty' (English and Mayo, 2012, p. 80). All this must be considered in addition to the 'credential inflation' as a result of which the price of labour involved diminishes or the diploma-holder has to make do with underemployment, especially in contexts when family concerns make it difficult to move elsewhere.

Transfer of skills

In a discussion of the Memorandum on Lifelong Learning and the documentation of examples of best practice with regard to this document, attention was drawn to 'the intimation that the skills required for success in the market economy are the same skills necessary for active citizenship' (Borg and Mayo, 2006, p. 23). I now draw attention to the intimation, regarding the linkage of creativity, entrepreneurship and innovation, that the qualities and skills required for social life are those required for economic success and vice versa. After all, the then commissioner for education, training, culture and multilingualism argued, in 2006, that 'the competences required by the jobs of the future are very much the same as those required by the citizens of the future' (Figel, 2006, p. 3), thus echoing the point just made regarding LLL.

Internationalisation

Perhaps the most serious recommendation made in arguably the most important communiqué from the Commission with regard to the modernisation of universities and HE institutions (CEC, 2006a) concerns the much-augured process of internationalisation. We witnessed a whole series of communications leading to this, starting with the communication concerning third countries (CEC, 2003). International students from outside the EU are meant to enhance the universities' and HE systems' stature in the world. They are also intended to provide the cash (generally exorbitant foreign fees charged by 'big league' players), which will enable European universities to compete with their USA counterparts, such fees becoming a significant source of revenue and foreign exchange. Universities and HE institutions are being encouraged to compete in a lucrative world-student market and increase their share of the takings. In a world characterised by the constant flow of labour and prospective labour from South to North, European universities could well be creating barriers, especially financial ones, for access to universities by migrants and their offspring. Furthermore, they could well be contributing towards the Third World and Eastern European 'brain drain' by possibly creaming off that small percentage of foreign students who, for a variety of reasons, fail to return to their country of origin.

Access in a social Europe

Access becomes an important issue here and it is laudable that much importance is attached to breaking down barriers for women, minorities and traditionally disenfranchised groups to enter HE institutions and pursue courses in the much-heralded areas of maths, science and technology. It is also laudable that importance is given to the universities' and HE's extension and short-course programmes in keeping with the spirit of LLE. It is equally laudable that the EU places emphasis on broadening access to HE institutions among school leavers. This has positive implications for reforms within the secondary and higher secondary school systems, reforms intended to do away with or minimise stiff selection processes and streaming (Borg, 2005, p. 32) purported to be based on meritocracy when, in effect, they constitute a process of social selection. To my mind, this is the most noteworthy aspect of many of the communications when viewed from the perspective of social equality and justice, which once again attests to the existence of a 'social Europe'.

With regard to women, however, the discourse is restricted to career advancement and individual mobility (Morley, 2008) – very much a traditional liberal-bourgeois concept. There is little about reconfiguring universities and other HE institutions to become inclusive of different ways of knowing, including women's ways of knowing (Barr, 1999; Belenky et al., 1986) – transforming them from patriarchal bastions into more gender- and ethnically inclusive institutions. It would be this inclusivity that would be a key element that would allow universities and HE to play their part in the development of a substantive democracy.

The public sphere

It is the *leitmotif* throughout this book that one way in which universities can engage in a meaningful process of access is by re-conceiving of their role as not simply being there to boost the economy, 'knowledge-intensive' or otherwise, but also to contribute to a regeneration of democracy and the public sphere (Giroux and Searls Giroux, 2004). In keeping with the EU's promotion of the concept of 'active citizenship', not one in which the individual is reduced to the intertwined roles of producer-consumer as mentioned earlier, we require institutions that support the efforts of those who have traditionally been swimming against the current. They seek ways and means of extending their roles as educators outside the university. They seek to build alliances with activists and popular educators in the wider communities, among youth, children and adults, doing such work against all odds and in the face of much risk. This community involvement is rarely rewarded in department reviews or, for instance, the previous research assessment exercise replaced by the present REF (Sayer, 2015) in Britain, despite the fact that 'contribution to the community' is listed as one of the criteria for promotion in a number of universities worldwide.

We often come across attempts by academics and educators, working inside and outside the academy (tactically inside and strategically outside?), who act beyond the traditionally perceived boundaries of their work, culture and social location to join forces with others (on whose terms?) in the quest for a substantive democracy. This is an aspect that I shall deal with further on this work. Engaging communities is a valuable if often obscured aspect of university LLL engagement. In small countries such as the one where I was born and raised, and still live, the community expects this engagement. The sense of *gemeinschaft* remains strong. Engaging with and in communities also provides academics committed to social justice, ecological sustainability and to the idea of knowledge as being there to be co-investigated and shared with others, with a greater sense of coherence – to 'walk the talk'. It lends further meaning to the concept of critical pedagogue. Issues concerning community education and action, and relations between 'insider' and 'outsider', with respect to community engagement, will be discussed in this book's penultimate chapter.

Conclusion

It is my contention that a substantive democracy would be ill-served by an HE discourse seeking to separate teaching from research and therefore undermine *praxis*, as suggested in certain EU circles. *Praxis* (Brookfield, 2005) is not to be confused with *practice* but involves reflection upon action for transformative change. Freire adopted *praxis* as his central philosophical and pedagogical concept (Gadotti, 1996). It is the key pedagogical vehicle for the process of 'coming into critical consciousness' or '*conscientização*'. This is the means whereby one can stand back from the everyday world of action to perceive this world in a more critical light. It is the sort of approach from Freire which another critical pedagogue, Ira Shor, calls 'Extraordinarily Re-experiencing the Ordinary' (Shor, 1987, p. 93). Educators and learners need to start from their existential situation. They then engage critically through *praxis*, the obtaining of critical distance, to uncover the underlying contradictions of one's reading of the world, history, specific situations, etc. The stimuli for this can be various: an extraordinary experience, critical questions posed by educators, a codification of aspects of this experience in the form of representative photography, a drawing, a play or a documentary (Freire, 1973). Whichever medium is used or experience is called into question, it must have the potential to allow people to stand back from the world they know in order to view it in a different light, the kind of light that allows for what Mezirow would call a 'perspective transformation' (Mezirow, 1978). There would be potential here, without any guarantees (I follow Stuart Hall's warning here with respect to socialism), for a person to develop a more coherent and therefore critical view of things.

Teaching and research provide some of the means to reflect, in a grounded manner, on what is meant to be taught or is being taught. New research sheds light on things. This allows for a fresh take on the topic or skill at hand. This is why we still need to retain institutions that combine both aspects and not have 'first' and 'second' category institutions, calling themselves a university, specialising in either one or the other or else devoting more time to one than the other. Reaching out to communities should not be divorced from research and teaching as new knowledge emerges and feeds into new research, which then feeds back into the teaching situation itself both in the extension community field and the mainstream. Ideally, teaching, research and community engagement would be inextricably intertwined as each feeds into the other. I shall return to this issue in the penultimate chapter on community engagement.

The discourse of separation of tasks among different types of universities, research and teaching universities, seems to appeal to some, especially status-conscious academics, students and officials. We often hear of the occasional vice-chancellor, in a university with a strong community extension tradition, urging students, administrators and academics, to think 'outside their country' and reach out to the world (read: see themselves as part of an institution seeking to be a 'world university', the much coveted modern day 'world class' university) – a contemporary HE version of *Weltpolitik*?

It is also my contention that such a democracy will be undermined by a discourse reflecting an obsession with the corporatised HE scene in the USA. This seems to suggest that the image of the 'competitor' has been internalised to such an extent, reflected in the constant references to what American universities do in communications by the EU and its commissioners, that one wonders whether it is this very same competitor that is indirectly shaping the discourse for higher education in Europe.

Notes

1 An earlier version of this chapter was published as 'Competitiveness, diversification and the international higher education cash flow: the EU's higher education discourse amidst the challenges of globalisation', *International Studies in Sociology of Education*, 19(2), pp. 87–103. See Mayo (2009). Permission to republish granted automatically by Taylor & Francis. To link to this article: DOI: 10.1080/09620210903257174.

2 See Douglas Proctor and Laura E. Rumbley (2018) for different aspects of internationalisation from outside the dominant English-speaking and Western European perspectives and with respect to next-generation views.

3 People are nowadays talking about a potentially different model with reference to what Klaus Schwab (2016), the chairperson of the World Economic Forum, calls the Fourth Post-Industrial Revolution or 4th IR. This follows on from the 1st IR characterised by steam power, then the 2nd IR just before WWI characterised by electric energy and mass production, the 3rd IR characterised by ICT and electronics and now the 4th IR characterised by a situation when 'the fusion of several technologies is not only automating production, but also knowledge' (Gleason, 2018, p. 2).

4 I find it too early to comment on what shape this 4th IR will take. I maintain a healthy scepticism in this regard. It is said that millions of jobs will be lost the world over to automation, which will have an effect on a variety of services including transport and health. Among the promises made, we are told that HE will change considerably, with open and blended learning already being witnessed, and virtual classrooms and practical work settings being anticipated. It is said that people need to be educated as life-long learners (Gleason, 2018, p. 7) – nothing new in this regard as we have been hearing this mantra for quite a while, as indicated in the previous chapter. The query to pose here is: is LLL, as conceived of here, another form of *responsibilisation* to blame those who are bypassed by this IR?

5 There is also talk, regarding HE in the 4th IR, of the importance of liberal arts (Lewis, 2018) and that a STEM education on its own is not sufficient for the challenges ahead (Gleason, 2018, p. 6). I find this heartening. I would argue that the liberal arts (note the attempt at a globalised American concept rather than 'arts and humanities') and social sciences are to be justified not only in the interest of capital but also for the promised growth in importance of critical thinking which, I would argue, includes

critical consciousness as advocated by Paulo Freire under the rubric of critical literacy (reading the word and the world). This is much needed in a post-truth society. This critical literacy is also necessary to hold to critical scrutiny many of the claims made by those heralding this 'brave new world' of the 4th IR. It is also hoped that public funding will be provided not only for STEM but also for the arts, humanities and social sciences to project this kind of education, as all education for that matter, as a public good. The arts and a liberal education (see Zakaria, 2015) are there to be justified not only in capitalistic terms (à la Sir Kenneth Robinson) but mainly in terms of critical citizenship. Furthermore the promise of more integrated knowledge underscoring connections between areas of enquiry is also welcome especially for the kind of LLL or social engagement programmes advocated in this book. Over-specialisation is fraught with the danger of generating expertise without ethical considerations and without a broader conception of things which, I feel, is a necessary prerequisite for critical consciousness and thinking.

6 We are told, with regard to the 4th IR, that qualifications and education programmes will not be strictly geared towards particular jobs but will have to contain areas that are wide enough to allow for flexible specialisation and skill and knowledge transferability. I consider this a positive thing. It could relieve us of the excessive economic-oriented mantras with which we have been swamped for years. There is also talk of these virtues being key to a sound education: critical thinking, which, as I argued, needs to be broadened to critical consciousness, creativity and use of the imagination, which should include what Gramsci calls the 'popular creative spirit'. There is an emphasis, in the 4th IR discourse, on teamwork and networking, which I would broaden to emphasise the collective dimension of learning and Global North and Global South HE relations. The latter can lead to a symbiosis of different knowledges including Western and indigenous/Southern epistemologies, one side learning from the other. Authors such as Joseph Stiglitz (2002) have argued that the benefits of globalisation have been enjoyed by some and not the majority of the world's population, especially in Southern countries, with the IMF and World Bank wreaking havoc partly because of their lack of transparency. All the different emphases I added to the projections for HE under the 4th IR will be tackled further on in this volume.

7 See the European Parliament and Council Recommendation on Quality Assurance in Higher Education in the Official Journal L64 of 4.3.2006. There have also been consultations in the context of the European Qualifications Framework (CEC, 2006a, p. 10).

8 'Social Europe' is a term used by those who point to an alternative way of doing European politics, one which extends beyond neoliberal market-oriented approaches to include social solidarity measures and safety nets. They often point in this regard to Europe's tradition of social welfare programmes and more recently the Social Charter. There is also a different 'social Europe', which refers to the network of grassroots agencies, movements, etc. that frequently operate outside the state's apparatus – a sort of 'social Europe', or more appropriately a 'social world' from below.

9 I am indebted to Professor Anna Maria Piussi of the University of Verona, for providing me with useful documentation for this point. Cantiere srl – Ufficio Stampa Università IULM.

10 According to Godfrey Baldacchino (2008), people from a selection of small jurisdictions in Europe, many forming part of or being EU member states, did not seem to have honed their entrepreneurial skills through their educational systems.

11 Eurostat Statistics Explained: Educational Expenditure Statistics, http://ec.europa.eu/eurostat/statistics-explained/index.php/Educational_expenditure_statistics.

12 Eurostat Statistics Explained: Tertiary Education Statistics, http://ec.europa.eu/eurostat/statistics-explained/index.php/Tertiary_education_statistics.

13 A recent case is that of De Paul University, Chicago, which sold its curriculum to the newly set up American University of Malta (AUM) run by the Jordanian construction company Sadeen Education Investment Ltd., www.depaulnewsline.com/features/faculty-create-curricula-american-university-malta.

4

Extending the EU's higher education discourse to the rest of the Mediterranean[1]

This chapter builds on the previous one to show how the HE discourse is extending from Europe and specifically the EU to other regions of the world. This chapter focuses on the implications of this discourse specifically for university continuing education in the Euro-Mediterranean, including Turkey and Morocco.

The discussion I carry forward draws on postcolonial theory. I devote special importance to the concept of internationalisation that, as explained in the previous chapter, is seen as an attempt to attract to EU institutions more people from the rest of the Mediterranean (the non-EU part) by attuning them, in their undergraduate work inside their homeland, to the EU mode of HE organisation via the Bologna Process. Issues concerning cultural imperialism are raised in this context.

This chapter refers to the way representatives of higher education systems in the EU make their way to countries in North Africa and elsewhere to influence higher education policies there (e.g., Turkey), spreading the Bologna gospel and earning themselves the tag, by certain Moroccan academics, as the 'Bologna missionaries'. The question that arises is: what effects would such a model have on community outreach programmes in these territories? I am here referring to outreach programmes such as, to provide one example among many, the Al-Quds University programme in Jerusalem concerning the empowerment of women (and not simply through labour market empowerment) within Palestinian society (for further details, see Silwadi and Mayo, 2014).

Union for the Mediterranean

Established in July 2008, the Union for the Mediterranean (UfM),[2] with its secretariat in Barcelona, is an 'intergovernmental organisation bringing together the 28 European Union member states and 15 countries from the Southern and Eastern shores of the Mediterranean'.[3] It was set up with a view to establishing 'a unique forum to enhance regional cooperation and dialogue in the Euro-Mediterranean region'.[4] It 'provides a unique platform to formulate regional priorities and decide on specific cooperation initiatives to be put in place'.[5]

Higher education and research

Among its initiatives is a higher education and research project meant to kindle debates regarding what initiatives ought to be taken in order to develop a common Higher Education and Research Area. A lot of research initiatives have been taking place around the Mediterranean including the development of a number of research journals focusing on the area and the setting up of research networks and societies focusing on different areas of research including comparative education. The idea of a common Higher Education and Research Area is indeed quite interesting. The larger Mediterranean requires some kind of entity that can help sustain projects in the area, although I do have a few concerns regarding what this might entail. The last thing one desires for this area is a new form of cultural imperialism through a higher education discourse from Europe that places emphasis on internationalisation, competitiveness and privatisation, what I have regarded in the previous chapter as the ingredients for a neoliberal framework for higher education and LLL in general.

The EU policy discourse is partly an attempt to provide a modicum of direction for and regulation of universities which have suffered in this part of the world in many ways. Many of the shortcomings of Southern European universities have been highlighted in the national press of several countries, not least being the need to reform what are perceived as archaic structures. Even universities located in the south side of the Mediterranean were judged to be in need of reform. As is often the case in a situation when a 'jobs crisis' is being presented as a 'skills crisis', educational institutions are made the scapegoat, and therefore their renovation or restructuring provides the potential panacea for many existing ills: unemployment, lack of attraction of foreign investment, Islamic radicalisation of youth and so forth. Pressure is placed by the Bretton Woods institutions (IMF, World Bank) on these countries, such as Morocco, to reform their higher education and vocational sectors. These situations make it attractive for Europe to extend its higher education space to incorporate countries from the rest of the Mediterranean. In Turkey, for instance, the Bologna Process is an important reference point in the policy discourses on higher education reconstruction in the country (Gok, 2009).

Some of these countries had indeed served as the venues for 'trial runs' with regard to, say, the Bologna Process (e.g., Morocco), currently being adopted throughout the EU. There is the danger therefore that standardisation and harmonisation become keywords as the so-called 'Bologna gospel' continues to be spread to the rest of the region within the framework of Euro-Mediterranean, or rather EU–non-EU Mediterranean relations. Would these countries, including countries such as Turkey, be allowed to develop their own institutions on their own terms and in synch with the specificities of their own cultures, geographical location and social and economic needs? This would be the challenge for any cooperation in this regard where countries from different sides of the region, EU members or not, are allowed to participate in a process of exchange and policy 'reinvention' on their own terms.

I would argue that simply extending the dominant EU discourse across the Mediterranean would be just another form of Eurocentric domination and invasion. As with the situation concerning the market-driven HE discourse in Europe, I would caution against any project that promotes guidelines characterised by a 'one size fits all' approach, an approach that rides roughshod over different traditions in the interest of harmonisation. One ought to guard against this proposed Mediterranean higher education project becoming the vehicle for the expansion of the European space into North Africa and the eastern Mediterranean, with the universities in these regions simply becoming institutions that internalise the image of their European counterparts (see Sultana, 1999, p. 35) – a higher education institutional version of Frantz Fanon's 'black skin in white masks'? And as I argued in the previous chapter, the European higher education system can, in turn, be a reflection of its competitor's image, that of the USA.

This form of 'cultural invasion' would also give rise to the suspicion that one of the main purposes is to facilitate the process of enticing potential labour power and students towards Europe and its universities. European higher education institutions are being called upon to engage in internationalisation, apart from Europeanisation. Internationalisation entails attracting students from outside the EU fold to EU universities as these universities are being exhorted to compete with their US counterparts in this regard. We have seen how the USA enjoys the lion's share in terms of attracting foreign students. Not only that, but US-style university education has a strong presence throughout the region, with American universities prominent in cities from Cairo and Beirut to Sarajevo, Paris and Rome. Istanbul's Boğaziçi University also has strong USA ties and instruction throughout is in English. This prestigious Turkish public university was founded, in 1863, as Robert College, the first American higher education institution established outside the USA. American schools in Italy, such as the American University in Rome, or overseas campuses of top US universities, such as Johns Hopkins' School of Advanced International Relations, set up in Bologna in 1955, were established, according to a particular interpretation, as a means to extend US influence in the countries.

What renders the US HE influence in the region even stronger is that there is at least one instance of a private university being set up that uses the name American University to denote that the style of operation is American (Scott, 2015). Philip Altbach, a key researcher on higher education and a regular blogger on *Inside Higher Ed*, warned of the danger of 'business interests starting universities to make money using the American brand.' (email reproduced in Scott, 2015). Whatever the motives, universities of this kind continue to render the influence of American-style university education pervasive throughout the Mediterranean. This influence may get even stronger as the heralded USA-driven liberal arts concept (Zakaria, 2015) makes its way into the region, in view of its being attributed great importance with regard to the 4th IR. A lot is being made of the institution for studies in this area set up in Singapore by Yale University and the National University of Singapore (NUS): Yale-NUS College (Lewis, 2018, p. 15); the Mediterranean area can easily follow suit.

It is against this kind of American influence that the EU seems to be competing. International students from outside the EU are being targeted to enhance the European universities' and HE systems' stature in the world. They are also intended to provide the cash that will enable European universities to compete with their USA counterparts, such fees becoming a significant source of revenue and foreign exchange. Universities and HE institutions are being encouraged to compete in a lucrative world-student market and increase their share of the takings (Mayo, 2009). And non-EU Mediterranean countries can prove to be a valuable and sizable market here.

The dominant EU discourse also promotes the idea of diversification. We have seen in the previous chapter how this includes having different types of universities:

1. premier league/*primeira liga* players dedicated to research;
2. teaching universities;
3. regional development universities.

The question that arises is whether there is a need for a separation of this kind. Should teaching be separated from research and international research contributions from regional development issues, so crucial to many parts of the Mediterranean?

Praxis

As indicated in the previous chapter, short shrift seems to be given, by this sort of separation, to a concept that owes its origin to a Mediterranean country, albeit one that lies on the European side of the region. I refer here once again to the ancient Greek concept of *praxis*, which, to repeat, entails action and reflection, theory and practice, none of which ought to be separated. Quite welcome for a few universities in this region would be a higher education project that enables them to provide an effective contribution to the surrounding communities, local, regional or national, without losing their international vocation as producers and disseminators of knowledge.

The other major issue that emerges from the EU discourse, as well as the larger global neoliberal discourse, is that of privatisation and the market. We have seen how large supranational organisations such as the EU promote this market-driven regulatory function (Dale, 2008). In this scenario, public and private boundaries in higher education, and other areas for that matter, are blurred. The state engages in policymaking and other action in concert with other agencies and organisations, including NGOs (governance rather than government), either through loose networks or through partnerships ('heterarchies') (Ball, 2010). Partnerships in this proposed Mediterranean area might well involve agencies from outside and possibly from the EU itself, working in tandem with national states (see Ball, 2010).

Privatisation (see Sultana, 1999, pp. 22–24) is also a feature of a scenario in which the state becomes a 'competition' state (Ball, 2007), helping to create or sustain, or both, a higher education market (Darmanin, 2009) as part of a market for LLL in general. This has been occurring in many countries of the Mediterranean for quite some time. One did not need to anticipate the creation of a higher education Mediterranean space for neoliberal tenets to creep in. They have been there for quite some time, assisted in certain cases by the adoption of military action (e.g., the 1980 coup in Turkey[6]). In many countries of the Mediterranean, privatisation of higher education results in lecturers, who are underpaid in public institutions, boosting their income by teaching part-time in private universities to the detriment of research since most of their time is taken up by a double teaching shift.

It is a way by which the state helps sustain the private competition sector, underpaying its employees in the public sector and allowing the best qualified to be hired by the private sector on a part-time basis and being paid part-time rates. This strikes me as being a 'win-win' situation for public and private employers, but much to the detriment of research and possibly to teaching quality as well. What contribution can a Mediterranean higher education and research project make to assist academics in countries lying in the southern part of the Mediterranean to remedy this situation, getting rid of the economic shackles, to become an integral and visible part of the world academic research community? Furthermore what contribution can such an area make to strengthen the already documented links between university and community in this region with regard to university continuing education?

Mediterranean universities' contribution to LLL

The oldest extant universities in the world can be found in this region starting with the University of al-Qarawiyyin in Fez, Morocco, followed by Al-Azhar University in Cairo, Egypt[7] and the University of Bologna in Italy. The region has furnished us with great intellectual figures. Connell (2007), Maniam (2016) and de Sousa Santos (2017) wrote of the importance of Ibn Khaldun in the social sciences,[8] a historiographer from Tunis said to be worthy of the same esteem as that granted to Western sociologists such as Max Weber and Emile Durkheim. Boaventura de Sousa Santos (2017) shows how he anticipates some of their key concepts, especially the concept of solidarity in Durkheim. Tunisia is also the birthplace of Albert Memmi, the French writer of Tunisian-Jewish origin, whose work – as that of the Martinique writer Frantz Fanon or the Palestinians Edward Said and Ibrahim Abu-Lughod – has shaped our thinking about imperialism and colonialism in different ways. Suffice to mention Memmi's and Fanon's influences on Paulo Freire's classic text for community engagement, *Pedagogy of the Oppressed*.

The Mediterranean is rich in the scholarly legacy of the Golden Age of Arab and Islamic culture, in centres such as al-Andalus, Cordoba in particular. The name of Ibn Rushd, known as Averroes, immediately comes to mind.

Mediterranean university adult education centres

As far as the particular focus of this volume goes, universities in the Mediterranean have well-known centres and institutes catering for adult education and extension. The Centre for Adult Continuing Education (CACE), now the School of Continuing Education, at the American University in Cairo comes to mind.[9]

There are several ways by which the Mediterranean universities interact with communities. When the region included the Yugoslavia of old, comprising the current independent states of Serbia, Croatia, Bosnia and Herzegovina, Slovenia, Montenegro and Kosovo, a noticeable contribution to industrial democracy was made. Yugoslav universities were encouraged to develop centres, programmes and faculties to foreground adult education or andragogy to assist in extending resources to the public for LLL, including learning to engage in self-management (Tonkovic, 1985, p. 141).[10] As I pointed out in a 2012 book I co-wrote with Leona English (English and Mayo, 2012, p. 92), more than 390 workers' and people's universities and more than 430 cultural centres were set up throughout Yugoslavia to provide the necessary skills for workers to participate in self-management (Tonkovic, 1985, p. 143). In the early post-war period, that is to say from 1945 till 1950, around 2.3 million people previously considered illiterate were taught to read and write, and more than 1,000 people's universities were opened throughout the country (Samolovčev, 1985, p. 47).

It is hardly surprising, therefore, that adult education is a feature of a number of universities in countries that previously formed part of the 'old Yugoslavia'. The legacy in this area seems to have outlasted the Yugoslav nation itself. While the EU seems to provide a more management-directed process of employability-oriented LLL, this former Mediterranean country promoted a notion of workers' education which, despite having its critics,[11] could well prove instructive for those involved in developing university LLL from a 'workers' education' perspective. It would be interesting to see how much of this experience is given prominence in the work of the Global Labour University. It certainly exerted its influence on one university continuing education agency with which I am familiar, the University of Malta's Centre for Labour Studies whose original name was the Workers' Participation Development Centre. Its setting up in 1981 coincided with the introduction of self-management experiences in Malta, including the Malta Drydocks (English and Mayo, 2012; Mayo, 2015).

Other contributions include the involvement of Italian universities in the '150 hours' experiment in working-class adult education, a right to education for employees obtained by the metal workers' union. This led to programmes geared to personal and social development, and not to satisfying the employers' vocational requirements. The experiment led, among other things, to universities developing so-called 'monographic courses' (short courses around a specific theme) by women for women – a landmark in women's education and feminism in Italy.[12] In the Southern Mediterranean, the major issue is literacy, and adult education involves work in this area. Adult education in the Arab world is characterised also by its dependency on the state (Mojab, 2005, p. 401; ETF, 2012, p. 36, UILL, 2009, p. 28), with some countries gaining funds from the EU because of close agreements with it and eligibility to participate in some of its programmes. A number of programmes at Bir Zeit University's Centre for Continuing Education at the heart of Ramallah, in the West Bank and under Palestinian authority, fall into this category. The Centre participated in the Tempus programme on 'Lifelong Learning in Palestine' coordinated by the University of Glasgow (Hammond, 2012). One also finds in this Tempus programme community education work. This work especially concerns women and involves community theatre, also prominent in other parts of the Mediterranean.

Community education work among Jerusalemites and other Palestinians is carried out by and through Al-Quds University, in Al-Quds/Jerusalem, through its Community Action Centre (CAC). This is located in the heart of the Old City, and tackles such areas as domestic violence (Silwadi and Mayo, 2014), a theme also addressed at Bir Zeit's Centre for Continuing Education.

> Individuals come to CAC to share their personal stories; they discuss their experience of denials of basic rights and they identify their struggles for their rights to health and education. This process is based on teamwork where individuals learn how to access their rights and interests and how to protect their rights and to live with dignity. At the community level public meetings are organised with community members from different backgrounds to learn about their story of now and to learn about the story of us, as a team we learn about the challenges that face the community members' interests, values, and why they are at stake... The focus is on obtaining knowledge and insights and engaging community members to realize change at the individual, community, and social levels. (Silwadi and Mayo, 2014, p. 77)

The Al-Quds community education project draws on the influence of Paulo Freire and Augusto Boal (Silwadi and Mayo, 2014, p. 78). It connects with a particular type of adult education found throughout the Mediterranean. It consists of a participatory type of education involving a variety of sites, not least outdoor sites – another climatically favoured type of provision in a region where dramatic representations have a strong 'outdoor' dimension (recall amphitheatres of the Greco-Roman periods, the carnival, fiesta or *Semana Santa*/Holy Week representations). The University of Malta, through its extension centre in an area with a recently recorded low mainstream university student intake, developed an educational project involving history, politics, gender issues, environmental issues, music appreciation (band marches, solemn music and rock), art considerations and spirituality, deriving from the annual Holy Week spirit, so strong in countries such as Spain, Malta and Italy and regions such as Sicily – more about this in Chapter 7.

One needs not be a person of faith to benefit from such an education as this represented a case of moving from what Don Lorenzo Milani calls the 'motivo occasionale' (occasional motive) to the 'motivo profondo' (profound motive) (Martinelli, 2007).[13]

Projects such as these connect with Catalan Joan Bofill's exposition of the role of the Universitat Nova in the Barcelona area in reviving the *fiesta* (non-religious *fiestas* were banned in Spain during the Franco era), rendering it a form of community learning that brought people together to learn about their own culture and surroundings (Bofill, 1985, pp. 59–60); the Universitat Nova is another alternative university rooted in popular culture.

While the EU HE discourse is hegemonic in the region and especially in Southern European states, there are examples of university extension and LLL with a social purpose dimension in both the southern Mediterranean, as I have shown, and the Northern Mediterranean. One famous example derives from the University of Barcelona through its Centre for Social and Educational Research (CREA) in Barcelona, led by an important critical pedagogue and sociologist, Ramon Flecha (2000). Among its many activities, CREA carried out literacy circles among different types of workers lacking a formal education. It involved a creative way of carrying out dialogue including literature, personal narrative and life history, as a result of which people with low formal education read works by great artists such as Lorca, Kafka and Dostoyevsky. The link between literary texts and university LLL is a recurring one, which this book will demonstrate especially in the following chapter.

We find examples of contributions by the University of Seville to the capacity-building of citizens for effective engagement with the idea of a participatory budget having originated in Porto Alegre, Brazil. Academics and associates from the University of Seville were also involved in working with activists in developing the 'history from below' project at the Manolo Reyes School in the Barriada 'Las Aguilas' district of Seville. The school ran a 'collective memory' project focusing on the Spanish Civil War and the 40 years of Franco rule. People of different ages collectively pieced together a painful 'oral' history. They did so through the use of different media (printed matter, film documentaries) and community research/learning strategies (Guimarães et al., 2018; English and Mayo, 2012, p. 137). In this project, participants developed a documentary of oral history featuring interviews with persons who lived through the period. One of the greatest challenges was their opening up on traumatic experiences including the loss of loved ones. As a guest of the University of Seville in May 2007, I attended one of the sessions and engaged in discussions with the participants concerning the project, having been asked to provide feedback on the work by members of the team and especially the university educator involved in agreement with the project participants who were insistent that I voice my reactions to the documentary and the work.

There is ample documentation of the involvement of universities such as the University of Verona in projects of 'social creation' and the social solidarity economy (see De Vita and Piussi, 2013; De Vita, 2009; De Vita and Bertell, 2004). One documented case concerns 'social creation' in the Veneto – community and environmental renewal in Verona. It involves graduates engaging in agricultural production to make available and affordable to a large number of people fresh land produce that would, under conventional situations, be bought as a luxury and therefore at a high price by a small amount of people constituting a small niche market (De Vita, 2009). Antonia De Vita and Anna Maria Piussi maintain that the Social Solidarity Economy also includes Social Solidarity Purchasing Groups and consumer associations. The two University of Verona scholar-activists state that these groups reveal 'great potential for self-learning that occurs within groups and for capacity building' (De Vita and Piussi, 2013 p. 304). The lessons drawn from this and the other more progressive university LLL examples are those of people learning to be not simply, once again, passive producers and consumers, but well-informed and critically disposed social actors striving to create change at their workplace and in the larger domain beyond, what is often called, following Habermas, the public sphere (Guimarães et al., 2018, p. 63).

Once again we come across the idea, in parts of the Mediterranean, of a commitment by academics, ensconced in universities, towards social programmes in concert with social organisations and movements. Earlier I demonstrated the connection between Italian universities and the feminist movement via the '150 hours' project. Anna Maria Piussi, together with Luisa Muraro and Chiara Zamboni, was actively involved in this project. She formed part of the group of Italian feminist philosophers Diotima, named after Socrates' muse.

The point to register, through these examples, from both the Southern and Northern Mediterranean, is the need for a 'two-way' dialogical approach when it comes to developing a common higher education area across the Mediterranean. The southern Mediterranean and Southern Europe have their own traditions of university involvement in LLL, often community-oriented, which can be instructive, in this regard, for other universities in other parts of the world.

Certainly the great degree of unemployment that characterises large swathes of the Mediterranean makes the countries involved, and their universities, more susceptible to seeking support from the EU and elsewhere regarding continuing education for 'employability'. This raises interesting issues regarding the danger of cultural imperialism and the provision of external models that are at odds with the contextual specificities of their Mediterranean recipients, not least their reflecting a rhythm of life and work ill-suited to the climatic conditions of the region (see Braudel, 1972; Mayo, 2017b). There is the added danger that those who introduce these models pay lip service to the traditions and events that capture the popular imagination in this part of the world. It is work built on what captures the imagination in Mediterranean communities. This work gives rise to, once again, an engagement with what Gramsci calls the 'popular creative spirit' (Gramsci, 1996, p. 57). Work of this kind, as I will show in the penultimate chapter, features among the best specimens of popular communal education in which various community organisations and universities in the Mediterranean are and can be engaged. I would argue that any Mediterranean higher education research project should foreground this type of university community involvement.

Notes

1 This chapter is based on an article which originally appeared as Peter Mayo (2010) 'The EU'S higher education discourse and the rest of the Mediterranean' on the website of the IEMed Obs (Observatory of the Euro-Mediterranean Policies), 3 April 2010, www.iemed.org/observatori-en/arees-danalisi/arxius adjunts/copy_of_focus/The%20EUs%20Higher%20Education%20Discourse%20and%20the%20Rest%20of%20the%20Mediterranean.pdf. This is a much revised version. I am indebted to Professor Mohammed Ezroura from the Mohammed V University, Rabat, Morocco for his detailed comments on a previous draft of this chapter when prepared as the article for the IEMed Obs. I am also indebted to Professor Fatma Gok and Dr Sezan Bayhan

from Bogazici University for their feedback on the preparatory draft of the IEMed Obs article. Professor Roger Dale and Professor Ronald Sultana, from the Universities of Bristol and Malta respectively, challenged me with some pertinent issues, also in preparation of the earlier published article. Any remaining shortcomings are mine.

2 The UfM was established at the Paris Summit for the Mediterranean. This union, for which the former French president Nicholas Sarkozy and the then Spanish PM, José Luis Rodríguez Zapatero, strove hard, was intended to strengthen the Euro-Mediterranean Partnership (Euromed – referred to as the Barcelona Process).

3 http://ufmsecretariat.org/who-we-are/.

4 http://ufmsecretariat.org/who-we-are/.

5 http://ufmsecretariat.org/who-we-are/.

6 The coup occurred on 12 September 1980, a remarkable occurrence given that the Chile coup, also to introduce what today can be called neoliberal market economics, occurred on 11 September, seven years earlier. Actually the first introduction of neoliberal policies into Turkey occurred with decisions taken on 24 January 1980; that is, before the coup. The person behind these decisions was Turgut Özal, a former World Bank official, later to become prime minister. He was then undersecretary of state planning. As with Chile, the Turkish coup once again represents a bold attempt, this time by a US satellite state in the Eastern Mediterranean spanning from Europe into Asia, to set the conditions for the onset of neoliberal policies.

7 Al-Azhar University is very much engaged in university LLL via online learning offering courses in such areas as the Arabic language and Islam among others, http://alazhar. today/. At the 2006 conference of the Mediterranean Society of Comparative Education held at the Alexandrian Library in Alexandria Egypt, Ibrahim Marai and Mohamed Fathy from the Al-Azhar University proposed a renewed role for this Muslim university. This entailed e-learning for training of Imams all over the world. Being so topical in light of events in the Western world, this presentation led to a huge debate concerning the nature of Islam and the role of Imams; www.um.edu.mt/__data/assets/pdf_file/ 0009/39915/About_MESCE.pdf.

8 The late Maltese philosopher and former University of Malta Rector, Peter Serracino Inglott did much to spread Khaldun's thinking among university students in the country in the 1960s and 1970s. I am indebted to colleague, Professor Mary Darmanin for this point.

9 http://datacenter.aucegypt.edu/jmc471/ezines/caravanian2006/news,%20CACE.html.

10 As with cooperatives, self-management entails a great degree of educational preparation. Stipe Tonkovic defined 'education for self-management' as education that animates, stimulates and prepares workers for decision-making, develops their critical attitudes and analytical faculties, and encourages them to seek change and improvement. This process relied, for the most part, on the case-study method, verification or practice, and criticism of inadequate solutions and inappropriate attitudes and behaviour (Tonkovic, 1985, p. 141). Education for self-management also included delivery of lectures, and the holding of summer schools, discussion groups and evening courses (English and Mayo, 2012, p. 91).

11 There have been those who criticised what they felt was the strong ideological character of education for self-management. This, they felt, consisted of education about issues centring more on the Communist Party and its ideology, than about professional issues and management. I am indebted to Professor Katrina Popovic, from the University of Belgrade, for this and information in the previous footnote.

12 I am indebted to Professor Anna Maria Piussi, University of Verona, for this point.

13 A pedagogical approach that seizes upon aspects of life as an 'occasional motive' (Martinelli, 2007) is just a conduit that gradually takes the learners into the heart of those disciplines containing knowledge that is 'really useful' (a contentious term that raises the issue: who decides what is useful?) in the outside world. The intention is to take learners to that higher level, to 'take ... students beyond their experience and enable them to envisage alternatives that have some basis in the real world' (Young 2013, p. 107).

5

Mainstream and alternative HE discourses in LLL[1]

Introduction

In Chapter 3, I analysed the EU discourse on HE (see also Mayo, 2009) mainly through its policy documents on universities and other tertiary-level institutions. I highlighted key doxa in this discourse notably 'knowledge economy', 'competitiveness', 'entrepreneurship', 'lifelong learning', 'access', 'mobility', 'outcomes and performance', 'quality assurance', 'innovation and creativity', 'diversification', 'privatisation', 'internationalisation', 'autonomy' and 'business–HE relationships'. Once again, this is by no means an exhaustive list.

I also argued that the overall tenor of this discourse is that of HE for employability and also spoke about the agenda of industry gaining the upper hand with the emergence of documents geared towards a more structured relationship between universities (important institutions within HE) and business. The chapter highlighted the underlying neoliberal tenets of this discourse even though I tried to indicate the tension between neoliberal tenets and the idea of a social Europe, the latter to be regarded in both its formal realisation in the welfare tradition, the European Charter, EU and state-funded social programmes and so forth, and in its informal sense, at the grassroots level – social Europe from below involving local, regional and international networking.

This chapter

In this chapter, I would like to reiterate that HE LLL is an important terrain where this tension is played out. I will, however, focus, for the most part, on those institutions that have potential for furnishing people with further and lifelong learning opportunities outside the mainstream 'lock-step' approach. Many of the experiments in HE that serve as a radical alternative to the mainstream can provide LLL opportunities, in that they can attract students who otherwise cannot benefit from full-time attendance at a higher learning institution.

I shall start off by pointing to the most prominent forms of HE in evidence today, focusing on their connections to the market and underscoring the neoliberal tenets that underlie much HE practice worldwide. The second part will deal with alternative approaches to HE, including university education, indicating, borrowing from Carl Boggs, the 'prefigurative' nature of much of this work (i.e., embodying those practices that constitute the ultimate, long-term vision of a future university or HE institution). The third part will consist of a series of considerations around alternative discourses in HE LLL with references to past and present.

Many of these attempts point to alternative discourses to the generally accepted hegemonic one of a market-oriented and neoliberal LLL approach in HE. This alternative discourse affirms HE as a public good and the need for learning at this level to be accessible to most people irrespective of whether or not they have the wherewithal to benefit from it. It is primarily not learning *for* the economy and the market but learning to *engage critically with* society in general (this of course includes the economy). This alternative discourse is, for the most part, still in its embryonic form and the institutions that embrace it face major challenges regarding acceptance and recognition. I argue, however, that these pockets of alternative provision convey some idea of the direction struggles for a more democratic approach to HE can take.

The alternative conceptualisation of HE they provide is reflective of a whole critical discourse in the history of education where education is seen as potentially contributing to the further development of a democratic, critically inquiring public sphere. Learners, for their part, are once again seen as social actors rather than people who, as stated earlier, simply produce and consume. This discourse, conceiving of HE as a public good and as a repository of critical thinking accessible to all, provides the guiding thread for my analysis in this chapter and throughout the rest of the book.

Implications of the EU HE discourse for LLL

The EU HE discourse has several implications for adult continuing and LLL. The EU's focus is primarily on the 20/25–65 working-age bracket, despite other references to LLL as spanning life 'from cradle to grave'. The emphasis on work and employability encourages provision of continuing education for the economy's purposes, and this despite the fact that a person's 'employability' does not necessarily translate into that, namely, as argued earlier, a person's 'employment' (Gelpi, 2002) or 'desired level of employment' (Brown et al., 2010).

Colleges of further education, providing education beyond that received at secondary school, that is distinguished from university-based HE, are likely to provide courses purported to lead to a variety of 'prospective jobs'. These are often supported by funding from employers (CEDEFOP, 2015). Incentives for this purpose, including tax deductions for investment in employee training, are often provided by governments.

Universities, for their part, are more likely to invest in continuing professional education/development (CPE or CPD) programmes, funded by prospective adult learners. This applies to the North and South Mediterranean as well as the rest of Europe. They include those who can afford the fees involved, who take loans for this purpose or who benefit from 'sponsored mobility' accorded by their own employers to obtain the qualifications that suit that higher rank in the firm earmarked for them. The added qualifications, say an MBA or DBA, also convey status to the firm that has them on its books. These credentials tend to look good on the company's letterheads.

As for broader domains of learning, this is often governed by the market and by the ability of people, seeking coveted qualifications in say ICT, management, the arts and social sciences, to pay for courses leading to them. The classic example here would be the University of London's External Degree provision, the prices for which have shot up exponentially since the 1980s. These qualifications are often also obtained through a process of 'sponsored mobility' for teachers working in different institutions, including colleges of further education. Of course, this consideration does not necessarily apply to all nations. Suffice to mention that the English Open University model has taken root in a variety of places, as has the London External Degree model. The former differed from the latter as it traditionally provided a more structured course, with modules and assignments, while the latter was, for years, based solely on the candidate's performance in a final summative exam, with a possible allowance for one or two papers to be taken in advance. The London system changed considerably in more recent years, so that it is now modular, college/school/institute-based, with branded 'International Programmes' and designed to take advantage of recent technological developments. Of course, in the past, many students in the University of London External Degree programmes enrolled in correspondence programmes provided by independent colleges (e.g., Wolsey Hall College, Oxford; Extension College, Cambridge), that prepared people for these exams – some even attended the odd residential seminar offered by the University of London or by the preparatory independent college itself.

A non-UK institution, the University of South Africa (UNISA) that offered external degree courses somewhat on the lines of the old London External Degree model, although more structured, charges what is believed to be reasonably affordable fees. It has a longstanding provision of external degree course programmes. Nelson Mandela is arguably its most celebrated graduate, having studied for a UNISA external degree when incarcerated on Robben Island (UNISA, 2017). He also studied with Wolsey Hall College through correspondence education to prepare for his London External LLB degree while also in confinement.

As far as open universities are concerned, a few stand out. I can refer to the 2006 launch of the Open Universiteit in the Netherlands. We also find Athabasca University in Alberta, Canada; South Africa's UNISA, established in 2004 as a result of the merger between the old UNISA – from which Mandela graduated – and Technikon Southern Africa with the incorporation of the Vista University Distance Education Campus, Vudec); the Open University of Israel; the Universitat Oberta de Catalunya with its headquarters in Barcelona; the Palestinian Al-Quds Open University (QOU) with its headquarters in Jerusalem/Al-Quds (not to be confused with Al-Quds University mentioned earlier); the Hellenic Open University; and, more recently, the Open University of Cyprus (English and Mayo, 2012). This distance learning model, one of many models whereby universities and other HE institutions can provide forms of LLL, testifies to the widespread use of open learning platforms. This effort in reaching people in different localities has come a long way since the days of 'correspondence education'/'home study' (e.g., Wolsey Hall College, which, although autonomous, prepared people to take London External Degree and other academic bodies' exams) involving conventional snail-mail communication and printed course material with model answers to set questions (see Fisher, 1983, p. 2). The EU and the larger hegemonic discourse of ICT have arguably had their greatest impact on university continuing education in the area of online distance learning.

Access and the public sphere

The expenses vary among the different institutions, often to a large extent. The issue of access becomes relevant in this context. One way in which universities can engage in a meaningful process of *access* is by re-conceiving of their role as being there to not simply boost the economy, 'knowledge-intensive' or otherwise, but contribute to a regeneration of democracy and the public sphere (Giroux and Searls Giroux, 2004), a recurring theme in this volume. We have recently witnessed the development of MOOCs – Massive Open Online Courses – taking root not only in the USA but now also across Europe and especially the UK. MOOCs are considered an important feature of the 4th IR (Xing and Marwala, 2017). During their inception, much of what passed as MOOCs constituted a form of open access learning. Certain universities and consortia of universities from different parts of the world place their entire course material online, free of charge. People who sign up for a MOOC study unit can carry out the various tasks required of course participants and receive feedback. For the moment and in the majority of cases, they are barred from receiving the official university credit that can result in a degree. Some universities provide the option of obtaining an official testimonial of the course undertaken (Edx.org, 2017a) – a certificate – against a nominal charge (Edx.org, 2017b). This form of provision appears *prima facie* to be a way for the university or institution concerned to contribute to the public sphere. It appears laudable from an 'access to knowledge' perspective, a form of 'socialization of the means of knowledge production' (Livingstone, 2013, pp. 51–52), if you will. It remains to be seen what trajectory this type of provision will take in future – simply 'testing the waters' in the marketplace of knowledge dissemination and acquisition? The jury is still out on this. Sarah Speight (2017) indicates, in great detail, however, the manner in which some MOOCs are gradually becoming mainstreamed, becoming part and parcel of degree courses for which expensive fees are charged. This applies also to elite institutions such as Oxford and Harvard. As with the criticism once levelled at England's Open University, Speight posits that MOOCs attract people who are already in possession of a good education in which familiarity with basic learning platforms and modalities, as well as facilities, has been acquired. One also needs to have the wherewithal or the backing to follow certain courses 'with profit', which also implies being in possession of state of the art and therefore expensive ICT equipment. For this reason, Speight questions the degree of accessibility involved with respect to MOOCs. It seems to her to be a question of giving more to those who already have. MOOCs are more likely to constitute a form of continuing education for professionals. One simply has to search the fee structure for certain courses that can be accumulated towards a valuable qualification, often complementing 'on campus' learning to appreciate further the point made throughout Speight's (2017) chapter.

Alternative models of HE as a public good

As for the idea of HE LLL as a public good, much will depend on the nature of the institution concerned. There will always be those politically committed institutions or consortia of such institutions that seek to retain vestiges of university continuing education as a public good. In short, they would prioritise access for those not expected to form part of the traditional constituency for universities. Social class is an important factor in this thinking. Today one also broadens the profile to include people for whom traditional university settings can be disabling or people of an ethnic orientation and culture different from those of mainstream students. The Mediterranean chapter has already allowed me to provide examples of UCE as a public good that forms part of the history of education emerging from the countries involved where there is a tradition of linking education to community struggles. However, the linkages between universities and communities, social movements and the rest of the 'public sphere' do not end there. Pockets of inspiring and innovative practices in this regard are found everywhere. They existed in the past and exist at present.

One would expect the public good factor to feature prominently in the work of the Global Labour University (global-labour-university.org), with the International Labour Organization (ILO) among its institutional consortium members. It involves universities working in tandem with trade unions. A consortium of this type would be expected to strive to retain the notion of a workers' education programme in the tradition of those programmes that once represented, in the UK and elsewhere, the best of adult education in its democratic extension mission. This is the tradition associated once again with the likes of R. H. Tawney, Raymond Williams (McIlroy and Westwood, 1993) and E. P. Thompson. This tradition is associated with Ruskin College,[2] Plater College, the Plebs League (Waugh, 2009) and the Oxford Delegacy for Extra-Mural Studies. One can also mention, in this context, what Sharp et al. call the '[r]epressed historical tradition of independent working class education' (Sharp et al., 1989; B. Simon, 1992; Waugh, 2009).

In this respect and in keeping with the EU's promotion of the concept of 'active citizenship', we require institutions that support the efforts of those who have traditionally been swimming against the current.

HE, universities and social movements

We often come across attempts by academics to engage the academy in popular education, to forge partnerships with grassroots activists, as evident in the

Ontario-based projects, NALL (New Approaches to Lifelong Learning) and subsequently WALL (Work and Lifelong Learning), or PEN (the Popular Education Network), coordinated from Edinburgh. They involve engaging the academy in communities, including, in the Ontario case, engaging in communities of workplace learners in different sectors of the economy (WALLNET[3]). These and other initiatives in various parts of the globe can provide signposts for future directions that a truly vibrant HE institution can take. See, for example, attempts at forging links with social movements and other social organisations. This is the sort of link augured by Boaventura de Sousa Santos when providing proposals on which the Popular University of Social Movements (UPMS) was set up at the World Social Forum in 2003. The UPMS, a collective asset, holds workshops, preferably of a couple of days involving discussions, study and reflection periods and relaxation activities (Alice.ces, 2017). One classic example of social movement involvement in higher education is provided by the MST (Movimento Trabalhadores Rurais Sem Terra [Landless Peasants Movement][4]) especially through school it supports, the Escola Nacional Florestan Fernandes (ENFF) in Brazil, named after a working-class sociologist (Mayo and Vittoria, 2017, pp. 93–95). It has a main campus and also holds itinerant sessions throughout the country. It trains people in connection with the peasant movement and takes pride in the fact that, on completion of the course, the graduates return to their communities (de Sousa Santos, 2017, p. 407). It is recognised, by the Brazilian government, as a school with levels of learning equivalent to those of a university. It remains to be seen, however, whether, as a result of the impeachment of President Dilma Rousseff, in what has been perceived as an indirect 'coup', we shall witness the withdrawal of this recognition, given the Brazilian Right's opposition to the MST. The signs are definitely not good. As Boaventura de Sousa Santos (2017) states, shortly after the *golpe blanco* (white coup) against Dilma Rousseff, 'various police forces invaded the ENFF campus in an action of intimidation.' (p. 409). Second, the present incumbents at the helm have been seeking to deny Paulo Freire the title of Patron of Brazilian Education and have introduced the new mantra of 'Escola Sem Partido' (School without Party) (Mayo and Vittoria, 2017, pp. 100–101), an affront to Freire and those many others, myself included, who maintain that education is politics and that there is no such thing as a neutral education. The present Brazilian government's actions in seeing education as 'neutral' does not augur well for schools who argue to the contrary; Freire and others have argued that claiming neutrality is in itself a political act since it means siding with the dominant. On the other hand, emphasising the non-neutrality of education is tantamount, according to the government's view, to offering a form of political indoctrination. The ENFF strikes me as being an easy target for the right wing Brazilian government

In these most innovative of institutions, such as the ENFF, one finds parallels with other grassroots experiments in HE emanating from such movements as the Occupy Movement in the USA (Piven, 2012) and Europe or protestors in Turkey (Gezi Park), Greece and Italy who set up university tents and itinerant libraries. These provide a taste of what an alternative, popular higher education would look like. Other initiatives include the Global Centre for Advanced Studies

(GCAS)[5] founded by Creston Davis (Critical-Theory.com, 2017), which includes established academics/cultural workers such as Alain Badiou, Oliver Stone, Gayatri Spivak and Antonio Negri. This institution carries out its seminars in a variety of countries, including France and Cuba. It seeks to bridge the gap between theory and action by working with activists in connection with such movements and parties as Podemos, which was founded in Spain in the aftermath of the 15-M/¡Democracia Real YA! demonstrations.

Nostalgia for the Humboldtian model?

Most of this work can be regarded as providing an alternative to the neoliberal university. When confronting the neoliberal university, people often nostalgically lapse into exalting some 'golden age', including that in which the Humboldtian idea of the Prussian/German university was raised. One would pose the question of whether, for all its virtues, the old, still much-evoked Humboldtian concept of the university is still relevant, as society has changed significantly since the time when the idea was conceived. This in a way recalls Gramsci's 'epitaph' to the old, Italian classical school, which was once effective but could not continue to be so in his time since the society it was meant to serve had changed by then (Manacorda, 1970). What form this newly required university institution takes depends on the political values and orientation to knowledge production and dissemination that underlie the concept being carried forward. There are resistances to the hegemonic market-driven concept at hand. Some occur within the neoliberal institutions themselves, lending credence to the Gramscian view that hegemonic institutions contain, within their interstices, the spaces in which the relations involved can be challenged and renegotiated. Earlier I pointed out Foucault's view that resistances are not external to the power structures in place.

One finds resistance in the experiments of bringing together world-renowned intellectuals, academics and cultural workers in institutions making degrees available to persons who cannot afford high-quality university education on a full-time basis. These institutions cover areas of knowledge not easily associated with 'instrumental learning'; that is, learning for the economy. One can refer, as an example, to the fee-charging European Graduate School (EGS), a not-for-profit degree-granting institution in the social sciences and humanities, which has just received EU-wide accreditation through Malta's National Council for Further and Higher Education. Students, many in full time employment, meet in one of its two campuses (Saas-Fee, Switzerland and Valletta, Malta) for intensive two to three week periods working with such high calibre academics, artists and directors as Judith Butler, Slavoj Žižek, Jean-Luc Nancy, Margarethe Von Trotta, Achille Mbembe and Giorgio Agamben.

They do this in addition to writing research papers and working for a much longer period on their dissertations at MA and PhD levels. I recently attended Von Trotta's workshops on her films concerning courageous historical German female figures including the Ensslin sisters in *Marianne and Juliane*, Rosa Luxemburg, Hannah Arendt and the medieval mystic St Hildegard. Some of the sessions took the form of a cineforum in which the showing of the film was followed by inter-active discussions involving Von Trotta, EGS students and guests like myself. This took place a week after Achille Mbembe taught at the EGS Malta campus.

The Global Centre for Advanced Studies (GCAS) also seeks to depart from conventional university modes of operation. It has its degrees accredited by the Bologna Accords (Europe) through the Institutum Studiorum Humanitatis (ISH) and previously also through the Alma Mater Europaea–ECM.

The Cooperative Institute for Transnational Studies (CITS) (Coop-its.org, 2017) is another institution pursuing a non-conventional approach to LLL in HE. In this cooperative, one member has one vote in the decision-making. It is cre-ating higher education as the commons, neither public/state-funded nor private, but self-run. It was founded by Greek scholar and activist Maria Nikolakaki, pro-fessor at the University of Peloponnese, Greece and formerly of GCAS. It features such scholars and academics as Jacques Rancière, Étienne Balibar, Tariq Ali, John Holloway, Raquel Gutiérrez and Peter McLaren.

CITS collaborates with institutions such as the Autonomous University of Puebla, Mexico, for accreditation, and the California Institute of Integral Studies, Mexico Solidarity Network, the Social Sciences Centre at Lincoln, UK, and the Universidad de la Tierra[6] at Oaxaca for its projects. This, especially the Oaxaca connection, indicates the urge for these types of alternative institutions to collab-orate with social movement activists from all over the world. In fact, the issues of collaborations and the partner institutions involved constitute a bone of con-tention within these alternative agencies for continuing education and LLL. This has, at least in one instance, led to a fall-out, with a group leaving the institution to set up another on the grounds that the slightly older institution strayed from its original goals.

With no fees charged and no formal distinction drawn between students and staff, the Social Sciences Centre in Lincoln, England provides a radical alternative to the widespread marketisation of higher education. Lying at the heart of the city, it is housed in local county council premises, as indicated in an interview with Mike Neary (Opendemocracy.net, 2017).

Many of the above initiatives are born out of dissatisfaction with the way uni-versities have been developing in the USA and Europe over the years, especially their neoliberalisation. Needless to say, these resistances and re-conceptualisations meet with countless obstacles when it comes to recognition of qualifications and funding. We have grown accustomed to seeing a negative reaction 'from above' to anything highly innovative, especially those coming from the grassroots. These alternative projects are striking at the foundations of institutions that have, for the most part, been conveying privilege. Those who unlearn and give up privilege freely are few and far between. However, the establishment and general recognition of a radical social justice-oriented HE institution or university requires a 'long revolu-tion', to borrow the term coined for wider usage by Welshman Raymond Williams (1961). It is the revolution to which the GCAS, CITS, UPMS, MST (Florestan Fernandez School) and Lincoln projects aspire and contribute. The same holds for those setting up Tent University in London and Tent State University (a movement in the USA and Britain) when occupying squares and streets, reclaiming them as public spaces (Earl, 2016; Chun, 2017). Christian Chun writes extensively about his volunteering as a faculty member of the People's Collective University (Chun, 2012) during Occupy LA in 2001 (Chun, 2014) with their online hubs (Chun, 2015, p. 70). These types of alternative HE agencies focus on collective learning and activism, captured in CITS' slogan 'Occupy Knowledge'.

As I argued in an 'op ed' piece (Mayo, 2017c, p. 37), the germs of the new societies are found in the old ones. I argued that it takes a 'long revolution' to change a well-established concept of the university and other HE institutions into a radically democratic one. The revolution might have already started, although it is still in its embryonic stage. It might even be the 'proto' stage with regard to whatever shape the democratic university takes in future. The pockets prefiguring it, anticipating a development that is not happening yet, are there for those exploring different ways of doing HE, even inside current and established institutions (Mayo, 2017c, p. 37). The exploration is for more ways to render the HE/university space a democratic one.

Teaching and research

To return to a point made in Chapter 3, I argued that such a democracy would be ill-served by an HE discourse seeking to separate teaching from research and therefore *praxis*. This separation, between research universities and teaching universities, was proposed in certain EU circles (CEC, 2006a).

This is the direction the current EU HE discourse seems to be taking, as the university seems to have found itself at a crossroads. It sought change from the 'old ideal', popularly denigrated as that of the 'ivory tower', and chose the market-oriented one, albeit with some social-democratic trappings. Several of the above initiatives, certainly the more progressive ones, many in their embryonic stage, are born out of dissatisfaction with this choice. They provide an alternative that exalts criticality in education. They privilege accessibility – one's being able to further one's education without having to forfeit the need to earn a living at the same time. One is allowed to do so at a very affordable nominal charge by some of these institutions whose main concern is to foster the advancement of knowledge and not the 'bottom line'. These institutions' concept of knowledge is broad enough to embrace concerns with developing not simply the economy but a healthy democratically inclusive environment. That these pockets of alternative approaches exist has just been documented. That they are not mainstream HE institutions indicates that they prefigure a university not as it is but as it can and, depending on one's values, should be – a plausible alternative to the neoliberal paradigm. At the moment, these projects involve marginalised and at times 'subaltern' HE work. In their accessibility and alternative way of doing things, they constitute a form of LLL that prefigures what can prove to be the democratic university of the future. Their birth pangs can be painful. These alternative HE initiatives are met with stiff resistance and possibly derision and contempt (Mayo, 2017c, p. 37).

Implications for the social context of university or HE LLL

Like MOOCs, a number of the so-called alternative third-level education programmes on offer and mentioned above are likely to benefit those already in possession of a university education who cannot afford full-time continuing education at graduate level. They cannot afford to leave their partners, dependents and job for long stretches throughout the year. Those attending the EGS programme are a case in point. This school is providing alternative higher education at EQF 7 and 8 levels for those who already 'have'. This imposes limits on the degree of accessibility that is noticeable. In contrast, the tent universities or open learning spaces of the Occupy and other movements are more accessible, seemingly open to all. They are, however, of short duration, more likely to simply provide a foretaste of what this kind of education can be in the future than serve as a permanent source of learning for different people – those who have been 'initiated' and those who are 'uninitiated' in higher education.

In the latter case, alternative HE LLL requires preparatory work to help people develop some of the skills that will enable them to partake of the experience 'with profit'. This strikes me as being an important task for any agency or movement seeking to render HE accessible to large swathes of people who would not normally be associated with universities and HE in general. Foundation work is a prerequisite for this purpose.[7] On the other hand, innovative and democratic approaches to learning that engage the learner's experience have the potential to render this foundational and subsequent work more accessible.

Hopefully the centres and agencies involved would provide settings where learners are conceived of as lifelong learners. The emphasis is as much on knowledge acquisition as on knowledge exploration in individual and, most importantly, collective ways. This approach would echo the old UNESCO writings on LLE concerning a new conceptualisation of the school and other learning institutions: schools and institutions with an ethos that helps in the grooming of students as lifelong learners. As Dewey would argue, one teaches democracy by not simply talking about it but by practising it. By the same token, one teaches LLL by not simply talking about it but by practising it – treating participants as lifelong learners, capable of taking charge of present and future learning. LLE is not just one activity, among others, of a school or institution but its core activity – it is conceived holistically within a lifelong education framework. Likewise, EUCEN, the European University Continuing Education Network, has called on universities to develop as LLL institutions (EUCEN, n.d.); from university LLL to LLL universities. LLL would not be simply one, among many, of the branches or units of the university but the all-encompassing concept at the heart of its workings as a research and educational institution.

In the kind of pedagogical philosophy that inspires some of the institutions mentioned above, notably the critical/Freirean pedagogy-inspired ones, participants learn to be able to take charge of their own learning not simply individually, as self-directed learners, but also as collectively directed learners. The latter concept would fall within the best critical traditions of education (Freire,

Lorenzo Milani, social movement learning). Alas, this notion of collectivity is, for the most part, given short shrift in the contemporary LLL discourse. The concept of the self-directed learner can, as I argued in Chapter 2, easily fit into the neo-liberal mantra of 'responsibilisation' – LLL being a matter of individual rather than social and collective responsibility.

The collective dimension is that which would distinguish an alternative discourse around LLL from contemporary mainstream ones. In my view, entities such as the Florestan Fernandez School, embracing landless peasants,[8] often organised into cooperatives (cooperative management is one of the areas covered by the school – Mayo and Vittoria, 2017, p. 93), and the Cooperative Institute for Transnational Studies (CITS) lend themselves to this kind of approach. This approach to knowledge discovery is the antithesis of institutions that are 'top-down' as has recently been the case with some universities in Denmark, a country traditionally well-known for its 'bottom-up' approach to knowledge and organisation (Elkjaer, 2017, p. 291). Such a top-down approach, involving the presence of a board, above council and senate, consisting of people from outside the university,[9] was also mooted in Malta in 2017, with respect to a new University Act, and contested; the idea of its adoption in Malta was dropped as a result of clear opposition to the proposal.

Proponents of the more participative alternative HE discourses would, in their eagerness to stress process, ignore the importance of 'powerful knowledge' at their peril. Powerful knowledge is the term I borrow from Michael Young (2013). It refers to that knowledge that, although not ideologically neutral (no knowledge is), has served to empower people over the years. There is always the danger that one short-changes participants by not devoting sufficient attention to that knowledge that can enable them to 'crack the power codes', power here used in its positive sense. Writing on the university extension service in Alberta, Canada, Dennis Haughey (1998) drives home the point: 'largely lacking in contemporary... practice is the ability to function fluently in the language of the dominant culture so as not to be relegated to the periphery of political life' (p. 211).

Gramsci, for instance, insisted on the need for the subaltern classes to learn the standard language even though this was an imposed language, not a 'national popular' one. It had to be learnt for people not to remain on the margins of political life. Of course, one can argue, from a social justice perspective, that it needs to be learnt in a manner that provides an awareness of its ideological underpinnings – its colonial function and the way it serves as a means of social differentiation, among other things (Mayo, 2015).

Powerful knowledge provides the tools that can render people effective politically. Gramsci, in his criticism of the education reforms introduced by the fascist government of his time, was wary of the excessive emphasis on participation, without any substance, in reaction to the old Jesuitical school. He saw this as typical of the 'romantic' school – unbridled freedom for the learner – which, he argued, needed to enter its 'classical' phase, striking a balance between participatory democratic learning processes and rigorous mastery of certain knowledge (that of power) (Gramsci, 1971, pp. 32–33). Of course there is an argument to be made regarding how to balance all this with knowledge outside the mainstream, the knowledge of the specific communities and others, denigrated or dispossessed through a process of primitive accumulation, including 'cognitive accumulation' (dispossession and appropriation of, mainly Southern, subaltern knowledge) – more on this in the chapter that follows (de Sousa Santos, 2016; Hall and Tandon, 2017). After all, Gramsci indicated, a point also to be developed in the next chapter, how workers can assume responsibility for their own organised collective education.

On the other hand, many fields of practice, although capable of generating different forms of learning, knowledges and different insights, captured in the commonplace phrase – or should I say, the rather outworn cliché? – the 'University of Life', are also said to have both their strengths and limits. This has been argued with regard to schools where learning from the 'drift of life', although necessary as a potential starting point, is often deemed not sufficient in itself to provide the kind of knowledge necessary to partake fully of what life itself can offer (Young and Muller, 2010). Seizing upon aspects of life as an 'occasional motive', as indicated in the previous chapter, the occasional starting point is just a means to the end of taking students to the heart of the disciplines and beyond their experience into higher-order thinking that emerges from connecting with other experiences and knowledge, documented or otherwise (Young 2013, p. 107). It is argued by some that this is what justifies the effort of attending a school, no matter how unorthodox it is in its overall approach (think Barbiana and Lorenzo Milani – Batini et al., 2014) rather than simply learning from life itself.

The same applies to adult education projects including university LLL where the strength derives from the confrontation, centring on mutual respect, between the different perspectives and knowledges that come together in a genuinely democratic learning setting. One might argue, along the same lines, that we need institutions or settings that allow us to take steps forward and which provide knowledge that, although ideally having their basis in the real world, cannot be learnt simply from everyday life without some professional or significant intervention by teachers and others, including peers. Adults are said to have a broader range of experiences than children, which hence provide further reasons why their experience must be engaged (although I contend that this should be a feature of education at all levels). This is where the old Socratic maxim, as reported by Plato in the *Apologia*, gains importance: an unexamined life is a life not worth living. Practice on its own, without suitable conditions and stimuli for reflection and examination, besides imaginative elaboration of thought, does not necessarily 'make perfect'. In Freire's view, action without reflection is mere activism. What really 'makes perfect', or more appropriately takes us forward, in the views of many (notably Iram Siraj-Blatchford, 1994), is, as indicated in Chapter 3, *praxis*, reflection upon action for transformative action.

Marginalisation, *praxis* and imagination

The foregoing indicates that so many factors come to bear on the process of working ethically and in a socially committed manner, with adults in the field of

LLL. This applies to all areas of educational provision by universities, not only LLL. I have argued, time and time again earlier on, that many of the structured forms of LLL provision emerging from universities and other agencies are very much market-oriented, including such areas as foreign and local language teaching. Other marketable areas are connected with business and ICT, as indicated earlier. This does not preclude educators involved in these areas from bearing in mind the concerns about the nature and provenance of knowledge and power, and the issue of relevance. The same applies to those involved in the teaching of the humanities and social sciences.

There is a strong tradition of adult education concerning subaltern groups being connected to the arts and social sciences. Historically LLL or extension education in the arts and social sciences and the teachers who taught them were considered marginal to the work of the universities. For instance, work in connection with the Oxford Delegacy for Extramural Studies was considered marginal in the context of the University of Oxford's overall academic provision. Some refer to it as having been a means of appeasing the working class in its quest for higher education. As John McIlroy argued, regarding the status of extra-mural lecturers in Raymond Williams' time:

> In 1946 tutors did not enjoy the same tenure, facilities, or opportunities for pro-motion as internal lecturers. But by 1961 assimilation was advanced, although it was only in 1960 that Williams secured a form of promotion. This reflected and reinforced the marginality of university adult education. Critics felt that this work 'is not of university quality'. It was noted that 'extra-mural tutors, many of whom work at places remote from the university have little effective contact with their internal colleagues and are not in fact regarded as of equivalent status'. At Oxford, Frank Jessup recalled staff tutors in the post-war period as being connected with the uni-versity but not of it, 'irregulars skirmishing on the periphery'. (McIlroy, 1993, p. 275)

This attitude by the universities' authority smacked of tokenism, the same tokenism Gramsci commented upon with respect to the popular universities in Italy at his time, describing them as reminiscent of the early English merchants in Africa trading 'trashy baubles' for 'nuggets of gold' (Gramsci, 1971, p. 330). The Workers' Education Association at the heart of this provision, although having the workers' interests at heart, was often criticised for being 'ameliorist' in approach and not challenging the nature of society itself (B. Simon, 1992, p. 22),[10] the alter-native radical position to this coming from the Plebs League (Waugh, 2009).[11] Luminaries such as Raymond Williams and Edward P. Thompson later took advantage of the liminal spaces existing on the margins to connect different areas of knowledge with the participants' lifeworlds – working-class lifeworlds for the most part. History, economy, communications, popular culture, literature and other areas were brought together in a manner that was inconceivable in the main-stream HE provision. That 'trendy' area called cultural studies had its origins in this work on the margins of university life, in university LLL if you will. The point to register is that, in these marginal spaces and pockets, an alternative discourse can be born – alternative ways by which different threads are connected to provide holistic and potentially more critical engagements with knowledge and 'readings of the world' (see Freire and Macedo, 1987). As Raymond Williams observed:

> [W]e are beginning, I am afraid, to see encyclopedia articles dating the birth of Cultural Studies from this or that book in the late fifties. Don't believe a word of it. That shift of perspective about the teaching of arts and literature and their relation to history and to contemporary society began in Adult Education, it didn't happen anywhere else. It was when it was taken across by people with that experience to the Universities that it was suddenly recognised as a subject. It is in these and other similar ways that the contribution of the process itself to social change itself, and specifically to learning, has happened. (Williams, in McIlroy and Westwood, 1993, p. 260)

All this occurred well before the area's elaboration at the famed although alas defunct Centre for Contemporary Cultural Studies[12] at the University of Birmingham, comprising, *noblesse oblige*, Stuart Hall who subsequently made important contributions to university LLL as a sociologist via the Open University, Milton Keynes.[13] Cultural studies continues to feature prominently in certain programmes of university distance learning such as those provided by Athabasca University in Canada and the Open University of the Netherlands.

Raymond Williams, for his part, indicates that there is therefore the potential in the alternative sites to not only organise learning differently but also develop different approaches to knowledge, connecting with the concerns and preoccupations of the communities involved. Tom Sperlinger (2015) makes this point with regard to the teaching of literature in a specific setting, Palestine, a country under occupation. This approach helps the material discussed (co-investigated) connect with the 'structures of feeling' (to use Raymond Williams' expression) of the learning community – sentiments that have been felt, often deeply, but have not always been articulated in specific communities.

Flexibility or the smothering of imaginative impulses?

Flexibility is of essence in this regard, although much depends on the commitment and imagination of the educator/s involved. That flexibility is alas threatened if not diminished in many university settings these days with their over-bureaucratisation as the administration has gained the upper hand over the academic and student bodies. Everything has to be accounted for on paper as educators are primarily seen as service providers and the students are seen as clients. Fears of stepping out of line and credit over-consciousness are often held to be features of academic life these days, among faculty and students respectively. These fears are even stronger in situations when tenure is denied or rendered increasingly difficult to obtain and when the institution relies on a high percentage of adjunct faculty suffering from precarious conditions of employment; the latter applies to many engaged in extension LLL programmes.

There has often been criticism of certain faculty members themselves seeking kudos by becoming part of the institution's extended bureaucratic arm. They earn power and titles, in the form of full professorships, once reserved for academic achievement, through their sitting on committees, including ethics review committees, which allow them to control the work of colleagues. This situation favours the 'control freaks' among them. University leadership gestures in the direction of business administration. The work of top position incumbents, once entailing sound and inspirational academic direction, becomes more befitting of a corporation's CEO than a university leader. Legal rational bureaucratic authority, in Max Weber's terms, becomes a much more palatable proposition than academic stature or gravitas.

Situations such as these can lead to the stifling of imaginative impulses among faculty and students. While not belittling the importance of university administration in the smooth functioning of an institution facing several challenges in an age of intensified globalisation, one has to constantly question whether its modus operandi and its effects on the daily lives of faculty and students allow space for the imagination to 'take flight' and flourish (see Barnett, 2013). Approaches to learning, resulting in cultural studies of the type affirmed by Williams, require a strong sense of imagination.

Today one has to question every decision for satisfying either simply bureaucratic exigencies or academic ones. Does the decision simply serve to keep the wheels turning and dissuade anyone from attempting to do things differently or does it enhance the educative and research role of a university that looks forward imaginatively and refreshingly in its pursuit of academic excellence and furthering knowledge? We have even reached a stage, in certain universities operating on neoliberal lines, when obtaining a room for an innovative academic activity, or an extra-mural class or event, becomes a major consideration and a decisive one at that. Rooms are rented for such activities in a situation characterised by the constant commodification of public spaces. All this militates against the flexibility to try things differently, that flexibility LLL requires if it is meant to contribute to making a difference to the lives of universities, people and communities. Hopefully the alternative HE agencies discussed in this chapter operate on more flexible grounds; in many instances, the people involved have embarked on these projects for this reason, among others.

I envisage that things will become trickier when the students of these 'alternative' agencies seek international recognition for their qualifications. This would, in turn, lead to external pressure being placed on the agencies to conform to international trends and procedures. This will be a stern test for the alternative providers of HE. It takes use of the imagination to circumvent bureaucratic hurdles. Happily, some university community members prove remarkably adept at this. It is these kinds of people who serve the cause of making university LLL refreshing in its approaches.

It is the resourcefulness of academics who engage in a Gramscian 'war of position' (tactically inside and strategically outside the system) that is key in LLL programmes intended to engender new knowledge(s). They would take other knowledge forward while acknowledging their original sources, Western or other. In doing so, they open up new spheres of enquiry and develop new approaches to knowledge acquisition and exploration. Working for change through LLL, possibly effectively 'in against the system', requires social commitment on the educators' part. Do the lecturers/educators involved require preparation for this task? Some of the best experiments in adult education emerged from individuals and groups who learnt from encounters with the realities of ordinary people. Some were dubbed 'amateurs out to change the world' (Welton, 1995), in the positive sense that some of the major landmarks in the field involved people with no adult education training, people who were not concerned with professionalisation – not buying into its ideology (how professionals present themselves rather than how they actually are).

This notwithstanding, we are witnessing preparatory pedagogical courses for newly hired academics, some on tenure track, who are inducted into the art of teaching and supervising adolescents at tertiary level. Not everyone is a born and inspiring teacher, and qualifications in a specific subject, on their own, are no guarantee of success in teaching the area at undergraduate and other levels. There is room for preparatory work in these programmes not simply to, for instance, conduct differentiated teaching, a key skill at all levels, but also to work and learn with adults (English and Mayo, 2012). Anticipating the plethora of academic and professional journals on adult education and on community development in existence, the *Tutors' Bulletin* served as the resource journal for those involved in the Workers' Education Association classes in which contributions by Raymond Williams, E. P. Thompson, Karl Mannheim and Richard Hoggart were published. Even then it must have been felt that tutors, irrespective of their qualifications and experience, required supporting pedagogical material to aid or stimulate reflection on their area of adult education practice.[14]

LLL is, however, also offered by people connected with the university who are driven by their strong social commitment and who want to place their knowledge and acquired skills at the service of different communities. These might involve both academics and university students from different fields. At times, some engage in this work through the momentum generated by a political development, say the Second Republic democratic period in Spain, before Franco's rule, which led to several cultural and education missions. Students such as the great Andalusian poet and playwright Federico García Lorca were involved in adult education this way. When a law undergraduate, Lorca and his troupe of university and other actors, *La Barraca* (the Shack), engaged in community theatre throughout Spain and even in Harlem, New York City. This represented an attempt by university students to take theatre back to the people (Flecha, 1992), an initiative that led to a belief in the theatre of social action.[15] University theatre students can take and have often taken a leaf out of Lorca's book, as can students in a variety of other fields. They can engage in working outside the university walls with different communities. This is a form of university LLL engagement carried out both through support from or connection to a university structure or as a personal or group initiative. Initiatives such as the latter should also be considered as part and parcel of university LLL provision. For academics under pressure to publish, this can provide an opportunity for different forms of community research in different disciplines, such as community arts, in tandem with community members, at times also involving innovative and subaltern forms of enquiry as participatory action research (research in which community members are directly involved and which concerns issues directly related to the community itself). Academics carrying out this socially committed educational work break with the age-old stereotype of the 'ivory tower' university intellectual, immersed in books, to become either public or more specifically organic intellectuals in the Gramscian sense. In the latter case, the term 'intellectual' is defined not by any immanent features but by the function the person performs in and with a specific community, political movement or social movement. The function involved is that of either cementing or challenging relations of hegemony. In Gramsci's specific case, one either served the workings of capital or in challenging it served to transform (a long-term process) the relations that keep it in place. Working and engaging with communities, in a critically engaged LLL process, is the subject of the next chapter.

Notes

1 This chapter builds on P. Mayo (2017), 'Alternative higher education (HE): discourses in lifelong learning (LLL)', *Journal of Comparative International Higher Education*, 9, pp. 1–7, https://static1.squarespace.com/static/59de47487131a5734282c4b7/t/5a2583 21e4966b9c06669d7e/1512407842230/Mayo+Fall+2017.pdf.

2 Ruskin College, a trade union-oriented residential college for workers, was connected for a long time of its history with Oxford University. Like Plater College (Christian workers-oriented), it prepared its students for the University of Oxford's Diploma in Social Studies, which subsequently allowed the successful student to proceed to one of the colleges at Oxford University to study for a degree. According to Thomas Hardy, Ruskin was likely to be called 'the college of Jude the obscure' (in Alvarez, 1963, p. 115). The reference is to the character of Jude Fawley in his *Jude the Obscure*. One of the book's themes is frustrated, unrequited passion, including Jude's thwarted passion for learning within the walls of academia owing to his background as a tradesperson – a letter of rejection from the university (Christminster is the fictitious name) denies him entry on the grounds that the place is not suitable for a person of his station and calling.

3 WALLNET programme at OISE/University of Toronto: www.oise.utoronto.ca/clsew/ Research/Work_and_Lifelong_Learning.html.

4 The MST in Brazil focuses on dispossession and landlessness. As part of the colonial process, settlers drove people off the land and some of the latter's descendants continue to live an impoverished landless scenario (Young, 2003, p. 45). Popular education, in the Latin American tradition associated with Paulo Freire and others, is an important feature of the all-embracing educational work of the MST (Kane, 2001). They establish connections with dispossessed and landless people throughout the world including the Palestinians.

5 globlcenterforadvancedstudies.org.

6 The Universidad de la Tierra (UNITIERRA) has several campuses or locations as indicated by Boaventura de Sousa Santos (2017, pp. 403–409) with its main one being at San Cristobal de las Casas Chiapas where it is popularly known as the Centro Indigena de Capacitación Integral Fray Bartolomeu de las Casas (de Sousa Santos, 2017, p. 403). The university started operating in 1983 and declared its autonomy from the state in its connection with indigenous struggles in Chiapas, gaining strong support from leading liberation theologian Bishop D. Samuel Ruiz, forced to resign as head of the diocese by

the Vatican in 2000 (de Sousa Santos, 2017, p. 403). Its presence in Oaxaca occurs under the direction and leadership of Gustavo Esteva whose approach, as indicated in one of his books (Prakash and Esteva, 1998), has great affinities with the ideas of Ivan Illich and not so much with those of Paulo Freire. As Boavantura de Sousa Santos indicates, 'UNITIERRA is consciously a subversitivity; it begins from the idea that the term university must be resignified and liberated from its illegitimate appropriation by the conventional universities. It offers an alternative for training and earning that encourages respect for the land and its people, and promotes the search for technologies that are adequate to serve the interests of local communities' (de Sousa Santos, 2017, p. 405).

7 There has been a long series of debates around ways and means of evaluating and validating practice, especially in the area of prior learning assessment and recognition (PLAR). Validation packages have also been the outcomes of projects for this purpose. A lot of adult education takes the form of attempts to learn to be able to tackle issues concerning people's lives, both individual and communal. Hence relevance becomes an important feature. By relevance one means a strong connection between learning and life or rather the lifeworld (*lebenswelt*) of the participants involved

8 The idea of alternative rural universities is quite prevalent in the history of adult education and higher education. Two great writers, one from Europe and one from India, were involved in setting up educational centres for farmers, Tolstoy on the one hand and more significantly, in the context of universities, India's national and Nobel Prize-winning poet Rabindranath Tagore. The latter's contribution was his rural or agricultural university, the institute he set up which became Visva Bharati University. The idea of rural universities has been taken in up in Spain and Portugal as part of the Plataforma Rural to educate people in a bid to stem the tide of internal migration from hinterland to the coastal areas (see Guimarães et al., 2018). Projects are currently occurring, involving university, to prevent the colonisation of aspects of vanishing lifeworlds, namely skills and crafts, by the system world (Lucio-Villegas, 2017).

9 The 2003 University Act stipulates the establishment of a governing board consisting of people external to the university.

10 The object of the dissatisfaction was Ruskin College and this quote from *Plebs*, the organ of the Plebs League, sums up the concern among those who sought a different form of workers' education: 'Ruskin College has ceased to fulfil whatever useful function it did perform for the Labour Movement. Henceforth the object of the "Plebs" must be to assist in the establishing of a new educational structure definitely controlled by organized Labour]' (as quoted in Waugh, 2009, p. 24).

11 The labour colleges in the UK which formed the Plebs League (see B. Simon, 1992; Waugh, 2009) provided the radical response. They provided an approach to education that investigated knowledge from the proletariat's vantage point. This effort at radical working-class education can be seen in the context of a larger, radical alternative adult education to 'bourgeois education' that, as stated earlier, is known as independent working-class education, a movement found in many other places such as Scotland, Germany and Australia. The struggles in adult education and the working class reflected larger struggles and currents within and beyond socialism. The Plebs League survived until the 1950s before it petered out mainly but not exclusively as a result of the Cold War climate in which Britain found itself (see English and Mayo, 2012, p. 87).

12 It is well-known that cultural studies was much later taken up at universities across the Atlantic and in Australia, as well as at Goldsmith's University of London, the last mentioned institution striking me as the leading centre for research and study in this area in Britain today.

13 See Hall's interview, where he dwells on his pedagogy at the Open University (de Peuter and Hall, 2007).

14 Copies of this journal are archived at the TUC Holdings in the Library of London Metropolitan University, and constitute a boon for anyone seeking a broader understanding of the workings of this early form of university LLL provision in the UK.

15 The idea of linking theatre with social action is quite popular. It has been taken up in various places by a variety of playwrights (e.g., Edward Bond in England) and groups including popular education groups and movements in Latin America. Later, Augusto Boal, echoing the work of his friend Paulo Freire (with whom he shared the experience of exile following the 1964 coup), developed the theatre of the oppressed (Boal, 1993). This is based on the popular education initiatives one associates with Freire and on learning through *praxis* (English and Mayo, 2012, p. 136). The whole purpose is to enable participants, notably people from different communities, to gradually unveil the contradictions lacerating society. University students frequently engage in this type of theatre, which takes them out of the academy into communities, thus providing another form of university LLL. I experienced such a situation among theatre students at the University of Bologna in 2000.

6

University/HE LLL and the community

University LLL has always presented opportunities for community engagement. The activities involved can be carried out via departments and centres
or individuals/teams of people connected with them, people in full-time or part-
time employment. In this chapter, I will propose – drawing on insights from
key educators, such as Paulo Freire, Jane Vella, Lorenzo Milani and Ivan Illich –
signposts for a critical engagement between universities or educators connected
with them and the surrounding communities. I will also draw on insights from
my own experiences in this regard, once again writing from the vantage point of a
university academic in adult education located in Southern Europe.

Historical preamble

Extension service or extra-mural studies (taking place outside the precincts of
the university), as we have seen, constituted one of the most prominent forms,
although not the only form, of engagement in this regard. There are those who
would trace the history of this provision back to Cambridge University's establishment of extra-mural studies in the late nineteenth century. This is regarded as an
important landmark. I would, however, be hesitant to state that it marks the oldest
type of university public or community engagement, as there might have been
similar activities or ones that approximate this kind of provision elsewhere. As far
as the English-speaking world goes, however, existing documentation refers to the
Cambridge scientist and politician James Stuart as a pioneer in this regard. He is
recognised as being the key historical figure in this context. In the late nineteenth
century he delivered a course of lectures, under Cambridge University's aegis, in
different cities (Barlow, 2012, pp. 18–19). This university has been offering extra-
mural or extension courses until the present day, with an institute for this purpose located in Madingley, Cambridgeshire. The idea spread to many other cities
in Britain – by 1891 there were 464 outreach programmes frequented by around
45,000 students (Stromquist and Lozano, 2017, p. 786) – and the English-speaking
world. The concept of extending the university's reach through delivery of lectures
in different localities was taken up by institutions as recently established as the
University of Cyprus, which started functioning in 1992 (see Phtiaka, 2003).[1] There
is documentation (Stromquist and Lozano, 2017, p. 786) of university outreach

efforts taking place elsewhere, especially in France, Italy and Spain, as well as in Latin American countries. Quite indicative was the university student movement in Cordoba, Argentina in 1918. It placed demands on universities to embark on changes including that of providing university extension services to workers in the spirit of solidarity with the proletariat (Stromquist and Lozano, 2017, p. 786).

A cursory Google view of university extension or 'public engagement', to use the phrase adopted in England, indicates the plethora of university–community engagements in countries ranging from New Zealand to cities such as Mumbai and Nairobi. Many universities have their departments of outreach, extension studies, extra-mural studies or continuing education, now often subsumed under the all-embracing term LLL. The last mentioned is at odds with the idea that LLL should be the guiding principle throughout the whole university or HE institution rather than simply the concept governing just one of its single branches or centres. Needless to say, distance education plays an important role in this provision. At times even Universities of the Third Age (U3A) are connected with established universities, thus following the original French model (University of Toulouse), rather than, for instance, the British model where U3As are separate autonomous entities adopting a 'self-help' approach, with the first of their kind established, once again, at Cambridge, England (Formosa, 2013, pp. 229–231).

There is a strong tradition in Europe and elsewhere of popular universities that vary in their activities and nature, many autonomous and funded by the municipality or state, others private. Some include a modicum of vocational education but the majority hold a concept of university different from that emphasised in LLL in official EU discourse, more community-oriented and embracing a variety of areas covered, mostly centring around citizenship and communal needs (see Stromquist and Lozano, 2017).

There are also all-age universities such as Italy's Università della Libera Età. The notion of 'university' being used here is the old medieval notion of a gathering of scholars. These are primarily adult education centres. Established universities can take a leaf out of their book with regard to their outreach work. The huge presence of these popular universities or similar centres indicates the social craving or rather community craving for knowledge in its wide variety of forms and not for simply instrumental learning. Taking a leaf out of this book does not mean, however, finding ways of colonising these spaces. This would contradict the argument with which I conclude this chapter. Learning communities functioning autonomously and smoothly should be left to do so.

This consolidates the view that people have the potential to organise their own education as part of their lifeworlds. Many are those who guard these lifeworlds against their colonisation by the system world that, in this case, is represented by universities, public or private.

This century we have been witnessing the growth of university–community engagement movements with several networks to boot, including the Popular Education Network (Crowther, 2013) initiated by academic-activists such as Mae Shaw, Ian Martin, Jim Crowther and Vernon Galloway – at Moray House School of Education, University of Edinburgh (the initial conference was held at the

University of Edinburgh in 2000), PASCAL (http://pascalobservatory.org/) and the Talloires Network. The last-mentioned network arose from a 2005 meeting at the Tufts University European Centre in Talloires, France, which brought together 29 university presidents, vice-chancellors and rectors from 23 countries spread across six continents (Bacow, 2011). Its work is best captured in a fine contribution providing case studies of the network's member universities involved in community engagement (Watson et al., 2011). The institutions ranged from the Shreemati Nathibai Damodar Thackersey Women's University in Mumbai and another women's university (Ahfad University for Women), this time in Sudan, to the Petro Mohyla Black Sea State University in Ukraine and the Universiti Kebangsaan Malaysia. The compendium includes universities from the Middle East, namely the University of Haifa and Al-Quds University. Al-Quds University carries out work of this kind through the Abu Dis campus and the Community Action Centre in the Old City of Jerusalem, the latter given prominence in the previous chapter. One of Al-Quds University's features is its Centre for Jerusalem Studies, which offers courses from certificate to Master's in the area – in short, a centre for the study of the university's surrounding city from a multidisciplinary perspective.

One prominent university, included in the network, is the University of Dar es Salaam, Tanzania. I say 'prominent' because the establishment of this university and its forerunner, the University College forming part of the then University of East Africa, were given prominence in international discussions on education and development with respect to Julius Kambarage Nyerere's signature concepts of 'Ujamaa Vijijini' and 'Education for Self-Reliance'.

In his writings, including his address at the official opening of the University, Nyerere, the Tanzanian president addressed reverentially as 'Mwalimu', underlined the contribution that the university and its academics are expected to make to the wider community. The effort is intended to enable the community to tackle its challenges. Nyerere argued for a genuine exchange between both sides, in which there should be no distinction between manual and academic workers. He argued that academics and other intellectuals educated at popular expense should not hold society to ransom for their services and that there should be a reciprocal exchange between academics and peasants as the latter have much to offer through their insights and first-hand knowledge of the agricultural field (Mayo, 2013, p. 112; Mayo and Vittoria, 2017, p. 171).

As cited in Watson et al. (2011, p. 153), Nyerere is on record as having stated, during the founding of the University of Dar es Salaam's forerunner (University College, University of East Africa):

> For let us be clear; the University has not been established purely for prestige purposes. It has a very definite role to play in development in this area, and to do so effectively, it must be in, and of, the community it has been established to serve.

The Watson et al. (2011) book highlights one very important point, namely the importance given to universities and community engagement in the Global South. The late Dave Watson, a key writer on the issue, and his colleagues (Watson et al., 2011), find much purchase in Global South examples where the concern at most universities is that of response to immediate communal needs. Nyerere is instructive in this regard, arguing that the purpose of universities in countries like his, characterised by poverty, is to help alleviate this situation through knowledge.

The community's taxes have been channelled towards supporting a public university because the community expects to benefit in return, hence the connection between higher education and communal development. He states:

> [A] university in a developing country must put the emphasis of its work on subjects of immediate moment to the nation in which it exists and it must be committed to the people of that nation and their humanistic goals…and it is this fact which justifies the heavy expenditure of resources on this one aspect of national life and development. Its research, and the energies of its staffing particular, must be freely offered to the community, and they must be relevant. (Nyerere, 1968, p. 183)[2]

This idea of the socially engaged university is opposed to that of many contemporary Western universities and their preoccupation with moving up the global ranking ladder/'pecking order' and therefore with being competitive (Laing, 2016), the ultimate aspiration for some being that of becoming a 'world class' or 'blue chip' university. This is often to the detriment of expanding 'civic engagement and social responsibility programs in an ethical manner, through teaching, research and public service' creating 'institutional frameworks for the encouragement, reward and recognition of good practice in social service by students, faculty, staff and their community partners' and fostering 'partnerships between universities and communities' (Talloires Declaration in Watson et al., 2011), all this constituting what the Italians call the universities' 'Terza Missione' (Third Mission).[3]

Community/ies

The words 'community' and 'communities' have had different meanings, rendering the concept involved quite fluid and complex. They can refer to a variety of people brought together through national, regional or municipal boundaries, among many others. They can be bound by some common characteristics. Raymond Williams (1976) stresses the relational aspect of community in its older meaning and also its association with the commons, i.e., common people as opposed to those of rank. We are told by Williams that around the nineteenth century, it took on a 'sense of immediacy or locality' which was developed 'in the context of larger and more complex industrial society' (Williams, 1976, p. 75). It also referred to a community of alternative group living (Williams, 1976, p. 75).

The classical sociological notion is that of Ferdinand Tönnies' *Gemeinschaft*, signifying what has been perceived as the old traditional way of living together tied by communal bonds – intimate, enduring, in which every person knows his or her position and role in society, where institutions such as churches and family prescribe these roles through a given culture (Mann, 1983, p. 143). Williams (1976) sees this as referring to the more direct, more total and more significant relationships of community as opposed to the more formal, more abstract and more instrumentalised relationships of *Gesellschaft* (p. 76). Territories can feature in some meanings of the word and feature less when referring, for example, to the 'Muslim community', 'Jewish community' and so forth,[4] although, in certain places, districts can be found that are associated with the presence of communities where the word is used in this sense (e.g., quarters, ghettos, diamond centres; such as Little Italy in New York City, Corso d'Italia in Toronto, 'Little Kinshasa' in Brussels, El Barrio in New York City, etc.).

Raymond Williams (1976) refers to 'community' as a word that has never been used 'unfavourably and never to be given any positive opposing or distinguishing term' (Williams, 1976, p. 76). Many have argued that community has taken on different interpretations since the time of his writing this, some of which having pejorative connotations, often denoting exclusivity. This is, for instance, found in work that is critical of 'social capital', the term used in the Putnam (2000) and Coleman sense.

In this chapter, I shall draw on different meanings attached to the words 'community' or 'communities', although the overriding sense in which the words are used is that of relations (a common aspect of most of the foregoing definitions of community) among common people within particular boundaries of locality. Of course I try to avoid any romanticised notion of community, and, more importantly, any essentialising and monolithic views in this regard. Based on some experiences I have had in this regard, in work connected to the university where I have been employed for the past 30 years, I refer to community with respect to people living in a certain locality and its surroundings characterised by some general features but, as always, with social difference at the core.[5]

Giving 'community' favourable connotations risks leading to idealistic representations besides the danger of not recognising difference and the dynamic nature of the territory, with its contestation often occurring through the changes brought about by immigration from outside the locality or from outside the country, entailing portability of cultures and knowledge traditions. Certain communities also have had knowledge traditions that are different from those promoted at established institutions such as universities and other HE providers, as Carlo Levi (2006) has shown with regard to particular interpretations of history, lying at the furthest remove from those of the mainstream versions.

If we search for a genuinely democratic approach to university/HE LLL engagement in this context, then we need to recognise the complexity involved where the old system of simply 'extension' needs to be ditched in favour of one suggesting a more reciprocal approach. This would be one where the university and its personnel learn as much as the target learners themselves. I highlight some facets of the alternative approach involved, drawing inspiration from Paulo Freire, Lorenzo Milani, Ada Gobetti, Jane Vella and a host of other educators within the emancipatory education tradition.

In keeping with the tenor of the book, especially the previous chapter, it is one where learning is interactive and dynamic. While involving the epistemological investigation of different kinds of knowledge, including the already discussed 'powerful knowledge', not to keep anyone on the margins of political life, it is also one that is inclusive of the different knowledge traditions brought to bear on the community as a result of its changing demographics, reflecting different sources of thinking and wisdom (see, for instance, once again, the importance of a major Arab social science pioneer, Ibn Khaldun, as discussed by de Sousa Santos, 2017).

Pedagogical approaches and strategies for teaching and learning with adults in the community

The first step entails learning about the community, as education is always context-based. Learning in this context would entail reading material and discussing with informed contacts, preferably from the community, about the locality in question. Perusing literature on and around the community requires critical engagement. One should be alert to identify any stereotyping, self-fulfilling prophecies and any degree of pathologising. The identified key informants can include social and community workers already engaged in the area. Again the information derived should be held to the same level of critical scrutiny as in the case of the literature. At the same time as flagging up instances of deficit approaches, one should also avoid romanticising communities and their cultures. This in my view applies to all cultures and not just those of the subaltern. These would constitute the preliminary stages of community research. This research does not need to be carried out in a formal sense but in the manner explained by Paulo Freire in his early work.[6]

Where and when possible, one can invite potential learners for informal meetings to discuss the community in pairs or groups. This involves mixing with people in and from the community. It entails learning through listening carefully (Vella, 2002), understanding speech patterns and an exploration of what captures the imagination of several members of the community. This would serve as the starting point for the projects in question, as indicated in the previous chapter, drawing from Lorenzo Milani's 'occasional motive', the initial step before moving on to 'higher order' mutual inquiry, a gradual entrance into the nature of any subject intended to be taught. In my view, some of the best examples of community education are those that build on that which by and large captures the community members' imagination; there will be those who have different interests in this regard. Given my location as a person born and raised in Southern Europe, outdoor activities such as *festas* with rituals and related spectacles rank among the activities that bring people together, often imbuing them with a sense of collective identity. This applies to localities in Spain, Greece, Malta, Italy, Portugal, Croatia, etc. These activities are conditioned by the climate of this part of the world and the 'rhythms of life' it generates (Braudel, 1972). Earlier I gave examples of how adult education projects have built on these interests. The reference to Joan Bofill and the work in Catalonia also indicated how a collective sense of belonging was perceived as a threat in certain contexts, in this case, Franco's Spain, or Estado Español, as the Catalans would call it. Franco's regime was bent on centralisation as opposed to regional autonomy and difference. These activities, which can spark off educational projects, are connected with aspects of many people's identity – they constituted forms of resistance to 'top-down' impositions in centralised policymaking. Any religious significance these activities originally might have had can be subsumed by their communal significance, which, in my view, can appeal to atheists and people of different faiths, the feasts being cause for communal togetherness.

This becomes all the more important in situations when new members from outside, with different traditions, join the community. It does, however, raise other issues. One should be on the lookout for what divides the community – any sectarian strains in a community often manifest in a variety of related institutions such as feasts in certain localities, support of football teams and religious/ethnic adherence (Glasgow as an example)? This is where awareness, tact and prudence must be shown, the sort of prudence Lorenzo Milani sought to show in the locality of San Donato di Calenzano when facing a politico–religious split between the Christian Democrats and the Communist Party, or rather the Church and the Communist Party (Batini et al., 2014). This situation was satirised by Giovanni Guareschi in his *Don Camillo and Peppone* vignettes of life in post-WWII Italy. Here 'big' ideological confrontations trickled down to parish pump politics in the locality of Brescello.

This leads to a consideration of an important feature of a local community, its social class composition. This has implications for a variety of approaches highlighted in the sociology of education literature, which one needs not rehearse here. I would limit myself to just a couple of important features: moving pedagogically from the concrete to the abstract rather than vice versa, the latter often very much the approach adopted with mainstream students at universities, students who have made it through a system favouring specific forms of cultural capital and language codes and registers.

This is one aspect that community educators, especially university educators, ought to bear in mind and be prepared to learn about not solely from the existing sociological literature but from any interactive process itself, one that allows space and confidence for the learners to express themselves in a manner that reflects their own framework of relevance. My experience interacting in adult education sessions with people on a labour studies course in the late 1990s, comprising shop stewards and other personnel in the trade union movement, taught me a lot in this regard. The advantage the people in question had was that they acquired and developed the confidence, over the years, in their bargaining with management, not to be deferential towards authority. They had the confidence and assertiveness to bring their own terms to bear on the interactive co-learning process involved. This experience would stand me in good stead with others who have not had similar trade union experiences.

I have to say that once my university and other colleagues and I helped to provide the right setting and sense of trust, there was a similar amount of participation by parents, mainly women, in a project of adult education concerning parental involvement in children's education. This project has been documented in the international literature through a qualitative case study (Borg and Mayo, 2006).

Of course, there was always the danger, in the labour studies sessions, that, like the trade unions themselves, the areas of workers' and trade union education became male bastions, a standard critique over the years of this kind of adult education provision (Taking Liberties Collective, 1989). I sought to address this theme in a published case study, involving qualitative research, concerning the workers' education programme in question. This engagement occurred through the University of Malta's Centre for Labour Studies (formerly the Workers' Participation Development Centre). The case study tackled aspects of social relations of the education process. It also tackled the nature of the contents provided or co-investigated, giving prominence to the gender considerations involved (Mayo, 2015).

Gender therefore remains a key issue. The elementary question for the preliminary community research is to identify the gender composition of the community, treating the area in its broadest dimensions. It is important for the university itself, where and when possible, allowing for ineluctable situations, to be inclusive in the teams of people it employs to carry out community engagement projects. It is important for educators to have sensitivity to women's ways of knowing (Belenky et al., 1986) and to provide all the safeguards to ensure that the learning setting and experience does not become another example of patriarchal subjugation, a main criticism of workers' education programmes. There is need for greater sensitivity to the entire range of identities in the LGBTQ continuum. One major issue is: who takes up most of the space in these learning settings and who is favoured by the times when and localities where the activity takes place? Whose worldview is being given prominence in the sessions?

One important area in the preliminary community research concerns the ethnic composition of the community. This is an ever-growing feature of life in communities, with migration occurring on a large and, in certain parts of the world, unprecedented scale. As Leona English and I argue in a piece on LLL and SDGs (English and Mayo, forthcoming), we shall witness an exponential increase in migration from South to North, and from South to South. Capitalism, via corporations, exacerbates the 'greenhouse effect' as individual sustainable living has minimal effects on climate improvement when contrasted with efforts expected of corporations and other similarly powerful entities. It is predicted that climate change will render life unbearable for people in the South. The year 2015 was the hottest thus far and the UN Intergovernmental Panel on Climate Change envisages a 1.5 degrees centigrade increase, with 20–30 per cent of the planet's species at risk of extinction. During the 2015–2016 summers, southern Africa faced unprecedented droughts, causing starvation for millions.

With the worsening of climate change, there will be an increase in famine, calamitous weather conditions, heatwaves, droughts and floods affecting millions. Diseases such as malaria will become even more widespread, which will hit countries untouched by them thus far. The disputes over resources will, in all probability, lead to wars (Empson, 2016, pp. 1–2), fuelled further by a Western-based arms industry. Many will risk life and limb to emigrate. Leona English and I point out that droughts are often not assisted by appropriate famine relief from Western powers and corporations lest the market prices become destabilised. This is a capitalist practice of long standing, a practice that historically led to tragedies such as the Irish potato famine in the nineteenth century (Empson, 2016, p. 17). All this points to a massive increase in migration into Europe and other places in the forthcoming years.

Many will manage to enter the so-called 'fortresses' such as 'Fortress Europe' and other Western places, others will be left stranded in transit places such as Libya. There are those who live on the margins of the Western context, without papers (*sans papiers*) and with deportation crooking a beckoning finger at them. Those less fortunate will have drowned in a sea, the likes of which some had never witnessed before. Others will have perished in such barren lands as the Sahara Desert, their bones serving as a stark reminder to those who follow in their footsteps of the fate that awaits many. In short, migration will grow on a massive scale and this is bound to touch and alter the demographic composition of communities.

Those who survive and manage to join these communities (alas, many remain marginalised within the communities) will have their own stories to tell, both tragic and less so; stories that indelibly affect the complexion of what they have to say on aspects of politics, economics, sociology, health and several other areas that might be discussed in the community learning setting.

This is one of the most challenging aspects of university community engagement where the 'established' knowledge of universities, at times Western and Eurocentric, meets the new learning being brought into the community from countries and regions with a wealth of knowledge and whose people have different perspectives on things. This knowledge had been dismissed through colonial and neo-colonial forces or else appropriated and patented in what has been referred to as a process of cognitive (mis)appropriation and accumulation (Hall and Tandon, 2017; Odora Hoppers, 2017).

One task is to seize the opportunity to question the 'established' origins of certain knowledge and challenge the misconceptions and omissions, the latter, for instance, including Islamic and Arabic (not to be conflated[7]) civilisations' contributions to 'Western' civilisation. The communal research indications would place one on guard with respect to the point made earlier regarding whose social and cultural capital is valorised and whose is excluded, hence whose culture and knowledge is engaged, represented and how.

Once again, quite beneficial would be a dialogical approach that allows spaces and the confidence for people of different ethnic backgrounds, including the 'autochthonous' community members, to participate and bring their own cultures and knowledge traditions to bear on the learning encounter.

It can help break with the conventional Eurocentric tradition of confining the learning to the 'official' knowledge (Western 'regimes of truth'). This does not mean that we replace one knowledge tradition with another. It means, to the contrary, that an enriching cultural experience can be provided by the bringing together – perhaps in a complementary fashion, and at times also in confrontation with one another – of different knowledge traditions. Of course this approach to knowledge applies not only to interethnic communities but to even purportedly 'ethnically homogenous' communities. It revolves around the issue of whose knowledge we teach and share and which knowledge we leave out. Leaving out huge chunks and traditions of knowledge, often because of their subaltern/subjugated status, represents an impoverishment of what is learnt and a falsehood when it comes to the real historical origins of what we mistakenly attribute to 'Western civilisation'. These encounters can well become a decolonising experience. Needless to say, this represents one of the greatest challenges in this day and age. For this challenge to be met, we must be prepared to relearn that which we think we already know.[8]

Another key feature of the preliminary community research would be the age composition of the community with special attention attached to knowledge as endangered species. This often entails appreciating and engaging the skills and oral history of people involved to be contrasted with mainstream history and other recounting of events. This oral history is not to be dismissed as 'misconception', 'preconceived ideas' and so forth. Older persons have much to teach the younger generation in the same way that the latter have much to teach the former. Intergenerational learning is an important feature of adult education. University community engagement can therefore draw on this aspect of epistemological enquiry. This also has implications for sciences especially regarding indigenous sciences, indigenous medicines and applied sciences of older adults in their former work environments. One final key point in the community research fact-finding mission is the availability of learning settings and whether they provide enabling or disabling environments for potential learners.

Freirean approach

Earlier, I remarked that one need not follow Freire's approach to the letter. Education is context based, so the codification–de-codification process is something that can be approximated in spirit. His is not a method or blueprint to be followed or project to be transferred cargo-cult style. Freire emphasised this time and time again with his famous remark: experiments are not to be transplanted but must be reinvented. Don Lorenzo Milani said very much the same thing when he stated categorically that the School of Barbiana began at Barbiana and ended at Barbiana.

This notwithstanding, there is much inspiration we can draw from Freire and Milani in community outreach. If critical university engagement is what we are after, and I make no bones about the fact that this is the kind of approach to education that I favour, based on a commitment to an education for social justice, then Freire's codification underlines the importance of *praxis* in any engagement with these ideals in mind. This is a central concept in this volume, as readers will have realised by now given its recurrence throughout the chapters. I realise that certain subjects or areas of concern lend themselves to this approach more than others. *Praxis*, as I remarked earlier, entails enabling the learners to gain critical distance from the everyday to be able to perceive it in a more critical light – hence the codification of what is gathered from researching/exploring the community into an educational prop or device, maybe a play, a set of photographs, a piece of graffiti, which 'distances' the participants from what is being presented.

Through dialogue around the work itself and with judicious and timely prompts, people can potentially begin to realise that what is being represented is an aspect of their own everyday life, an aspect they take for granted but that, once again in the words of Ira Shor, now appears extraordinarily to them. Collectively they can come to appreciate that and begin to problematise the issue. This process, as adopted by Freire, is based on two very important aspects which universities ought to take on board.

One is the degree to which learners can be engaged in co-developing material, as in the Seville project involving collective memory with regard to 40 years of Franco rule. Works of art by community members themselves can prove valuable in this regard. A piece of artistic work or graffiti can reveal aspects of their present life. This should be availed of by the university educator.

The second related point is that of starting from the learners' concrete exist-ential situation – everyday life in the 'here and now', that is to say, the human beings' current situation 'from which they emerge, and in which they intervene' (Freire, 1970, 2000, p. 85). This is how Freire expressed the view in *Pedagogy of the Oppressed* and re-elaborated it in *Pedagogy of Hope* (Freire, 1994), which was meant to be a revision of the former work – echoes once again of Lorenzo Milani's much cited reference, in this volume, to moving from 'occasional motive' to the 'profound motive'.

The adult education experience should help learners move beyond this; other-wise we remain where we are – denounced by Freire and others as populism or 'basismo'. He argues that, in remaining there and not moving beyond (through co-investigation of the object of inquiry), one would be engaging in 'basism', the romanticisation (or 'mythification') of the vernacular (see Freire, 1994, p. 84). Freire's insistence that we start by connecting with the learners' 'concrete con-text' (1994, p. 78), including their dreams or possibly nightmares, marks a gradual and tactful entry into the disciplines. They then engage critically through *praxis* to uncover the underlying contradictions of one's reading of the world and its construction through various narratives, historical accounts, specific situations, etc. This can help a person develop a more coherent and therefore critical view of things.

Educators must tread carefully here, being aware of the proper nature of the knowledge systems engaged with, allowing for different traditions from different territories to be brought to bear on the discipline, especially by those who carry them into the community.

The Freire approach highlights one other obvious thing that warrants repeti-tion. It concerns the need to develop material that is sensitive with regards to cul-ture, age, social class, ethnicity and gender. One needs to avoid the temptation of using texts suitable for mainstream 'lock-step' students, arguably a truism. Once again relevance is of essence in this regard. Depending on the background of the different community members, this process of induction to the material should occur gradually, starting once again from the members' albeit differentiated existential situations. The more one knows about the community, the more one is in a position to select material that suits different members and the different knowledge traditions they bring with them. Texts, as Michael W. Apple and many others have shown, give legitimacy to certain knowledge traditions at the expense of others represented in the learning setting.

Carefully chosen relevant texts provide wonderful opportunities for participants to appreciate difference also in the views and standpoints available. Participants should also be allowed to contribute in this regard by bringing material to be shared with the rest of the group. Once again a genuine process of dialogue and interpersonal communication would also allow for different perspectives and narratives, spoken and written, to be brought to bear on the educational encounter.

The notion of outreach, in the great university tradition of providing learning experiences beyond the walls of the university, captured in the term 'extra-mural', leads us to explore, with rest of the participants, different sites with potential for learning. The challenge here is to ensure that they are enabling sites for a variety of learners on the recognition, as mentioned earlier, that, although the community is bound by some common element – for example, living in the locality – one needs to eschew a monolithic view of it.

Apart from giving the university or other HE institutions visibility in specific communities, satellite university sites enable partnerships to be forged between university personnel and the community. These include partnerships between the university educators and the community members who frequent or are involved with these sites. We have interesting examples of the use of such local sites, especially municipal sites. A case in point is the way the EGS makes use of a public municipal site in Saas-Fee, Switzerland, for one of its intensive periods of teaching and learning. We have seen how the Lincoln Social Sciences Centre project is carried out in local county council premises.

While the Paulo Freire and Jane Vella approaches lead us to be as interactive and dialogical as possible, it is also important to follow the former's lead when he states that there are moments where one has to be 50 per cent a traditional and 50 per cent a democratic teacher, mixing instruction where necessary and unavoidable with asking questions.[9] Elements of the old pedagogy can co-exist with the new, provided the overall climate is one that fosters democratic relations. As stated earlier, avoiding powerful knowledge would sell the community learners short and so this presents a good reason to strike a balance between instruction and dialogue. Furthermore, community learners would have trust in the educator's competence and therefore bestow a certain authority on her or him which, however, should not be allowed to degenerate into authoritarianism, a point Freire repeats over and over again.

Freire stressed the notion of educators who *dare teach* (1998b). He underlined that they do not act as coddling aunts (*profesora sim tia nao*, in the official Brazilian title of Freire, 1998b) and are not simply 'facilitators', the latter a term he had used in his early work but which he stopped using later because of its connotations of laissez faire pedagogy and the danger of shirking one's responsibility to teach.

My experience in adult education, including university outreach or workers' education, indicates that the learners in question want to make ample use of the time allotted for learning and would brook no time wastage. Prison inmates, who I taught in the late 1990s, as part of a university extension project inside the precincts, would immediately detect a suspect educator just as they would 'smell' a person attempting to con them on the streets. My local experience suggests that they would not think twice about calling on the prison school authorities to have him or her removed. Competence is what learners expect of the university educator as they would not allow themselves to be short-changed.

The Freirean approach to dialogue is also nuanced. It also requires preparation. Freire advocates that the questions posed are searching and intended to stimulate critical and imaginative thinking. These would not be the sort of questions that simply elicit 'closed' answers. They should also be, in the Freirean sense, of a problem-posing nature, which engages the group's critical acumen, sense of imagination and emotional reactions. This is the sort of dialogical approach meant to arouse epistemological curiosity.

There are limits to simply problem-solving. The hallmark of a good university encounter is that which allows the student to develop a healthy scepticism, to fear 'certainties', to question given assumptions and to realise that there is no clear answer to every question posed. Questions generate further questions as 'different takes' on things, often reflecting different ways in which community members are located discursively, because of their class, gender, ethnic and other backgrounds, among other things. These questions lead one to call 'all in doubt', to echo John Donne's statement regarding 'The New Philosophy' affecting the early seventeenth century in England, hence problem-posing or, once again, problematising.

Depending on the nature of the object of co-investigation, learners can be assigned preliminary or audio recordings to be equipped to engage in dialogue and to contrast what is being proposed or professed against the background of their own experience and knowledge deriving from their lifeworlds. In short, they are encouraged to 'rewrite' and 'reinterpret' the texts involved. This process of rewriting and reinterpreting is what had led Gramsci (1971), in his notes on the 'Unitarian School', to question the existence of a 'passive recipient' of knowledge. Once people are kept alert by a stimulating learning process, they reconstruct things both before and after the pedagogical encounter.

They also go through the same process of reinterpreting and rewriting during the encounter itself. 'Banking education' suppresses these different interpretations in the sense that it allows little space for them to be voiced and listened to, while a genuine dialogical education – authentic dialogue, in Freire's sense – allows these rewritings to be voiced, challenged and developed further, rendering the co-investigation ever-more nuanced.

Humility

Humility is one virtue that is given prominence in the Freirean lexicon. It is highlighted in Paulo Freire's major works and a recurrent theme throughout his oeuvre. I have often heard ministers and other persons, including influential opinion leaders, criticise university academics on these grounds. Whether this criticism is fair is open to debate and depends on context. What, however, sticks in the perception of these detractors of university academics is the idea of the academic as a know-it-all figure, a fount of expertise on specific matters to which students are deferential. This smacks of the pre-1968 university and not the post-1968 one. I am once again using this year as a tentative watershed, a year characterised by upheavals and contestations, including contestations by the radical Left in various places (Williams, 2018). The riots in France and the rest of the continent are said to have put paid to the 'top-down' approach to university lecturing. There are of course lecturers and lecturers as there are school teachers and school teachers, but old habits occasionally die hard.

In adult education, however, there exists a progressive tradition of a democratic educator, a tradition to which Paulo Freire and Jane Vella, as well as a host of other influential educators, have contributed. Learning to listen is presented as an important aspect of this tradition. This requires a degree of humility.

Humility on the part of the official educator is called for in this tradition, which I have been attempting to follow in this volume. Earlier, I stated the importance of the educator being ready to teach and not sell students short – however, without allowing the authority bestowed by the learners to degenerate into authoritarianism. I also mentioned that one should always be disposed to relearn what is thought to be known through engaging the learners' thinking and reactions, which can lead to one's gaining new insights on the matter, if not also revising preconceived ideas.

All this is based on recognition of the learners as being teachers at the same time, as people who have much to offer and who might well have first-hand experience of the topic and context being co-investigated. In my book, humility should be a feature of all who partake of the learning process, which is not there to be abused – dialogue, Freire warns us, is not to be abused or, I would add, hijacked. Neither is there room for patronising attitudes towards others

'Have you seen, guys, how the bourgeois people are? They teach China to the Chinese', Don Lorenzo Milani quipped in reaction to a friend from Florence who corrected a Chinese priest speaking about China at the Barbiana School.[10] What can be inferred from this and other episodes, such as the one disclosed by Paulo Freire regarding an experience he had with impoverished people in a Brazilian community (Freire, 1994),[11] is not to try to 'teach the community' to those who form part of it. One should have the humility to outline one's limitations when, for instance, being invited to lead a session on, say, Paulo Freire to a group of students in Brazil or on Gramsci to a group of participants at a seminar in Sardinia, situations in which I have found myself over the years, given my work in these fields.

I try, in these circumstances, to engage the group's first-hand knowledge of the community. Together, invited university educator and community members, the latter assuming the role of co-educators, can co-investigate the community further by building on this knowledge and the different knowledge traditions involved, doing so critically. The prudent, 'As an outsider working with this community, I observe that...' is how I tend to precede statements made in these contexts.

Recognising one's limitations is a great challenge for the university educator engaged in such learning settings.

And yet the recognition of one's limitations has always appeared to me to be the mark of true scholarship, despite the fact that, in the highly competitive environments that university and HE have become, this can be perceived as a weakness. The most progressive educators, however, are those who are willing to swim against the current or, to put it differently, echoing the late Roger I. Simon (1992), to 'teach against the grain'. Community engagement by university educators allows ample opportunities for doing this.

Learners are not *tabula rasa*, as indicated time and time again in this book. They often reveal manifestations of the 'popular creative spirit' or, simply, creative spirit, popular or non-popular. A healthy reciprocal university–community LLL relationship would involve engagement with this spirit, which can also be a resource for the university itself in the same way that university engagement can make available to communities publicly funded resources allocated to the institution. Community arts education and engagement offer endless opportunities, in this regard, in the interest of broadening cultural democracy. As Mae Shaw and Rosie Meade remind us, cultural democracy:

> is vibrant, public and discursive… It asserts that diverse citizens should and do communicate their views and understandings of the world through a range of processes and in multiple spheres. Cultural democracy positions cultural production as both central to human experience and as a necessary site for democratisation. In other words, citizens are seen as creators as opposed to mere audiences or spectators, whose active engagement in the making, consumption and distribution of culture should be acknowledged and supported. (Shaw and Meade, 2013, p. 198)

As the two Irish authors state, 'community arts and development processes can contribute to a more nuanced understanding of how ordinary people', part of the 'commons' (Williams, 1976), 'navigate their identities in consumer society' (Shaw and Meade, 2013, p. 201). A university community engagement project can openly embrace and promote these processes, more so when seeking to engage the social differences within the community, for example through the inclusion of recent members, such as migrants who bring different artistic traditions with them, allowing for possibilities of artistic fusions.[12]

In this regard, one should avoid limiting oneself to what Italians call *assistenzialismo* (simply, welfare programmes, often decried for conceiving of community members as 'deficits'). In the Freire sense, the community members as well as the university educators are to be conceived of as *subjects* and not *objects* – another and possibly the most basic reason to eschew 'banking education' (Freire) or what Dewey calls 'pouring in', and to engage the learners' active reconstruction of meaning.

Collectivity and ownership

The more socially conscious educators involved would attach importance to individual and collective learning. Gramsci praised workers, who attended a proletarian school within the context of a politics having collective working-class emancipation as the goal, for their determination to learn, despite their tiredness after a day's work. According to Gramsci, what added to their merit was that they learnt not simply for personal social mobility, as with bourgeois schools, but to help realise their dream of a better society (Gramsci, 1967, p. 290). Freire, for his part, argued that we carry out the task of becoming more fully human not on our own, as it is not an individualistic endeavour, but in concert and solidarity with others (Freire, 1970, 2000, pp. 85–86). This task, therefore, 'cannot unfold in the antagonistic relations between oppressors and oppressed' (pp. 85–86). Freire argued, in this context, that when we take an individualistic approach to being authentically human, we would be barring others from attaining the same state.

This individualistic endeavour would entail a dehumanising process of 'having more' (Freire, 1970, 2000, pp. 85–86), in Eric Fromm's terms, rather than 'being more' (*ser mais*). The same applies to the work of Lorenzo Milani who, like Freire, emphasised the collective dimensions of learning. Learning was intended not as a means to possess a positional good, something that very much applies to today's neoliberal world where even education becomes a consumer product, but as something to share with others. This was seen as part and parcel of a social class' struggle to acquire the collective means to confront privilege and class domination in society.

Logistical constraints led him to devise a system whereby the older boys were both teachers and learners as they taught the younger ones, thus gaining the confidence to not only to learn subjects that they failed at school but also be sufficiently equipped to teach this to others – a tremendous boost to their self-esteem. They would not move to the next stage of what is being learnt unless every single child in the class mastered the task at hand. The time spent by the students in racking their brains to put concepts across to their peers enhanced their own learning and mastery of the material at hand. It was no waste of time for those who might have been perceived to have had their wings clipped in this process.

The students at Barbiana even learned to read (the day's newspapers and other materials) and write collectively in a process reminiscent of Mario Lodi's approach to cooperative education which in turn drew on the work of Célestin Freinet (Batini et al., 2014). 'Peer tutoring' with learners acting as teachers as well as learners, sharing what they are learning with others, is a key aspect of this approach, which can be traced back to the Lancaster schools in the UK and calls to mind Lev Vygotsky's concept of 'Zones of Proximal Development'. It was encouraged by Maria Montessori for infants. If this approach can apply to infants then there is all the more reason to expect it to apply to adults in the community with their greater wealth of experiences.

Learners learn more about something through the effort of conveying this to others. Co-ownership of the programme becomes the key operative phrase here. It constitutes a popular approach to different forms of adult education, including university engagement programmes in prisons, communities and clubs.

Progressive university educators engaged with communities can therefore see learning as a means to collectively engage in action for change and not simply for individual advancement, although this cannot be ruled out. This is once again 'learning for democracy', in John Dewey's sense; that is to say, fostering a democratic ethos by rendering it an aspect of the learning setting itself. Again, one learns democracy by doing it, just as one learns LLL by doing it, not only in the individualistic self-directed sense but also in the collective one. There is a long history, in adult education, of promoting and encouraging the collective dimensions of learning. Examples abound in the areas of workers', popular and radical adult education in general.

Weaning off

This brings me to an important point for which there is mileage in the history of twentieth-century radical adult education. In my view, the most critical approach to university/LLL within the community is that in which it is recognised by the providers that people, given the right support and confidence, are capable of taking charge of their own learning – collective learning or, more appropriately, once more, collectively directed learning. I feel that there is the need for universities/HE institutions and those working with communities to respect that and the tradition that exists in this regard. There comes a time when the university educator/s might have to withdraw. The university provision involved might just serve as a catalyst to bring people together. These people gradually wean themselves off the institution and start providing their own co-teaching/learning. This was the case with the School of San Donato di Calenzano, which continued functioning after the Curia in collusion with the local power brokers, forced Milani away from the town into 'exile' at a distant place in the mountains. It happened with the projects in which Gramsci was involved where many were teachers and students at the same time both in the workers' education circles and in the prison school at Ustica, the island where Gramsci and other detainees awaited their trial under the fascist regime. It happens among prisoners in concentration camps (see Sacco's 2007 account of collectively directed learning among Palestinian prisoners at Ansar III in the Al-Naqab/Negev desert) and many other paces.

Mixed communities, sometimes including formally educated persons and others not so formally educated, come together and organise their own collectively directed learning. This might consist of one person, irrespective of her or his formal education background, being given a week or two to prepare a presentation on a topic that serves as a stimulus for debate with the rest of the group. Those teaching and attending the school set up by Gramsci and Amadeo Bordiga, among others, on the island of Ustica, were of mixed academic backgrounds. Many participated in preparing lessons and attending others, and among the participants were members of the Ustica community itself who collaborated with the prisoners (while many were political detainees there were also hardened criminals) who brought 'education' to their shores. This informal process of community engagement is said to have been a catalyst for the development of education on the island (Mayo, 2015).

Gramsci, Illich and his followers (see Prakash and Esteva, 1998) and more recently Ranciere (1991) have all underlined their belief in communities, including subaltern groups, being capable of organising their own education away from formal institutions. The greatest contribution a university/HE LLL effort can make towards an emancipatory community education is simply to serve as a catalyst, when asked, for this to occur. The institution and its educators would help, where and when necessary, to set the ball rolling but be prepared to leave when the time is right and the community itself has felt the confidence to 'go it alone'.

This sounds a logical approach in view of the ability of people throughout history to organise their own learning around their own knowledge traditions and beyond. This all depends on who is behind the university/HE LLL involvement and for what purpose this effort is being carried out. If it is HE LLL meant as a public good, then one can hope that such prudence will be shown. If HE LLL is seen simply as a consumption good and as a university PR exercise, then one faces the danger that such a community's weaning will not take place unless the community members themselves make their move in this regard. They can restrict the institution or its educators, in whom they retain confidence, to a consultative role, including that of allowing the community to access university/HE resources often born, in the case of public institutions, out of its members' taxes.

They can, through this acquired confidence and through certain developments, such as the university failing to continue to support the project, decide to make use of the communities' internal resources, learning from their own shared knowledge traditions and concerted preparatory efforts by their own members. They can also invite guest presenters who expose the subject before allowing the community members to take up issues with them based on their own experience or through some remote preparation. The Lorenzo Milani inspired Friday Conference at San Donato di Calenzano operated this way where the community prepared beforehand to pose questions to the invited speakers on issues such as employment relations, etc. The possibilities are legion.

A tall order?

The list of desiderata drawn up in this chapter might appear overwhelming for those engaged in community engagement. Work carried out on top of day-to-day teaching in mainstream university education can be very stressful. Having the image of a person with an axe right behind, ready to clamp down on any 'slip up' adds to the stress of the conscientious educator. One does not expect all of the above to be accomplished, as we all have our limitations. More realistically, the points are not intended to make one lose heart in one's work with community members, work that involves a great deal of negotiation between the different parties, as described in symbolic interactionist research. Realistically speaking, these points are more likely to serve as part of a checklist for critical self-reflection with regard to work in this area of university engagement. They can help one in the task of avoiding complacency in this area and in the struggle to, as Freire (1997) put it, become less incoherent, les incomplete as a 'person in process' working in and with communities.

It has always been my contention that the critical university educator, just as any critical educator for that matter, is constantly involved in a struggle to move between two ends of a continuum – criticality and prescription. The socially committed educator would strive to move to the 'critical' end of the continuum while being buffeted towards the other conventional prescriptive end by a number of forces. In the university educator's case, they would include university audit cultures, feasibility studies, harmonisation specifications, programme validation requirements and so forth, in an age when administration has gained the upper hand in the academy. Being critical also entails accepting the tension arising out of the ongoing struggle involved.

The chapter that follows sheds light on a community project I helped organise as a member of the board of the University of Malta's extension programme in a particular region, a historically impoverished (in terms of material wealth) region in the southern part of my home country, surrounding the docks which, for many years, were the mainstay of the country's economy and the heart of what was the closest thing the country had to an industrial working class.

The context for this project is the Republic of Malta, the EU's smallest member state, which has historically absorbed an array of convergent and divergent influences from the Arab world, Spain and Italy (especially, in the case of these two Southern European influences, during the time of rule by the Sovereign Order of St John), besides its last coloniser, Britain.

I shall focus here on a project that connects with a series of manifestations that capture the imagination in various towns and villages in the Maltese Republic but especially in this region, the Cottonera region comprising three cities: Birgu, Bormla and Isla. The reflective chapter on this project is meant to explore the potential for transformative community learning in a project of this kind carried out by the country's leading public university, the University of Malta.

Notes

1 In view of the earlier reference to *Jude the Obscure*, would this sort of provision have whetted the main character's appetite for organised learning or that of his creator, the learned Thomas Hardy, an architect by profession at a time when architecture was not a university area of specialisation?

2 Opening speech of the World University Service General Assembly held at Dar es Salaam on 27 June 1966. The title of the speech was: 'The University's Role in the Development of the New Countries' (Nyerere, 1968, p. 179).

3 I am indebted to Professor Budd L. Hall, University of Victoria, BC, Canada, for providing me with lead information with regard to the above section.

4 I am indebted to a friend and colleague, Michael Grech for this point.

5 It is more in line with what the Italians call *territorio* (Allulli, 1990) in this context, and specifically the contexts of adult education and socio-cultural work, to refer to a specific place and its surroundings.

6 Recall that the approach involved a preliminary phase in which educators/animators spent time in the community, exposing themselves to the people's universe of knowledge. This included their vocabulary and speech patterns. They would be involved

in 'an arduous search for generative words' at the level of 'syllabic richness' and high 'experiential involvement' (Goulet, 1973, p. 11). One, of course, needs not follow Freire's approach to the letter but can reinvent it in the specific context in question, capturing some of the spirit in which it was carried out in Angicos and elsewhere.

7 Arabs constitute only one tenth in a billion Muslims and not all Arabs are Muslim.

8 We need to be wary of building on certain aspects of the community culture that capture the local people's imagination. Building on folkloristic aspects when involving immigrant members of the community can be fraught with problems. A classic case is that of building on parades or puppet shows (e.g., the Sicilian marionette shows) that celebrate popular lore that can be offensive to immigrants – the marionette shows in Sicily hearken back to the age of the Crusades. In these shows, Crusader knights are shown confronting and defeating the Saracen 'other', normally wearing black and of swarthy complexion – all this in the presence of an immigrant population including many of Muslim faith. This is a problematic form of popular culture in the Southern European region where I live. The same applies to building educationally on the communities' artistic heritage steeped in a politics of (mis)representation that renders the Turk or Moor an object of demonisation and exoticisation. There is also the issue of gold and silver in such heritage sites as palaces and churches in this part of the word. This raises questions about human disposability in terms of the extermination of the indigenous of the Americas and other places, forced to extract the precious minerals concerned, suffering entombment, disabilities, slow deaths and many other human indignities and atrocities. The work of Eduardo Galeano (2009) is very revealing here.

9 The educator can alternate between traditional and progressive teaching. It is as though Freire seems to be saying that, in such difficult circumstances, dialogue should be introduced only gradually (see Horton and Freire, 1990, p. 160).

10 My translation from the original in Italian. The original reads: 'Avete visto ragazzi come sono i borghesi? Insegnano la Cina ai Cinesi.' This episode was also disclosed in a RAI TV (Italy's national TV station) interview with his student, the recently deceased Michele Gesualdi (Corradi, 2012, p. 5).

11 He was told in no uncertain terms that they did not need him to come and tell them how impoverished and oppressed they were. They knew this only too well.

12 This recalls recent African-Neapolitan experiments in music.

7

University community engagement project: engaging the popular imagination and the 'Holy Week' culture[1]

During February–March 2016, the University of Malta's Cottonera Resource Centre held a community education project focusing on 'Holy Week', a theme that served as the springboard to delve into different areas of enquiry and knowledge.

The centre was set up as a university outreach site; what led to the university opening this centre was the consistently low number of students at university, over the years, hailing from these areas. It was once argued by sociologist Godfrey Baldacchino (1999, p. 210) that research showed a person from the Cottonera region in the south of Malta (recall that it consists of three historical cities) having a 20 times less chance to enter the university than someone hailing from one of the country's affluent, upper-middle-class 'Three Villages' (Attard, Balzan and Lija). The Cottonera region, once the heart of the British naval base and home to the Drydocks, had, since the end of WWII, fallen on hard times. It is now going through a process of gentrification in view of its historical surroundings, impressive waterfronts and harbour facilities offering lucrative possibilities for investors; it now incorporates a yacht marina. The opening up of what used to be Dock 1 as a public/private space, while ridding the surrounding community from the effects of grit blasting and other environmental hazards, has led to private investments in the form of setting up 'state of the art' cafés and restaurants besides the main premises for the Jordanian-financed American University of Malta (AUM).

It can be argued that the setting up of the university outreach centre represents an attempt, hopefully not the only one, at making the University of Malta visible and present in different districts throughout the Maltese islands; it has a centre in Gozo.[2] As a member of the board for this centre, I bear this question in mind: on whose terms is the engagement taking place? This explains the need to draw on motivating factors such as events and issues that capture the communities' (and I stress the plural) imagination. Hopefully other outreach 'community engagement' programmes will continue to be carried out by the university, availing itself of some excellent community premises in various localities, including local council premises. The challenge, in my view and in keeping with the tenor throughout this volume, is to have a two-way engagement regarding choices of project and pedagogical approach. In my view, the aspiration would be to add a 'polyphonic' dimension (de Sousa Santos, 2017, p. 378) to a university that has all the makings of a traditional one, assailed by a neoliberal discourse. Emphasis was placed by the then rector in office on developing a culture of entrepreneurship at the university. The slogan adopted at the commencement of the academic year 2006–2007, which marked his coming into office as rector, was 'Towards an Entrepreneurial University'.[3] As far as the *doxa* is concerned, this university was not immune to the neoliberal tenets that have marked the international higher education discourse for the past few decades. And yet, the University of Malta, as any other public university, is not monolithic, with humanities and social sciences, for instance, being in a relatively healthy shape. University education has continued to be seen primarily as a public good; no fees are charged to full-time students who also benefit from a government stipend. The centre allows possibilities for the university to be open to polyphonic voices. It offers possibilities for doing things differently in a manner that involves use of the imagination, sensitivity to different voices and knowledge of what captures the people's imagination in this part of the country.

Popular creative spirit

Communal celebrations or commemorations, with their plethora of different forms of artistic expression and craftwork, as well as culinary delights, are a boon for popular creativity – once again Gramsci's notion of the 'popular creative spirit' (Gramsci, 1996, p. 57). What strikes me as most relevant is the potential to turn this form of communal expression and manifestation of the 'popular creative spirit' into an educational event about matters concerning people's lives. The 'popular creative spirit' is quite evident in this part of the island historically characterised by a seafaring community displaying a range of craftsmanship and technological skills in areas such as boat-building, to mention one example. One area where this 'popular creative spirit' is evident is in the Holy Week events that take place in the region around the end of March or April.

Holy Week, in the Christian religious tradition, comprises an important series of events that take place in spring in many communities in the Mediterranean, Latin America and beyond – events commemorating Jesus Christ's entry to Jerusalem, his last supper with the Apostles, together with his passion, death and resurrection. These commemorative events extend well beyond religious devotion and piety.

Beyond the spiritual

This project was conceived in such a way that it should appeal to believers of different denominations and non-believers alike. It so happens that this, the first project of its kind chosen, had a religious ring to it. Another theme chosen in future may not have any religious dimension at all. It might, for all I know, centre round the popular 'Regatta', which offers possibilities for tackling knowledge of both a social and technical nature.[4]

A central question concerning the chosen 'Holy Week' project had to be addressed: how does one build educationally on what really 'gets the communities going'? What is the 'occasional motive', to echo, once again, Italian critical educator Lorenzo Milani (Martinelli, 2007), and how do we move beyond this to explore, together, a broad range of knowledges (plural intended)?

Festas, communities and political education

Festas or *fiestas* are an important feature of outdoor communities in many parts of the Mediterranean as witnessed in several parts of Spain, Italy, Portugal and Greece. They constitute an important form of community action and learning, an outward form of communal action/learning, in this part of the world. This has a very long history. Witness the Greco-Roman amphitheatres or megalithic remains as examples. Religious and fertility rituals, temple dancing and theatre come to mind, albeit with some degree of exoticisation.

Outdoor activities in the form of village or town celebrations continue this tradition and have been the subject of social science research (Boissevain, 1993). Novelists such as Ernest Hemingway have done much to highlight events such as the feast of San Fermín in Pamplona with the well-known *encierro/los toros de San Fermín* (the bulls of San Fermín).[5] Again romanticisation and glorification of the macho element involved are evident in these fictional works, often captured in film. Painters have often highlighted the foibles observed, as with Francisco de Goya's depictions of seemingly inebriated *campesinos* celebrating the feast of San Isidro,[6] their patron saint.

The studies and artistic interpretations, whether satirical or not, do reveal one aspect of these celebrations or commemorations. They are part and parcel of communal identities. In certain communities, religion and religiosity intermesh with issues of identity, being part of the dominant – to avoid a totalising discourse – popular culture. The two elements are inextricably intertwined. As sociologist Mary Darmanin argues, in a commentary on three photos regarding the solemnity of outdoor Holy Week processions in Malta, 'Together, this trio [of photographs] neatly condense much of the complexity of Malta's religiosity. It is collective in combining a national with a religious identity' (Darmanin, 2012, p. 85). In these situations, we need to eschew any binary between Catholic religiosity and dominant community identity. This situation is true of many contexts, not only the Maltese one. It is true, for instance, of many parts of Italy, Spain, Greece, Mexico and the rest of Latin America.

This identity aspect is carried by migrants from these communities to countries such as Canada and Australia – 'portability of cultures'. John P. Portelli writes about the Mater Dolorosa procession among members of the Maltese community at Dundas St W-Runnymede (also known as the Junction) in Toronto (Portelli, 2012, pp. 206–209). This is as much a show of devotion as an affirmation of ethnic identity which connects with other identities such as those of members of the Italian, Portuguese and other Latin communities. They converge on 'Little Italy' on College, Toronto to participate in the Good Friday procession that starts from St Francis of Assisi Church. The spectacle involves processional statues, band marches and people dressed as Roman soldiers, Christ, personages from the Passion narrative and, to underscore the Italian presence, Carabinieri (Carabineers).[7]

In Spain's *Semana Santa* processions, the events often highlight identity issues connected with the *barrio*, municipality, region and nation. It is common for a float emerging from a church to be greeted with brief strains from the Spanish national anthem before the band switches to the specific fanfare for the occasion. Arab-Latin fusions, typical of the cultural heritage of Southern Spain, can be found in the *Saeta*: public lamentation, reverberating from vantage points such as a damask-decorated balcony and centred on the processional statue of the suffering Christ or Madonna. The *Saeta* is characterised by its *jarcha*[8] origins, a wailing tone (one denotes strong Arab legacies in the intonation), typical of *Al Andalus*. A consideration such as this indicates that there is more to the *Semana Santa*, as an educational moment, than simply spiritual education. There is much that is political in the broader sense possible, in this case the cultural politics of life in and around Mediterranean cities always marked by hybridisation with regard to cultural fusions involving Arab, Muslim, European and Christian influences. As Michael Grech and I argued, in an op-ed piece (Grech and Mayo, 2018), many of these events have political ramifications. They may perpetuate, consolidate or challenge existing relations of power in various sites.

Earlier in the volume, I remarked that *fiestas* were often banned by autocratic regimes such as the one led by 'Generalissimo' Francisco Franco in Spain; in this specific case, non-religious *fiestas* such as carnival.[9] They are banned for bringing people together and fostering communal identities in contrast to the totalising national identity politics propagated by the central and centralising government, echoing, in this regard, one of the main principles of the Spanish National Syndicalist State outlined by the founder of the Falange Party, José Antonio Primo de Rivera, son of the Dictator Miguel Primo de Rivera. This partly explains their re-emergence with a vengeance, as in the Barcelona area, following the collapse of the authoritarian regime after the *caudillo*'s death – as indicated by my earlier reference to Joan Bofill (1985) and the Universitat Nova.

Politics and *fiestas* or communal remembrances such as the *Semana Santa*[10] are no strange bedfellows. Religious or otherwise, these manifestations are popular events where power relations within communities are displayed, reinforced, challenged, subverted, sublimated and renegotiated. As an example of consolidation or possibly renegotiation of power relations, we can note the presence, in Spain, of groups and lobbies in the form of *hermandades* –brotherhoods, confraternities – with a possible double entendre in the case of *del Gran Poder* (of great power), the brotherhood connected with Seville's famous *paso procesional* (processional statue or float) *Jesús del Gran Poder* – the majestic striding figure of Christ, in resplendent robe, bearing the cross on his back.[11]

In other countries, where religion or religiosity is part of the identity of several communities, religious and political images are often intertwined. Think of the juxtaposition of Che Guevara's image with that of Jesus Christ, the *Sangre de Cristo* (Blood of Christ) concept, in many parts of Latin America where this concept is deeply rooted. Think of political mileage being made out of religious texts in Latin

America, both conservative mileages as well as progressive ones. Popular education in the Christian Base Communities constitutes a fine example of the latter. Liberation theology in Latin America is born out of these readings of scriptures, to which pre-Colombian myths and traditions are added as professed by Bishop Samuel Ruiz, Óscar Arnulfo Romero, Ignacio Ellacuría and Gustavo Gutiérrez. The same can be said of black liberation theology.[12]

In Malta there were cases, during a 1960s politico-religious dispute involving the then socialist Labour Party, of elections being held before or after Easter. This led to accusations by this party that Lenten sermons served as an effective means of propaganda favouring the pro-Church Nationalist Party, the government incumbent then. The British governor general would make it a point to visit a prominent Last Supper display, in the Cottonera region – a form of populism? Even Labour politicians and supporters participated in the 1960s Holy Week activities as it meant greater connections with the party base, and this despite the fact that their party was, at the time, at loggerheads with the Church because of six points in their electoral programme that threatened the latter's hegemony[13] (see Grech and Mayo, 2018).

Political education

The strong connection between this type of religious/communal celebration and politics renders political education, drawing on these events and the narrative they focus on, quite relevant. Community activists interested in emancipatory politics can therefore use these manifestations for the purposes of community education. This type of education is meant to be critical not paternalistic, involve the community, and be channelled towards emancipatory ends. Political education, with a strong historical foundation, featured prominently in the 'Holy Week' project at the Cottonera Resource Centre. Since this was the first of what we anticipate to be a series of projects centring on themes that capture the communal imagination or rather the imagination of several members of the communities involved, we went for a safe subject that, we knew, would attract large interest.

We also selected people to direct the sessions not only on the basis of their knowledge of the field but also because of their manner of communication with different groups of participants, especially their ability to dialogue and engage with the voices present. We identified a few topics and also based this choice on various factors not least availability of personnel who are ready to give of their time and direct sessions.

The intention was for both session leader and rest of the participants to move 'from the known to the unknown' to adopt a well-known pedagogical maxim. Guest session leaders were informally briefed with regard to the project's ethos – helping to foster a co-learning experience. The range of topics demonstrates the potential that lies in developing projects around events capturing the popular imagination. I would like to think that this approach falls within the best critical traditions of community education. Alas, time constraints (timing is very important when drawing on things that capture the popular communal imagination) limited the number of themes that can be broached. The whole project had to be carried out during the Lent period, the time when the *Semana Santa* fever is at its highest – hence the connection with the popular imagination and framework of relevance. The downside to this, of course, is that those who are most engaged in *Semana Santa* work are less likely to turn up for the sessions, or are present intermittently, because of their direct engagement in the preparations for the commemorative activities.

One other major issue was finance, given the shoestring budget available. People chose to come because of their love of the subject and of sharing their knowledge with and learning from others. The themes consisted of: 1) historical overview of Holy Week in Malta and beyond; 2) Roman imperialism; 3) colonialism then and at present; 4) women, masculinity and Holy Week; 5) visual arts and Holy Week; 6) theatre and Holy Week; 7) film and Holy Week; 8) Holy Week and the environment; 9) spirituality and Holy Week; 10) music and Holy Week.

Spirituality is the obvious aspect underlined time and time again, with regard to Holy Week, in churches, the media, etc. This was certainly accorded its due importance in the project; in fact, I would say that it was a recurring theme. However, we went beyond that in keeping with the broad agenda of this project, as explained earlier.

The opening session by a university-qualified historian, involved at the popular level in these commemorative events, combined historical and spiritual aspects admirably. It set the context by providing a rigorous overview of the historical developments of outward Holy Week events on the island, at the same time provoking participants to engage in dialogue drawing on their own perceptions, some based on evidence and others based on hearsay. The latter was corroborated or rebutted through documented historical evidence. It offered potential for the coming together of constituted authoritative knowledge, which one associates with the conventional university, and popular knowledge. The session I led on colonialism was meant to follow the one, led by an archaeology professor, on Roman imperialism during the specific historical context in Jesus Christ's time and later periods. We ventured into a discussion on colonialism and neo-colonialism in later and present times, including the current intensification of globalisation with its colonising foundation and the plight of immigrants perceived as victims of a colonial legacy. Themes concerning different forms of colonialism, such as, for example, 'settler colonialism' (ironically in Palestine) or a country's 'internal colonialism', were broached.

Different genres

The project, particularly through its sessions on visual arts, music (solemn music, marches, heavy metal and folk rock) and theatre, offered potential for drawing out and discussing relations between different art genres – popular and those conventionally and perhaps problematically presented as being more 'highbrow'. The session on film highlighted different ways of representing episodes from the public life of Christ especially his trial, death and resurrection. This was discussed by juxtaposing Pier Paolo Pasolini's *Vangelo Secondo Matteo* (*Gospels According to Matthew*)[14] against Mel Gibson's *Passion of the Christ*[15]). Controversies were not glossed over; they were brought to the fore. There were discussions among people who held opposed views, being different but not antagonistic, as Paulo Freire would put it. One session, which led to an animated exchange, concerned the environment. The session focused on the practice of cutting down branches of olive trees or indeed small trees to recreate the Gethsemane scenes in pageants and especially floats. The cutting down of leaves for Palm Sunday is also common practice. This specific focus on the importance of trees for several well-documented and obvious environmental reasons connected with a current controversy raging in the country regarding the constant cutting down of trees to open roads and develop pedestrian areas. An environmental activist led the discussion, a person who was quite prominent for her public denunciation of this practice.

The overall project experience stimulated the imagination of all participants who expressed different views regarding how to take this initiative forward with regard to both a follow-up project with a new theme and any repetition of this specific Holy Week series of presentations and conversations. In the section that follows and drawing on material I co-wrote with my friend and colleague, Michael Grech, in *Counterpunch* (Grech and Mayo, 2018), I highlight some themes that can be taken up when this Holy Week project is carried out again. The topic is so popular in this region, where we can speak of the existence of a strong 'Holy Week culture', that it is most likely that there will be a demand for a further project around it.

Suggestions for the future

In our joint work, and learning from the above experience (Michael Grech also led a session, the one on film), we chose as examples the following themes: imperialism, political theatre, women and art to which I will add the theme of resurrection/regeneration. As evidenced from this chapter, we can also address more broadly the issue of politics and Holy Week, about which we need not dwell any further given the treatment provided in the main text and footnotes. Many of the themes to be discussed fall under the broad title of politics but they can be treated more specifically.

Imperialism

The specific historical context that provides the backdrop to the Passion of Christ is characterised by imperialism – Roman imperialism. Christ and many others in his day suffered death at the hands of an imperial regime and its collaborators. In many Good Friday displays, however, the splendour and the glory of the Roman Empire, rather than the brutality and suffering perpetrated in many regions, including Palestine, are emphasised. One can increasingly refer to the latter in activities and commemorations. Starting from here, one can then seek occasions to engage with such phenomena as the contemporary version of imperialism, as well as colonialism and neo-colonialism in later and present times. This would include a focus on such victims of colonial legacies as migrants from the Middle East and North Africa (MENA) and sub-Saharan Africa (SSA). We wrote:

> [W]itness the Palm Sunday processions organised by Maltese and immigrants (from Syria and Sub-Saharan Africa) in a particular locality, and the Lenten Talks addressed by migrants at the University of Malta's Sixth Form College. Here links between the ordeal of victims of colonialism in Christ's days – including Jesus himself – and the plight of modern victims were forged, in the latter case by the victims themselves. (Grech and Mayo, 2018)

We posed the following question:

> Is the local community itself being taken over by phenomena such as over-development, the loss of public spaces or the tranquillity that once characterised definite parts of localities, a case of loss of effective sovereignty by inhabitants of the community? (Grech and Mayo, 2018)

In short, we can tackle private/corporate encroachment on and commodification of public communal life and spaces. This is colonisation in one of its most manifest forms today as indicated in several writings by one of critical pedagogy's foremost exponents, Henry A. Giroux (see Giroux, 2001). We can also raise the issue of whose knowledge counts and whose knowledge is subjugated in colonial and neo-colonial contexts. This is pertinent given recorded and unrecorded cases of what, once again, Boaventura de Sousa Santos calls 'epistemicide' (de Sousa Santos, 2016), the 'killing'/attempt at obliteration of knowledge that does not fit the Eurocentric colonial paradigm, especially indigenous knowledge; in short, the 'killing of knowledge systems' (Hall and Tandon, 2017, p. 6).

The situation concerning 'official' and 'subjugated' knowledges would also include different interpretations of the Passion of Christ narrative, often reflecting different social standpoints. Whose narrative prevails and which narrative is dismissed as being devoid of academic authority despite providing a reading of events from the standpoint of a colonised subaltern group? Using the narrative of the Holy Week to underline the complex features of colonialism is in itself a subversive act, in line with Boaventura de Sousa Santos' reference to 'subversitivity' as a manifestation of a decolonising university (see also Mbembe, 2016, on this).

Political theatre

Many Holy Week activities involve theatre. In Malta, people, who have moved out of the locality where they were 'born and bred' maintain their connection with their home town through participation in festivities. These include eager participation as actors in the Holy Week pageant. There are actors who would attribute their initial interest in drama to these kinds of events.

The various pageants carried out on stage or inside the church or on its parvis, hearkening back to the Medieval Miracle plays in England and their equivalent elsewhere, are said to mark an important historical landmark in the development of European theatre. These activities occur not only in Malta but in other parts of the world, testifying to a tradition that goes back hundreds of years and that also influenced regions and countries outside the continent. Hamlet's advice, to the travelling players, not to 'out-Herod Herod', is a direct reference to these forms of theatre where Herod was, in the English Middle Ages and later, stereotypic- ally a swaggering ranting bully, a type of casting that must have led a few actors concerned to go 'over the top'.

There is mileage in these dramatic activities to enable one to dwell on the evo- lution of European theatre and, once again, to break the conventional binary of cultural politics involving so-called popular and so-called highbrow culture. The two are much more connected than one would imagine, especially at the level of communal village life. Most of the participants and the audience in the Maltese pageants are working-class people. With some important exceptions, this pageantry involves spectacular displays of a chain of events certainly not as they really occurred but as they are imagined to have taken place, albeit in a hyper-real way. Throughout the Good Friday processions in Malta we have our full gruesome spectacle of flashing whips and more *machista* delightful displays of Romans in shining armour.

Based on these spectacles, one would be forgiven for thinking that it took more than a legion to accompany the defenceless and ailing Nazarene and the equally defenceless 'thieves' to their execution. The probable reason for this excessive presence of men in Roman military garb is the huge demand for this role coming from the community's male sector (see Cassar, 2012), a situation also found in Spain where people pay to participate in the processions. Romans in splendid attire accompany Spanish floats such as the *Macarena*, the grieving Mater Dolorosa deriving its appellation from its surrounding Macarena *barrio* (neighbourhood) in Seville. In Seville, the emphasis regarding the Roman soldiers' pageantry is on choreography. In Malta, the emphasis is also on spectacle but is often perceived as an exercise in machismo tout court (Grech et al., 2015).

These events, however, can be used for emancipatory purposes, as is frequently the case with passion plays in some areas in Latin America. One can explore the link between machismo, virility and the culture of militarisation still prevalent today. Why are males so excited to join the phalanx (no pun intended regarding the Spanish Falange/phalange) of Roman soldiers in commemorations such as these? Does this reflect a fascination for the military and their bellicose posturing? Is this part and parcel of a global culture of militarisation that has escalated since 9/11?

One can also raise the question of poverty which led people, such as the two 'thieves' in the Passion narrative, to be imprisoned and executed possibly for simply stealing food, a recurring theme in European literature down to the eight- eenth century where authors such as Daniel Defoe[16] suggest that one can be hanged for simply 'stealing a handkerchief', to repeat the old cliché. This anticipated the recurring nineteenth- and turn-of-the-century Dickensian and Hardy-ian themes of 'justice' being done (or seeming to have been done)[17] – drastic sentences meted out only to the poor and powerless, as the law is there primarily to safeguard the interests and possessions ('private property' as Karl Marx and Friedrich Engels would underline) of the powerful members of the ruling class.

Several similar themes are present in the Good Friday narrative; Grech and I refer to

> public executions associated with people who could not afford to buy Roman citizenship, innocent people sacrificed at the altar of political expedience; the manner in which those who wield political/cultural power react when people threaten their hold or speak truth to their power. (Grech and Mayo, 2018)

I would add here that the image of the severed head of John the Baptist on a silver plate, carried by a girl dressed as Salomé during many Maltese Good Friday processions, offers a stark reminder of the fate awaiting those challenging the powerful.

Similar recurrent themes can be tackled in a way such that the links between what transpired then and what has continued to occur since are emphasised. One can explore several possibilities in this regard through theatre, and engage dialogically with the audience in the manner of Boal's street theatre or Federico Garcia Lorca's and Eduardo Ugarte's *La Barraca* (the shack) itinerant community theatre, the latter complementing the 'Pedagogic missions' of Spain's Second Republic led by José Castillejo, featuring itinerant work throughout Spain.

Women

We argue that:

> Though the main character of the Passion is Jesus, the Passion Narrative involves a lot of women as protagonists, even when males failed miserably (for instance at the foot of the cross). The Gospels narrate that a woman constituted the first witness on Easter Sunday. This account challenges then contemporary Jewish practice which did not recognise testimonies offered by women. (Grech and Mayo 2018)

There is mileage here for discussions concerning the historical status of women and citizenship throughout the years (barred from voting, from attending universities, etc.). In Malta's Holy Week events, one procession that involves great solemnity is that of Our Lady of Sorrows – the Mater Dolorosa (a key image evoked by Southern European playwrights and film directors, including Luigi Pirandello[18] and Giacomo Gentilomo[19]), organised one week before Good Friday. Our Lady of Sorrows constitutes a key figure in Holy Week processions in many parts of the Mediterranean and beyond. One of the best-known processional statues is the one from Seville I already mentioned, La Macarena,[20] a much revered paso. Great devotion is shown towards this typical Spanish doll-like wooden image of the *Virgen* (Virgin). She is regally attired in a long embroidered mantle and is sheltered by a canopy exhibiting different crests. A couple of exquisitely executed teardrops are exposed in the glow of light from the many candles ceremoniously surrounding this seventeenth-century image.

As for this solemn feast in Malta, many manage to connect the suffering of Jesus' mother to that of actual people in distress because of things that have occurred to them or to their loved ones. The procession in Malta's capital city of Valletta attracts a large crowd, including people from different social classes who walk behind the statue, showing great devotion and fealty: 'In this procession... [a] Minister's wife walks with the green grocer, the football player, the cleaning lady' (Darmanin, 2012, p. 85). The leading Neapolitan playwright, Eduardo de Filippo wrote a play, *Filumena Marturano* (originally scripted with his sister in mind as main actress) that gains some resonance here, with the Madonna's image featuring prominently – not the Mater Dolorosa but simply a statue of the Madonna in a niche, typical of Naples and other Southern European cities. The Virgin Mary constitutes the classic representative of the woman embracing that strong sense of responsibility in a patriarchal society: 'E figlie so' figlie' (Neapolitan – formal Italian: *I figli sono figli*) meaning: offspring are offspring. These are the words Filumena imagines the statue of the Virgin Mary to have pronounced as she walked past the shrine (Act 1). The Mater Dolorosa feast and other Holy Week events, therefore, foreground women's suffering, strength and hopes. This can be used to generate thoughts about the sufferings, challenges and hopes of women today, especially in local communities: the injustices that women are suffering in communities because they are women, and the signs of hope (the Sevillian Macarena is the Madonna of Hope – *la Virgen de la Esperanza*).[21]

In the case of the Cottonera and other Maltese regions, one can discuss the role of Cottonera women in not-too-distant colonial history, with their washing of UK sailors' clothes for a pittance, engaging, out of necessity, in prostitution to serve the garrison's needs. There were the occasional instances of the cause being young widowhood resulting from fatal tragedies befalling husbands during work on HM's ships at sea or in the docks. The several votive (*Ex Voto*) paintings (a form of popular art, imploring or thanking divine providence for the safe return, or cure, of a relative), in one of the Cottonera's parishes, attest to concerns about the well-being of seafaring family members in this historically maritime region. An image such as that of the Mater Dolorosa can evoke all sorts of feelings and identification and lead to discussions around the plight of women and the structural forms of patriarchy, and how the courage of women who appear in the narrative can be channelled in the direction of action, collective or otherwise, to help transform these structures. One can contrast the machismo showing off of males against the more humble and life-centred values surrounding women depicted in this kind of pageantry, an observation that can stimulate a variety of issues up for debate.

Art

Communal celebrations or commemorations such as Holy Week, with its plethora of different forms of artistic expression and craftwork, as well as culinary delights, constitute further manifestations of the 'popular creative spirit'. The way in which this spirit is manifested in Holy Week events and activities has changed throughout the years. Some of the recent forms involve such features as Eurocentrism and machismo. We argued that:

> Good Friday events can be activities where the art is valued critically; where the community itself would consider the limits and possibilities of this art not merely in

aesthetic terms, but with respect to the experiences and struggles that occur in local-ities, communities and nation at large. (Grech and Mayo, 2018)

One of the themes raised during the 2016 sessions was the freedom or otherwise artists have in reinterpreting and depicting instances from the narrative.

The issue of the Spanish Inquisition, with respect to details regarding the pos-ition of Christ's feet when nailed to the cross, was raised in one of the sessions. What is considered sacred and what is considered profane with regard to the forms of representation – politics of representation – in this day and age? One of the questions we raised is: 'Why (or if) are they happy with a blondish, blue-eyed and "larger than life" Jesus (Jeffrey Hunter being the prototype), even if the passion mysteries are supposed to celebrate a Middle-Eastern dissident who entered the lowest gutters of humanity?' (Grech and Mayo, 2018).

Resurrection/regeneration

This episode represents the culmination of the Holy Week narrative and is celebrated, outwardly in the streets and squares of certain localities, with great pomp. Viewed from a Christian perspective, to dwell simply on the Passion and tribulation of Christ without meditating on the significance of the resurrection, the Lord's triumph over death, is to miss the entire point of the Christian message of redemption and regeneration.

From a political education perspective, this represents an interesting theme insofar as emancipatory and transformative communal politics are concerned. One can dwell on the significance of Easter-Spring-Regeneration from both a Christian and non-Christian perspective. One recognises that this is a recurring theme in religious rituals dating as far back as at least the fertility deities of ancient Egypt – Adonis, Attis, Osiris and Tammuz. All represent yearly decay and life's, especially vegetable life's, regenerative force – dying and resurrecting.

The issue of death and resurrection can be discussed from both a spiritual and political transformative perspective, including transformation of communal life. One can discuss how the Easter metaphor is used with respect to people and communities undergoing a change – experiencing, in Paulo Freire's words, their 'Easter'. Carl Jung's notion of archetype of transformation is a useful conceptual tool, allowing for a collocation of ancient Egyptian and Christian rituals.[22] As shown by the ancient fertility deities and their recurrence through later religions, including the Christian one, the image of a god dying and resurrecting is an arche-typal one. Discussions can emerge around the meaning of regeneration in the lives of different members and sectors of the learning community at the Cottonera Resource Centre .

One can venture into a more global discussion regarding planetary con-sciousness and regeneration or the hope for 'another world that is possible', the slogan of the World Social Forum, in contrast to the current neoliberal mantra: 'there is no alternative' (TINA). Any consensus around this view would beg the question: what strategies need to be developed at the local and global levels for this consummation to occur? What kinds of utopias can be conjured by the group? Does the Cottonera Resource Centre provide one of the liminal spaces in this day and age for the expression, elaboration and intermeshing of heterotopias?

Conclusion: authority and authoritarianism – who speaks and who directs?

These are examples of possible political themes that a project such as the one centring on Holy Week can develop. These, of course, are Michael Grech's and my ideas. One never knows what other themes participants might come up with in a space where they bring their own cultures and learning traditions to bear on the subject of co-investigation. The main challenge remains that of collectively engendering a polyphonic space where different voices engage with the issue. Choosing the right personnel to direct the discussions in a manner that allows for this polyphony of voices is a key challenge. These voices must also condition the development of the project regarding choice of follow-up focus.

Choice of the follow-up project depends on discussions with the participants and hopefully several other members of the surrounding communities. In fact, the follow-up project to that of Holy Week centred on artistic expression in the region, based on popular demand expressed by people in the area reached by the centre itself through its networking channels. The major challenge, however, is whether the participants not only choose the themes but also take complete control of the sessions. The Cottonera Resource Centre ought to address this potential challenge, which raises different issues, since it would entail confronting the established university with its modus operandi. We have not yet reached this stage. The issue of authority and authoritarianism, raised time and time again in this book, comes into the reckoning.

I gathered that many participants wanted a session leader who had authority, in terms of knowledge of the subject and as a pedagogue, without allowing this authority to degenerate into authoritarianism. There is always the danger that, without a measure of control, one or two people among the participants will hog the discussion to the detriment of others. This is something I personally was fully conscious of when I conducted my session on colonialism and when I attended the others led by colleagues and friends. As project coordinator, making sure that everyone had a chance to express views partly fell within my responsibility.

Notes

1 I am indebted to Professor Eugenio-Enrique Cortés-Ramirez for information on the Spanish *Semana Santa* activities, which the present author followed through direct transmissions (en vivo-live) at often ungodly hours (no pun intended) of the various processions and accompanying programmes on TV Andalucía.

2 Gozo is the second most inhabited island in the archipelago of islands constituting the Republic of Malta. The inhabitants of Gozo are called Gozitans.

3 Maltese slogan: Lejn Università Imprenditorjali (Towards an Entrepreneurial University).

4 The Regatta involves rowing teams from different localities surrounding Malta's Grand Harbour, one of the island's two natural harbours which made the country attractive to its colonisers, including Britain, which used it as its Mediterranean Naval outpost. The Regatta takes place on different public holidays, the most prominent one being the 8 September national day, commemorating the 1565 repelling of an Ottoman onslaught on the islands.

5 One of the memorable settings in his novel *Fiesta/The Sun also Rises* (1926); also in *Death in the Afternoon* (1932), a nonfiction book on the art of bullfighting; and *A Dangerous Summer*, another nonfiction book on tauromachy, written between 1959 and 1960, and published posthumously in 1985.

6 San Isidro is patron saint of the city of Madrid and of farmers.

7 Footage available of the 2018 procession on College, Toronto, https://toronto.citynews.ca/video/2018/03/30/thousands-take-part-in-good-friday-procession/.

8 *Jarcha* is one of the most ancient wailing traditional songs in Spain. It comes from those Arabs who lived with Christians and Jews in times prior to the Catholic Kings, i.e., before the Unity of Spain in 1469. A *jarcha* is an Arabic song that is sung with Spanish phonemes and pronunciation. I am indebted to Eugenio-Enrique Cortés-Ramirez of the University of Castilla La Mancha (Cuenca) for this point.

9 Most of these forbidden *fiestas* were held in a clandestine and secret way during Franco's 40-year rule, like those in the Albaicin (Granada) or carnivals in Cadiz and the Canary Islands. I am indebted to Eugenio-Enrique Cortés-Ramirez for this point.

10 *Semana Santa* processions were established by the Holy Inquisition as a way of supporting Roman Catholicism as the true standard of living in comparison to Protestantism: colours, ornaments and a rejection of austerity (supported by the Protestant world) are the main traits of these processions – never forbidden during the Franco regime. As a matter of fact there are those who have highlighted insignias of different types connected with *franquismo*, including the sash belonging to General Gonzalo Queipo de Llano (said to be responsible for Federico García Lorca's killing) who was Franco's right-hand man in Seville and Andalusia during the Spanish Civil War. I am indebted to Eugenio Corté for this point. Llano is said to have been responsible for the killing of 1,400 people, in this war and immediate aftermath, in the Sevilla area alone. He heavily bombarded the barrio of La Macarena where he and his wife are buried (in the sanctuary erected in the 1940s to the Virgin of Hope) and this has created controversy generated by the Movement around Historical Memory, with the response from the specific *hermandad* being that they are interred there because they are both Macarenas and not for any connection with *franquismo*. Llano's sash has been removed from the statue of the Virgin not because it violates the memory of those who perished in the Civil War but for preservation purposes (Maestre, 2015). In a famous photograph, General Llano is shown at the forefront of the procession carrying the float of *Jesus del Gran Poder* in 1939, marking the end of the Civil War (Serrano, 2017).

11 This represents quite a contrast to the figure of the Redeemer, in Malta and other places, depicted as having collapsed under the weight of the cross or the contorted figure of the same suffering Christ at Mexico City's Cathedral. According to Eugenio-Enrique Cortés-Ramirez (personal correspondence), the *Jesús del Gran Poder* image was highly manipulated by Francoist General Gonzalo Queipo de Llano, who identified it with Franco to justify the military uprising against the Spanish Second Republic in 1936. This interpretation of the myth is currently supported by the extreme right in Spain.

The person believed to have held most influence on Franco, his *cuñato* – Serrano Suñer, was often referred to as El Senor del Gran Poder (Pavlovic, 2003, p. 14). The plane piloted by Ramon Franco, brother of the future *caudillo*, which was the first to cross over to the South Atlantic, was named *Jesús del Gran Poder* (Buckley, 2013, p. 30).

12 I am indebted to Eugenio-Enrique Cortés-Ramirez for the points regarding the *Sangue de Cristo* and pre-Colombian rituals in Latin American liberation theology.

13 The situation was marked by the Church's thundering an interdiction levelled at the party's entire executive and which involved spiritual blackmail – a vote for Labour is a mortal sin.

14 Michael Grech contrasts the sombre and spiritually lifting low-budget film (*Il Vangelo Secondo Matteo*) by the iconic P.P. Pasolini, with the gory and overstated *Passion of the Christ* by Mel Gibson (Grech et al., 2015). Pasolini casts close relatives and friends as personages from the Gospels, with his mother playing Mary and contemporary philosopher Giorgio Agamben playing the Apostle Philip. This film, set in Matera (Basilicata), in Italy's *meridione*, is the work of a man who seems to have had a tortuous relationship with religion but whose film, infinitely more than the one by Mel Gibson, managed to capture the sense of mystery and spirituality of the Gospels with regard to this and other episodes from the life of Christ. There is a strong sense of understatement about this film (nothing to be added to what is written in the Gospels, save for non-verbal gestures and cues), which renders it all the more intriguing. As Grech implies, this leaves us in awe of what appears divine – the less said the better.

15 Grech demonstrates how Pasolini's understated narrative contrasts with the 'Senecan' rendering, in the sixteenth- and seventeenth-century Elizabethan and Jacobean drama sense, of the same episode in Mel Gibson's film, based on lay sister Anne Catherine Emmerich's *The Bitter Passion of the Christ* (Grech et al., 2015). Gibson takes great liberties of direction. These include inserting an ever-intrusive and haunting fiend. Then there is the uncalled for violent scene in which a crow gouges the unrepentant thief's eye, the sign of a vengeful God, anathema to the spirit of the Gospels.

16 See Daniel Defoe's *Moll Flanders*.

17 See Thomas Hardy's *Tess of the D'Urbervilles*.

18 See the play *Sei personaggi in cerca d'autore* (*Six Characters in Search of an Author*).

19 See the 1943 film *Mater Dolorosa*.

20 Many Sevillanas are named Macarena, hence the popular Spanish pop music hit of the 1990s.

21 The other prominent Mater Dolorosa in Seville is that which belongs to the Triana barrio (the neighbourhood of Triana). It is the Nuestra Señora de la Esperanza Triana, also known as La Esperanza de Triana.

22 T.S. Eliot's long poem *The Wasteland* was a catalyst for my appreciation of this point, when I was an undergraduate a long time ago: 'That corpse you planted last year in your garden. Has it begun to sprout?' (Eliot, 1954, p. 53). The line is from 'The Burial of the Dead' in *The Wasteland*. The word 'collocation' of course echoes Eliot's (1954) reference to the collocation of two major representatives of Eastern and Western Asceticism, Buddha and St. Augustine, in his notes concerning 'The Fire Sermon' in the above long poem (p. 72).

8

Whither European universities and other HE institutions and LLL?

To sum up, higher education (HE) is deeply affected by forces of globalisation, especially including hegemonic globalisation and its neoliberal agenda. Rather than being widened to render the university and other HE institutions more responsive to the democratic needs of society, and engage with the preoccupations and concerns of specific communities, the discourse is being reduced to one regarding another form of business governed by the principles of the market. And yet one would expect these institutions to serve much wider purposes than those of the economy and employment, important though these are; they need to be addressed and students require job opportunities allied to their course choices. However, addressing this issue is one thing but rendering universities exclusively concerned with this aspect to the detriment of others is something totally different. It provides cause for concern. It can also prove illusory given the well-known difficulties involved in addressing the needs of industry so well in advance. This area affects LLL especially as far as 'outside the mainstream' courses are concerned. These tend to be more short-term and hence more likely to be adaptable to immediate needs. This kind of short course LLL provision is more likely to be successful in this regard. At the same time, it falls in line with the 'great skills crises' and 'training robbery' phenomena, serving as a safety valve, and HE money-spinner, to which people resort as their skills obsolescence renders them redundant at the workplace or else places them in the 'at risk' bracket of employees. *Précarieté* and the fluctuating job market makes VET and CPD important features of university and the rest of LLL in HE. Add to this the idea of career enhancement and the general officially structured university/HE LLL provision is primarily job-related, ranging from ICT-driven technology to business studies, middle management courses and others such as project management. Attempts at providing courses in the humanities and social sciences, unless there is an immediate economic return to them, are few and far between. One example was the Manchester-based universities (University of Manchester, Manchester Metropolitan University and Salford University) offering a joint online Master's in sociology. This was short-lived. Was it less attractive than courses in human resource development (HRD) and business management?

Alternatively, is the effort involved in writing courses for online provision and conducting them more difficult than one anticipates, especially given the nature of economic returns involved? I have heard people involved in these projects, often aborted after a short while, mention the existence of a false assumption that teaching online is easier than carrying out this teaching face to face in lecture or seminar rooms.

There has been much writing, internationally, lamenting the current trends in university/HE, let alone the LLL provision involved. The writing spells out the danger of these institutions' conversion into training agencies rather than serving as places that contribute to the generation of a healthy public sphere. This book has hopefully shown that much of what is written connects with what is going on in Europe and beyond, not least through the language and guidelines provided by the European Union, with alternatives from both the Global North and South.

This state of affairs has been and continues to be contested in many parts of the continent with protests, sit-ins and university occupations. This is an important area for alternative HE discourses (in the post-structural Foucauldian sense of including practices) to emerge, always, given the short duration of these experiments, in a pre-figurative sense.

It would not be remiss to regard these actions as an integral part of the many actions, occurring in several European countries, regarding 'debtocracies,' the limits of traditional representative democracy; political corruption; a politics devoid of morality; precarious living; and, to repeat at this late stage a point made earlier in the words of one student protester against university neoliberal reforms in Vienna, a situation whereby 'We will have higher educational degrees than our parents, but we will never attain their standard of living' (English and Mayo, 2012, p. 119).

Universities and other HE institutions are by and large being encouraged to undergo a transformation into places for 'entrepreneurship' and to prepare people for jobs. Harmonisation processes are being established throughout the European Union, as part of the Bologna Process. These changes bring with them a series of bureaucratic procedures. This has shifted the balance of power between academia and administration in favour of the latter. Measurement becomes a very important aspect of this situation where quality is judged primarily through the transform-ation of complex processes into quantitative indicators – everything is judged in terms of easily measured outcomes. These measured outcomes might well fail to capture on paper what is 'really' and 'qualitatively' going on – all that is solid melts into PR (Fisher, 2009, p. 44).

Courses once lauded for their length and depth of analysis have been shortened into credits and are outcomes-based. Academics are meant to be made account-able through compliance with time-consuming bureaucratic procedures. LLL courses are generally made to adhere to this process if they are to be presented as falling under the aegis of the HE institution/university. This situation places flexibility and the space for experimentation and exploration, in line with adult education principles, at a premium (small groups, specific times, participants' co-ownership of the programme; constant or halfway changes in the programme as a result of the teacher-student interaction and feedback involved, etc.).

Furthermore, most funded research by and large takes on the form of research and development (R&D), and is often evaluated in terms of the amount of money it manages to attract. Community work, the classic case of university/HE involvement in social-purpose LLL, is frowned upon or is, at best, confined to second- or third-class institutions in the proposed diversified system intended to classify higher education institutions into different leagues – world-class research, teaching and regional universities. Even community-oriented LLL's confinement to the latter institutions can be jeopardised by these institutions' aspirations to climb the prestige ladder. Unless there is a sense of political commitment to the cause by the personnel involved and unless these persons have much clout within the institution, community LLL might be the first casualty of any institutional attempt at upward mobility.

In the scenario of a classified HE system (one of the connotations of the 'diversification' aspect explained in Chapter 3), one also observes a possible separation between teaching and research. Privatisation is encouraged, and the distinction between private and public is blurred as public funds are often siphoned for private needs. All this has implications for academics who, in several universities, notably 'teaching universities', have to cope with large numbers of students and a huge teaching load. A small elite is ensconced in 'world class' universities, enjoying all the necessary facilities and assistance for research. Overburdening with teaching often results in few research opportunities and less time for contributions to the public sphere, hence next to no voluntary contributions to LLL. There is less time for involvement in initiatives providing open access to members of the community and to engage in outreach work within communities. There is less time to provide other contributions such as writing articles in a variety of media, some accessible to ordinary people well outside the coterie of academic peers or *cognoscenti*. And history has shown how reviews written in accessible language have always formed part of the adult education or LLL provision (think *Plebs*). Exercises such as RAE or REF exert pressure for one to publish in highly ranked journals ('high impact' journals is the operative phrase) to keep one's programme going and not simply for promotions. Time for non-rewarded but publicly useful commitments is at a premium. Much social justice-oriented LLL, falling within the level of academic commitment, is thus denied. Departments often become little more than appendages to companies and ministries that provide the funding.

The areas of LLL that survive in these contexts are those that generate revenue such as foreign language teaching or English as a Second Language (ESL) courses, hence the opportunity for people teaching in these areas to render the teaching of language as a means of raising political consciousness. There exists quite a literature on developing a Freirean or critical pedagogical approach to foreign language teaching that needs to be consulted. Once again, a great degree of political commitment is necessary among the teachers involved. Although a revenue provider for universities, this area of UCE often involves marginalised educators including graduate students, adjunct faculty or teachers not given the status of faculty or, in certain cases, educators (past retirement age) demoted from being academics to fulfilling a less prestigious teaching role.

This does not bode well for such areas as the humanities and social sciences that are vulnerable to alternative funding sources, such as those provided by corporations, that can apply brakes to the range and uses of research. The corporation can prevent the results of research from being published because they might appear damning to the company itself or possibly incriminating. As far as LLL research is concerned there is much emphasis on contract work involving LLL research suiting the provider's market needs. The researcher can dance to the HRD or market exploration tune played and called by the piper, including subcontracted firms generating data for larger entities involved in, for example, the combined areas of employment and training.

This scenario is not so different from that prevalent in the United States, identified, together with South East Asia, as one of Europe's main competitors with regard to 'internationalisation', which, as explained in Chapter 3, refers to the ability to attract students from outside the EU. These students can pay high fees and, therefore, help raise university revenue.[1] The onset of private universities in many countries, including countries such as Spain, Italy, Turkey, Cyprus, Estonia, Hungary and other new EU member states, renders the bottom line the key feature of university education provision. The signs all indicate that the universities' and other HE institutions' roles in contributing to a democratic public sphere are being severely curtailed. HE institutions continue to take on the roles of 'training agencies' in a system that fails to provide jobs, but that promotes the view that the fault lies with people lacking the necessary skills.

Areas that do not have an immediate utilitarian purpose suffer, and the relevant departments have to reinvent themselves in 'employability' terms. When the bottom line becomes the key factor, especially in private universities, with many of them benefiting from indirect state funding (e.g., scholarships for students, tax deductions and rebates), then much emphasis is placed on teaching to the test rather than on a balance between teaching and research.

And yet, many Europeans are not accepting this state of affairs. Much of the higher education discourse coming from the EU and member states is easily perceived by those embracing a social justice perspective to be neoliberal in overall tenor. In Central Europe, this has made a mockery of concepts, albeit elitist and problematic, as I have argued earlier, such as *Bildung* and the Humboldt conception of the university. If the old university is elitist and not in tune with present-day realities, it requires a transformation that renders it more democratic and expansive in conception. This would entail a broad LLL conception, allowing for both vocational and social purpose LLL. LLL provision should not be lean in the same way that the state is said to be 'lean' only in so far as social programmes are concerned; it is not lean when, as the Freire quote in the first chapter indicates, it bails out banks in moments of crisis. Criticality, an ingredient of a truly democratic critical citizenship, becomes a casualty in these circumstances. It would become conspicuous by its absence in university/HE provision. We have seen, in this regard, how its presence in the more progressive forms of LLL, including those involving Williams, Thompson, Tawney and more recently the alternative social and cultural theory driven agencies, renders the adult education or LLL provided exciting. It is significant as underlined in Chapters 4 and especially 5 in that it creates liminal spaces for alternative ways of doing things. Excessive control, top-down management, bureaucratisation and standardisation, all hallmarks of neoliberalism, restrict these spaces, hence the widely expressed dissatisfaction with the neoliberal university.

We have seen how students in Austria, Hungary, Croatia and other parts of Europe have understood this, and joined forces with academics, to mobilise against this state of affairs. This provides the context for some of the short-term pre-figurative alternative HE settings carried out by protesting students through non-formal LLL tents as occurred in Vienna during the unibrennt protests and other places – alternative university-connected LLL (carried out non-formally by students, academic staff and others) as part of a struggle. The mobilisation often becomes international, as with the case of the protesting Hungarian students who blocked a train of HE experts trying to make it to Vienna for a meeting; students in both countries coordinated their protest efforts. This echoed what happened in Greece on 8 June 2006, when 20,000 students took part in the largest student march for two decades. This march made its way through downtown Athens. HE becomes a public space for which it is worth fighting. Greece was one of the last countries to resist the reforms being carried out throughout Europe. As a result of resistances to the military dictatorship (1967–1974), Greek HE has been defended by large swathes of Greek society as a public good, a notion enshrined in the Greek constitution.

This situation was seriously being jeopardised by the ousted government's proposals for reform, which also had to be seen in light of the austerity measures being introduced because of the 'debtocracy'. As indicated in a statement issued by Greek academics and supported by a number of people worldwide, the previous government drastically cut down on public funding for education to the tune of 50 per cent. This was considered among the lowest in the EU. The government used the pretext of enhancing 'the quality of education' and its 'harmonisation' with 'international academic standards'. New hiring of teaching staff was to be carried out at a ratio of 1:10 relative to staff retirement. LLL in the form of extension ser-vices and adult education would be one of the 'frills' to be cut or to be ignored in future policies in such an austerity-driven programme. The bill was passed despite the protests from the Greek and international academic communities. Happily, it was later repealed as a result of popular pressure, a tremendous fillip for grassroots activism.

These types of scenarios, which were and continue to be writ large in the 'debtocracy' countries, provide the context for academics and students to stand out as a social movement. For many of the students 'Debt, in fact, becomes part of… everyday life, as a highly coactive element' (Maniglio, 2018, p. 146). The movement would forge alliances with other movements. This was the case in Vienna, with kindergarten teachers joining university students and academics (the two ends of the education spectrum) in the 'unibrennt' (university burns) actions. Outside Europe, this brings to mind the later protests in Chile and Quebec (Giroux, 2014b).

The coming together of various forces was presumably also the case with the 'debtocracy' protests of the *indignados* where higher education was included among many other issues, such as corruption, unemployment and the general impoverishment of several sectors of the population, as a source of indignation. It also provides the contexts for students and academics to stand out as public intellectuals.

One should not underestimate the students' role here. Students have played a significant role in furnishing countries with a stream of public intellectuals. The neoliberal reform of universities offers a splendid opportunity for academics and students to continue to join forces as 'public intellectuals' and not only denounce university neoliberal reform, but also turn what is already a public issue (education as a public good) into a broader all-encompassing public concern. This entails that we connect critiques of this reform with the broader critiques of the neoliberal reforms, reforms that have been sweeping across countries and continents, and which have turned society into one large marketplace. These reforms and developments often lead to public spaces being turned into commodities, to be bought and sold – spaces that are encroached upon by corporate forces. And these are the very same forces which have ushered in one of the deepest economic and social crises in the history of humankind.

Students as well as academics can also develop their alternative ideas concerning universities in the domain of university LLL services especially in continuing education provision. Graduate students hired as teaching or research assistants (TAs/RAs) have the option of being employed, at TA or RA rates, in the continuing education services field. They might engage in this area to not simply obtain the wherewithal to finance their studies but also explore different ways of sharing their knowledge and engaging with different members of the community, including immigrants who can be present in ESL or other language classes.

I recall student friends of mine, when I was a graduate student at OISE/University of Toronto, in the early 1990s, being employed to teach languages in the university's language programme for migrants. This presents a great opportunity for students to become agents of change through university LLL. Of course, those already exposed to the literature on and practice in adult education might have the right orientation and baggage to seek alternative ways of exploring knowledge with the participants in LLL programmes. However, programmes and departments of adult education (adult education seen as a discipline and area of practice) have been shrinking considerably in recent years. Happily, other areas such as sociology of education, curriculum studies, history and philosophy of education, social work, health sciences, the arts and sciences (natural and social), can lend themselves to generating the ethos of working with communities. This can predispose students to act differently from the mainstream in university/HE LLL.

Academics committed to the cause can also take the lead and create as well as help prepare teams of students to work on projects around university/LLL. The presence of students, many of whom hold out the promise of the future for universities/HE, is crucial. A number of them are students now but will become the academics of tomorrow. They can begin the long process of contributing to shaping the future of LLL and the universities/HE. We have seen how some of the most innovative projects in the past in adult community education were those

114

in which students were heavily involved. Federico Garcia Lorca and the *Barraca* team are those who come readily to mind. Once again this also calls to mind the students from Central /Eastern Europe in more recent years and students and young faculty in Italy's '150 hours' project, where some of the courses provided were attached to universities.

Academics, students and the population at large need to engage in a struggle for a rethink and renewal of HE as a vital public space within a democracy. It has been the mantra of this book that education is important not for simply employability but also for the development of a genuinely democratic public environment. The humanities and social sciences need to be defended at all costs. This struggle must also be complemented by action on the part of social movements and workers' institutions to create alternative forms of provision in these areas, many in association with university/HE institutions or with members of these institutions. This was the case, for instance, with personnel, from the doctoral school I attended, with regard to PEL[2] programmes in connection with the Canadian Automobile Workers (CAW) (Livingstone and Roth, 1998)

Some of the students protesting in Vienna and other students elsewhere have been exploring a variety of alternative paths to pursue. A number of educational activities were organised during the protest activities that attest to the emergence of albeit short-lived capillary forms of power within the context of grassroots democracies, the sort of situation being witnessed in other parts of the world, including Occupy Wall Street and Occupy London, the latter inaugurating Tent University and the People's Collective University in LA. These and others constituted an alternative, more grassroots-oriented site of learning (LLL from below in the form of 'Occupy Knowledge' to repeat Nikolakaki's phrase regarding CITS – Mayo, 2017c). Recall that 'unibrennt' (university burns) in Vienna gave rise to a 'student self-organized university':

> There was some kind of collective learning/ consciousness development… there have been a lot of activities: Founding of a student self organized university, a counter-meeting of activists from all over Europe when EU-ministers met in Vienna…Reading circles, students published several texts and books on topics of the movement and on the movement itself. (interview with activist, reproduced from English and Mayo, 2012, p. 119)

These paths lead us to contemplate pursuing several routes when developing LLL at universities and other HE institutions. This would include taking back many of the humanities and social sciences, as well as interdisciplinary studies (e.g., cultural studies), to their places of origin. These, according to Raymond Williams, as shown in Chapter 5, included adult education. This should, however, be a struggle on two fronts, the university campus and the community. The community provision outside the university should not serve as an alternative to university provision. It is not an 'either/or' situation except in the way learning settings are created and learning takes place – more flat, dialogical and participative than your conventional HE classroom setting. And even here we would conceive of LLL as being part and parcel of all university/HE provision whereby, ideally, the concept takes on its old UNESCO-driven, all-embracing meaning, not the one limited to the 25–64 employability age bracket as propounded nowadays. In this age of draconic cutbacks in these areas, community provision would keep indicating the importance of the humanities and social sciences in the ongoing process of social development. The best examples of progressive adult education, throughout history, draw from these fields, as well as agriculture and health. Academics and students committed to a democratic HE should play their part in this struggle and type of alternative provision, especially LLL provision on offer.

In sum

One cannot separate higher education from the issue of globalisation as, I hope, this book has shown. It is shaped by different strands of this process. It is shaped by both hegemonic globalisation predicated on neoliberal lines and, in its resistances to the market ideology and the offering of alternatives, by different other forms of globalisation. These include the globalisation of human rights in terms of the much-echoed claim that access to HE is a human right, made throughout several struggles, and also globalisation from below – the global connections between different practitioners and movements engaging, in different parts of the world, in alternative forms of HE, often taking the form of LLL initiatives.

University extension programmes often constitute a space for alternative projects of LLL to occur in what is a struggle against entrenched administrative procedures. The case study from Malta indicates steps taken in this direction. The pockets of alternative HE exist both within established institutions and outside them, thus rendering any binary between different forms of globalisation problematic. There are people working outside the established institutions or 'in and against' them. Some, as with the ENFF in Brazil, started outside but they now have the recognition (although for how long, in the ENFF's case?) of an established HE institution, albeit doing things differently than the mainstream. Once again, as with most rubrics/classifications, the different forms of globalisation serve a heuristic purpose as they often intersect. I have shown how the language of globalisation, as provided by such a non-monolithic institution as the EU, is caught in the tension of promoting specific terms we associate with neoliberalism – diversification, entrepreneurship, knowledge society, modernisation, quality assurance, innovation, governance, business–HE partnerships – and equity issues – access, creativity. One notices, from this discourse, as explained in Chapter 3, the tension between neoliberal tenets and the idea of a social Europe.

This discourse featured in attempts to reach out to countries and regions outside the European Union, including those situated in the southern part of the Mediterranean basin, to show how globalisation, as indicated by Stiglitz (2006, p. 9) and others with respect to the influence of 'Americanisation' on 'developing' countries, provides an extension of mainly Western models into other territories; globalisation is not an economic phenomenon that comes out of simply human instinct. Its fluctuations emerge from military conflict and competition among powerful blocs (Findlay and O'Rourke, 2008[3]). Recall that the EU wants to compete with the USA to attract the lion's share of international students. The effort towards developing a Euro-Mediterranean area in higher education, although hardly successful thus far, struck me as being in keeping with the hegemonic model of globalisation. And yet I have shown that the Mediterranean regions, which constitute the target of globalisation through higher education, have their own traditions which can serve as either a form of resistance or else, perhaps more productively, an important element of hybridisation which can change the model being imported from outside into something more contextually specific. We have seen how the Mediterranean is rich in its own higher education traditions with the oldest universities that are extant hailing from this region of the world, both within its Arabian and European shores. It is rich in its intellectual legacy, as show in the number of scholars and thinkers/activists of great intellectual stature hailing from the region. The region is also rich in its various experiments of university outreach carried by the institutions themselves and also by personnel attached to them who take their work outside their hallowed walls. There is potential for a symbiosis between local forms of knowledge, learning traditions and wisdom (Rhea, 2017) and elements coming from outside.

I have also shown that there has been a general groundswell of reactions against the neoliberalisation of universities in many parts of the world, a reaction where people cling to the idea of knowledge and learning as a public and not a commodified good (de Sousa Santos, 2017). It is my argument in this book that these forms of resistance and grassroots alternative HE experiments can be seen as part and parcel of 'globalisation from below', although never completely severed from 'hegemonic globalisation'. Although treated with contempt in certain quarters these days, if not derided as representing a mere pipe-dream, they can provide pockets anticipating a utopian view of a non-commodified university education and university social engagement that is still in its embryonic stages but which might well come into fruition as a strong viable alternative in the future. These alternative pre-figurative institutions already exist, as indicated in Chapter 5, and in the ultimate chapter of Boaventura de Sousa Santos' work (de Sousa Santos, 2017). These various institutions – which, indeed differ in their approach, some providing HE *gratis*, others charging fees – hold the promise of a different approach to higher education. They co-exist with the business-oriented commodified HE but, for the moment, constitute an alternative to the latter and conventional universities. They, for the most part, constitute a sector wherein knowledge in the arts and social sciences, promoted as important areas by those who herald the 4th IR, are given importance. There is recognition of their role in facilitating the sharpening of critical acumen, whereby learners are educated to not simply fit into society but *engage* with society in a critical manner. They also give importance, as with the ENFF, to areas that constitute the source of everyday work and living for members of the relevant social movement involved – in the ENFF's case, the MST.

There are those who provide or advocate an engagement with HE in a polyphonic manner (de Sousa Santos, 2017) in which different knowledge traditions come together – an 'ecology of knowledges' (de Sousa Santos, 2017, p. 229). These traditions, as I have argued, include knowledges that derive from different communities, historically relevant to people in their everyday lives. Alas, however, they are at the same time not considered worthy of inclusion in conventional academic settings. A large part of these knowledges are indigenous and have been subject to colonial attempts to discredit and 'kill' them – once again an act of epistemicide. Many, although not all of the alternative examples I provided, shed light on these types of knowledge which have occasionally been lauded for their relevance to, for instance, confront the planetary crisis we have been facing, indicative as, for instance, indigenous knowledges are in enhancing human–earth relations. Julius Nyerere once highlighted the everyday knowledge of farmers that contrasted with the 'one size fits all' knowledge, presumably of the type taught in the then Western 'metropole' universities, promoted by the colonial authorities. The colonial experts discarded indigenous knowledge concerning a Ground Nut Scheme (Nyerere, 1974, p. 10) to persevere with their prescription. This ended in an unmitigated disaster as it was knowledge that took no account of the specific environmental conditions at that time of the year. Only indigenous people from the specific Tanzanian area, with their knowledge of the terrain, would have addressed the situation adequately.

A progressive social justice-oriented higher education of the future, standing in contradistinction to the neoliberal model based on the market and on the production–consumption nexus, would therefore be a decolonising and hence a genuinely democratic process. It is one that would occur in settings, and through an approach where the emphasis would be not simply on imparting knowledge but also on listening (a HE institution that *listens* and *takes on board*), where different voices reflecting and expressing different cultures and knowledge traditions make their presence felt. It would also be one that sees knowledge emerging and developing from a process rooted in the learners' existential situation, centring, as in the case study from Malta, on themes that capture the popular imagination.[4] I hope to have shown how university–community partnerships built on mutual respect, including respect for different knowledge traditions, can have much to offer in this regard.

Notes

1 Sophisticated higher degree programmes such as the International Erasmus Master's programmes, including one on adult education for social change, provide clear examples of this drive. The provision of EU scholarships decreases from one cohort to another as the ratio of scholarship and self-funded students, many of whom outside Europe, becomes larger as the programme develops.

2 Paid educational leave.

3 See website https://fivebooks.com/best-books/globalisation-dani-rodrik/.

4 I take my cue here from the thematic complexes which were at the heart of the curriculum in São Paulo's popular public schools when Paulo Freire was education secretary in the municipal government for the city in the late 1980s.

Postscript

Rosemary Deem

Peter Mayo's book raises many significant questions about the effects of different types of globalisation under capitalism, especially hegemonic globalisation and what Mayo terms 'globalisation from below' on contemporary universities but with attention to sometimes somewhat less examined in educational contexts forms of globalisation such as globalisation of human rights or globalisation of the war on terror. Globalisation is indeed often referred to in contemporary analyses of higher education (King et al., 2013; Nerad and Evans, 2014). But Mayo's work is not simply a text that remains at the theoretical level, even though Mayo's use of social and political theories is highly skilled. He particularly explores different conceptions and definitions of lifelong learning and community learning. This is as contrasted with learning directed, as is much of the education of conventional higher education students, largely at enhancing that strange concept, employability, which assumes that universities have control over labour markets (Boden and Nedeva 2010) and that everyone enters a full-time post and not the gig economy.

Mayo asks important questions about how community learning and lifelong learning are operationalised, in whose interests and with what effects. The role of transnational bodies such as the EU in shaping current higher education discourse is carefully considered, as is where Mediterranean countries like Mayo's native Malta fit into these discourses and how different types of higher education institutions engage with them. There is emphasis too on the importance of taking both the Global North and Global South into account when policy borrowing or copying educational initiatives from one country to another. Mayo also provides valuable examples of university community engagement that he has used in his own higher education institution and ends the book by asking what the likely future developments are for both European and other higher education systems.

There are some major issues and concerns that are raised by this book that anyone who is or aspires to be a critical actor in a higher education or any other post school educational context would do well to ponder on. These are – what does higher education for the public good actually mean (McCowan and Deem, 2018)? Is the distinction between higher education *as* a public good and higher education *for* the public good a useful one (Locatelli, 2017)? Does it mean the same thing in the global north and global south (Leibowitz, 2012)? Is it just related to the debate about the costs of higher education and who should pay them? Can public good be taught or is it just another form of commodification (Deem, 2018; Marginson, 2007)? Who assesses whether members of the public find public engagement of science or hearing from a public intellectual relevant to their lives?

A second issue is about how academics and students in contemporary higher education institutions might be able to reject or reframe unhelpful national and transnational discourses about the purposes of universities in a way that is not just offering resistance but providing some alternative and viable ways forward. There are already some who engage with the resistance element (Collini, 2012) but less is said about the alternatives, although one or two writers try to do both (Delanty, 2001). A third issue is about the relationship between different groups of students – those from the host country, international students from the Global North and international students from the Global South and the relationships of power and inequality between them, unintentional or accidental students, young students, old students, female students, male students, transgender students, black and ethnic minority students, white students, students with disabilities, full-time students and part-time students. How does intersectionality between different social and cultural categories, so well-defined in gender politics (Acker, 1992, 2006) work in higher education, and are its effects always negative? How can we work with refugees and asylum seekers to provide a worthwhile and meaningful education for the rest of their lives? (Berg, 2018; Crea and McFarland, 2015)?

A fourth issue is about who shapes and benefits from different higher education and lifelong learning curricula. How can curricula be decolonised in all disciplines (Le Grange, 2016), not just in social sciences or humanities and who decides when this is sufficiently achieved? How do we capture communities of learners' imaginations and co-create knowledge when we devise curricula for community learning? This is scarcely a new topic as the historian Richard Johnson discussed a variant of this in the nineteenth century. A fifth issue is about using spaces inside higher education to debate and discuss things that affect contemporary principles of democracy (Habermas, 1992). How can we identify those spaces and how can we protect them (Calhoun, 2006), particularly in the face of attacks on democratic practice and values from far right political parties? A sixth issue is about the notion of a knowledge economy. Is there more than one knowledge economy (Shore and Wright, 2017)? Are there knowledge cultures as well as knowledge economies? Is higher education for a knowledge economy a good or a bad thing? What has happened to knowledge for its own sake – is that an unrescuable property? Should lifelong learning move well away from notions of knowledge economies? Finally, where do research and interdisciplinarity fit into lifelong learning? Is research only for the privileged academic staff and elite students or is it something everyone can engage in? Do you need to understand a discipline before you can consider interdisciplinarity (Falcus et al., 2019) or can the latter be an important part of learning on its own? Is the teaching of things like liberal arts an elitist preserve or for anyone (Kontowski and Kretz, 2017)?

Much of contemporary higher education has moved away from asking these kinds of big questions in favour of worrying about fundraising and league tables, but if we still believe in social justice then perhaps we need to come back to the fundamental purposes and principles of higher education and lifelong learning. As the HE system in England has recently begun to realise as a result of a recent prolonged strike by academics in research-intensive universities about significant cuts to their pensions, both home and international students may not always see strike action as something detracting from their education but rather may start asking awkward but pertinent questions about how to rescue higher education from the jaws of capitalism, too much emphasis on student fees, vice chancellors' pay and degrees as commodities. Perhaps such students will be able to come up with ideas about how to develop their own lifelong learning that also incorporates the fight for social justice.

Rosemary Deem,
Vice Principal (Teaching Innovation; Equality & Diversity) &
Dean of the Doctoral School;
Professor of Higher Education Management;
Executive Member, UK Council for Graduate Education;
Co-Editor, Higher Education (Springer);
Co-Convenor, Network 22 (Higher Education)
European Educational Research Association

References

Acker, J. (1992). Gendering organisational theory. In Mills, A. and Tancred, P. (eds.), *Gendering Organisational Analysis.* London: Sage.

Acker, J. (2006). Inequality regimes: gender, class and race in organisations. *Gender and Society* 20(4), pp. 441–464.

Berg, J. (2018). A new aspect of internationalisation? Specific challenges and support structures for refugees on their way to German higher education. In Curaj, A., Deca, L., and Pricopie, R. (eds.), *European Higher Education Area: The Impact of Past and Future Policies.* Cham, Switzerland: Springer.

Boden, R., and Nedeva, M. (2010). Employing discourse: universities and graduate 'employability'. *Journal of Education Policy* 25(1), pp. 37–54.

Calhoun, C. (2006). The university and the public good. *Thesis Eleven* 84, pp. 7–43.

Collini, S. (2012). *What Are Universities For?* London: Penguin.

Coop-its.org (2017). www.coop-its.org/.

Crea, T. M., and McFarland, M. (2015). Higher education for refugees: lessons from a 4-year pilot project. *International Review of Education* 61(2), pp. 235–245.

Deem, R. (2018). The current context of doctoral education: higher education systems, academic work, university purposes, mental health and the public good. In *Agência de Avaliação e Acreditação do Ensino Superior e O Centro de Investigação de Políticas do Ensino Superior 2018 Douro Conferencia [Doctoral Studies: Recent Developments, Challenges and Ways Forward].* Douro, Portugal: Unpublished paper.

Delanty, G. (2001). *Challenging Knowledge: The University in the Knowledge Society.* Buckingham: Open University Press.

Falcus, S., Cameron, C., and Halsall, J. (2019). Interdisciplinarity in higher education: the challenges of adaptability. In Snowden, M., and Halsall, J. (eds.), *Mentorship, Leadership and Research; International Perspectives on Social Policy, Administration, and Practice.* Cham, Switzerland: Springer.

Habermas, J. (1992). Further reflections on the public sphere. In Calhoun, C. (ed.), *Habermas and the Public Sphere.* Cambridge, MA: MIT Press.

King, R., Marginson, S., and Naidoo, R. (2013). *The Globalization of Higher Education.* Cheltenham and Northampton, MA: Edward Elgar Publishing.

Kontowski, D., and Kretz, D. (2017). Liberal education under financial pressure: the case of private German universities. In Deem, R. and Eggins, H. (eds.), *The University as a Critical Institution?* Rotterdam: Sense.

Le Grange, L. (2016). Decolonising the university curriculum. *Journal of South African Higher Education* 30(2), pp. 1–12.

Leibowitz, B. (2012). *Higher Education for the Public Good: Views from the South.* Trentham Books and Sun Media: Stellenbosch.

Locatelli, R. (2017). *Education as a Public and Common Good: Revisiting the Role of the State in a Context of Growing Marketization.* Bergamo, Italy: Bergamo University, unpublished PhD.

Marginson, S. (2007). The public/private divide in higher education: a global revision. *Higher Education* 53(3), pp. 307–333.

McCowan, T., and Deem, R. (2018). Understanding the role of university graduates in society: which conception of public good? In Ashwin, P., and Case, J. (eds.), *Pathways to the Public Good: Access, Experiences and Outcomes of South African Undergraduate Education.* Lancaster: Lancaster University.

Nerad, M., and Evans, B. (2014). *Globalization and Its Impacts on the Quality of PhD Education: Forces and Forms in Doctoral Education Worldwide.* Rotterdam, Boston and Taipei: Sense Publishers Rotterdam.

Shore, C., and Wright, S. (2017). *Death of the Public University? Uncertain Futures for Higher Education in the Knowledge Economy.* New York and Oxford: Berghahn Books.

References

Alice.ces (2017). The UPMS. http://alice.ces.uc.pt/en/index.php/upms/.

Allen, M., Benn, C., Chitty, C., Cole, M., Hatcher, R., Hirtt, N., and Rikowski, G. (1999). *Business, Business, Business: New Labour's Education Policy*. London: Tufnell Press.

Allulli, D. (1990). Italy: the territorio approach. In Poster, C., and Kruger, A. (eds.), *Community Education in the Western World*, London and New York: Routledge.

Alvarez, A. (1963). Jude the Obscure. In Guerard, A. J. (ed.), *Hardy. A Collection of Essays*. Englewood Cliffs, NJ: Prentice-Hall.

Ash, M. G. (2008). From 'Humboldt' to 'Bologna': history as discourse in higher education reform debated in German speaking Europe. In Jessop, B., Fairclough, N., and Wodak, R. (eds.), *Education and the Knowledge-Based Economy in Europe*. Rotterdam: Sense.

Bacow, L. S. (2011). Foreword. In Watson, D., Hollister, R. M., Stroud, S. E., and Babcock, E. (eds.), *The Engaged University. International Perspectives on Civic Engagement*. New York and London: Routledge.

Baldacchino, G. (1999). Recent developments in higher education in Malta. *Mediterranean Journal of Educational Studies* 4(1), pp. 205–214.

Baldacchino, G. (2008). Entrepreneurship in smaller jurisdictions: appraising a glocal elite. *Comparative Education* 44, pp. 187–201.

Ball, S. (2007). *Education Plc: Understanding Private Sector Participation in Public Sector Education*. New York: Routledge.

Ball, S. J. (2010). New states, new governance, new educational policy. In Apple, M. W. S., Ball S. J., and Gandin, L. A. (eds.), *The Routledge International Handbook of the Sociology of Education*. New York and London: Routledge.

Ballio, G. (2008). Lettera del Rettore sul Decreto Gelmini [Letter from the Rector regarding the Gelmini decree]. Alessandro Baffa It. www.alessandrobaffa.it/2008/10/28/lettera-del-rettore-sul-decreto-gelmini.

Barlow, A. (2012). *Extramural Literature and Lifelong Learning*. Cambridge: Lutterworth Press.

Barnett, R. (2013). *Imagining the University*. London and New York: Routledge.

Barr, J. (1999). *Liberating Knowledge: Research, Feminism and Adult Education*. Leicester, UK: NIACE.

Barrett, B. (2017). *Globalization and Change in Higher Education: The Political Economy of Policy Reform in Europe*. Basingstoke and New York: Palgrave Macmillan.

Batini, F. (2008). Competenze e Diritto all'Apprendimento [Competences and the right to learning]. In Batini, F., and Surian, A. (eds.), *Competenze e Diritto all'Apprendimento* [Competences and the Right to Learning]. Massa: Transeuropa.

Batini, F., Mayo, P., and Surian, A. (2014). *Lorenzo Milani, the School of Barbiana and the Struggle for Social Justice*. New York, Frankfurt, Bremen, Vienna and Berne: Peter Lang.

Bauman, Z. (2005). *Liquid Life*. Oxford: Polity Press.

Bauman, Z. (2013). Learning to walk on quicksand: lifelong learning in liquid modernity. In Mayo, P. (ed.), *Learning with Adults. A Reader*. Rotterdam, Boston and Taipei: Sense Publishers.

Beck, U. (1992). *Risk Society Towards a New Modernity*. Thousand Oaks, CA and London: Sage.

Belenky, M. F., Clinchy, B., Goldberger, N., and Tarule, J. (1986). *Women's Ways of Knowing: The Development of Self, Voice and Mind*. New York: Basic Books.

Berg, I. (1974). *Education and Jobs: The Great Training Robbery*. Harmondsworth, UK: Penguin Education.

Bhaskaran Nair, M., and Panikka, K. N. (2011). *Globalization and Higher Education in India*. Taramani, Chennai: Pearson India.

Boal, A. (1993). *Theater of the Oppressed*. New York: Theatre Communications Group.

Bofill, J. (1985). Participatory education. In Wain, K. (ed.), *Lifelong Learning and Participation*. Malta: University of Malta Press.

Boissevain, J. (1993). *Saints and Fireworks: Religion and Politics in Rural Malta*. Malta: Progress Press.

Borg, C. (2005). The public university and market hegemony: international trends and implications for the future of the University of Malta. In University of Malta (ed.), *University of Malta Annual Report 2004*. Malta: University of Malta Press.

Borg, C., and Mayo, P. (2004). Diluted wine in new bottles: The key messages of the EU memorandum (on lifelong learning). *Lifelong Learning in Europe (LlinE)* IX, pp. 19–25.

Borg, C., and Mayo, P. (2006). *Learning and Social Difference: Challenges for Public Education and Critical Pedagogy*. Boulder, CO: Paradigm; New York and London: Routledge.

Borg, C., and Mayo, P. (2007). *Public Intellectuals, Radical Democracy and Social Movements: A Book of Interviews*. New York: Peter Lang.

Borg, C., and Mayo, P. (2008). Globalisation, Southern Europe and European adult education policy. *Policy Futures in Education* 6(6), pp. 701–717.

Braudel, F. (1972). *The Mediterranean and the Mediterranean World in the Age of Philip II*, Vol. 1. New York: Harper & Row Publishers.

Brookfield, S. D. (2005). *Praxis*. In English, L. (ed.), *International Encyclopedia of Adult Education*. Basingstoke, UK and New York: Palgrave Macmillan.

Brown, P., Lauder, H., and Ashton, D. (2010). *The Global Auction: The Broken Promises of Education, Jobs and Incomes*. Oxford and New York: Oxford University Press.

Brown, R. (2007). *International Competitiveness: Competitiveness and the Role of Universities*. London: The Council for Industry and Higher Education.

Buckley, H. (2013). *The Life and Death of the Spanish Republic: A Witness to the Spanish Civil War* (reprinted version). London and New York: I. B. Tauris.

Calabro, R. (2008). Voci e storie dei ricercatori in fuga: 'Non ho più fiducia nella mia Italia' [Voices and stories of researchers on the move: 'I have no faith in my Italy']. *La Repubblica*. www.repubblica.it/2008/11/sezioni/scuola_e_universita/servizi/ricercatori-iniziativa/ricercatori-in-fuga/ricercatori-in-fuga.html.

Callinicos, A. (2006). *Universities in a Neoliberal World*. London: Bookmarks Publications.

Carlucci, D. (2008). Università – il crepuscolo dei baroni: Rivolta web nell'ateneo dei privilegi [University – The twilight of the barons: Web revolt in the athenaeum (university) of privileges]. *La Repubblica*. www.repubblica.it/2008/01/sezioni/scuola_e_universita/servizi/concorsopoli-atenei/concorsopoli-atenei/concorsopoli-atenei.html.

Carnoy, M. (1982). Education, economy and the state. In Apple, M. W. (ed.), *Cultural and Economic Reproduction in Education: Essays on Class, Ideology and the State.* London: Routledge and Kegan Paul.

Carnoy, M. (1999). *Globalization and Educational Reform: What Planners Need to Know.* Paris: UNESCO.

Carnoy, M., and Castells, M. (2001). Globalization, the knowledge society, and the network state: Poulantzas at the millennium. *Global Networks* 1(1), pp. 1–18.

Cassar, C. (2012). The 'centurions' take a break. In Borg, C. and Vella, R. (eds.), *Shooting Society: Documenting Contemporary Life in Malta.* Malta: Midsea Books.

Castells, M. (1999). Flows, networks and identities: a critical theory of the information society. In Castells, M., Flecha, R., Freire, P., Giroux, H., Macedo, D., and Willis, P. (eds.), *Critical Education in the Information Age.* Lanham: Rowman & Littlefield.

CEC (2000). *A Memorandum on Lifelong Learning.* Commission staff working paper. Brussels: European Commission.

CEC (2001a). *Making a European Area of Lifelong Learning A Reality.* Communication from the Commission. Brussels: European Commission.

CEC (2001b). *On Strengthening Cooperation with Third Countries in the Field of Higher Education.* Communication from the Commission to the European Parliament and the Council. Brussels: European Commission.

CEC (2003). *The Role of the Universities in the Europe of Knowledge.* Communication from the Commission. Brussels: European Commission.

CEC (2004). *Report on the Follow Up to the Recommendation of the European Parliament and the Council of 10 July 2001 on Mobility within the Community of Students, Persons Undergoing Training, Volunteers and Teachers and Trainers.* Report from the Commission to the Council, the European Parliament, the European Economic and Social Committee and the Committee of the Regions. Brussels: European Commission.

CEC (2005). *Annex to the Communication from the Commission. Mobilising the brainpower of Europe: Enabling Universities to Make Their Full Contribution to the Lisbon Strategy. European Higher Education in a Worldwide Perspective.* Commission staff working paper. Brussels: European Commission.

CEC (2006a). *Delivering on the Modernisation Agenda for Universities: Education, Research, Innovation.* Communication from the Commission to the Council of the European Parliament. Brussels: European Commission.

CEC (2006b). *Implementing the Community Lisbon Programme: Fostering Entrepreneurial Mindsets through Education and Learning.* Communication from the Commission to the Council, the European Parliament, the European Economic and Social Committee and the Committee of the Regions. Brussels: European Commission.

CEC (2008). *Decision of the European Parliament and of the Council Concerning the European Year of Creativity and Innovation (2009).* Brussels: European Commission.

CEDEFOP (2015). *CVET in Europe: The Way Ahead.* Luxembourg: European Centre for the Development of Vocational Training; Thessaloniki: CEDEFOP

Chevallier, T., and Paul, J. J. (2007). A tale of two reform styles. In Enders, J. and van Vught, F. (eds.), *Towards a Cartography of Higher Education Policy Change: A Festschrift in Honour of Guy Neave.* Enschede: Center for Higher Education and Policy Studies (CHEPS), University of Twente.

Chun, C. W. (2012). *Critical Language in Action.* Occupy LA Video, 19 November. Los Angeles: The People's Collective University. www.youtube.com/watch?v=bVHbuiaouyk Accessed 24 September 2018.

Chun, C. W. (2014). Modalities of a linguistic landscape at Los Angeles City Hall Park. *Journal of Language and Politics* 13(4), pp. 653–674.

Chun, C. W. (2015). *Power and Meaning Making in an EAP Classroom: Engaging with the Everyday*. Bristol and New York: Multilingual Matters.

Chun, C. W. (2017). *The Discourses of Capitalism: Everyday Economists and the Production of Common Sense*. Oxford and New York: Routledge.

Collins, R. (1979). *The Credential Society: A Historical Sociology of Education and Stratification* (third printing). New York: Academic Press.

Confederation of EU Rectors' Conferences and Association of European Universities (2000). *The Bologna Declaration: On the European Space for Higher Education, an Explanation*. Brussels: European Commission. ec.europa.eu/education/policies/educ/bologna/bologna.pdf.

Connell, R. (2007). *Southern Theory: The Global Dynamics of Knowledge in Social Science*. Cambridge: Polity Press.

Cooper, L. and Hardy, S. (2012). *Beyond Capitalism? The Future of Radical Politics*. Winchester, UK and Washington: Zero Books.

Coop-its.org (2017). www.coop-its.org/.

Corradi, A. (2012). Barbiana era una Scuola [Barbiana was a School]. Meeting with Rugani, N. and Vannucci, G. *Gli Asini*, 10 (June/July), pp. 1–10.

Crea, T. M., and McFarland, M. (2015). Higher education for refugees: lessons from a 4-year pilot project. *International Review of Education* 61(2), pp. 235–245.

Critical-Theory.com (2017). Chat with Creston Davis. www.critical-theory.com/inside-the-global-center-for-advanced-studies-a-chat-with-creston-davis/.

Cropley, A. J. (1980). Lifelong learning and systems of education: an overview. In Cropley, A. J. (ed.), *Towards a System of Lifelong Education: Some Practical Considerations*. Oxford, Pergamon Press; Hamburg: UNESCO Institute for Education.

Crowther, J. (2013). The international Popular Education Network: its purpose and contribution. *Rizoma freireano/Rizhome Freirean* 14. www.rizoma-freireano.org/the-international-popular-education-network.

Dale, R. (1999). Specifying globalization effects on national policy: a focus on the mechanisms. *Journal of Educational Policy* 14, pp. 1–17.

Dale, R. (2000). Globalization and education: demonstrating a 'common world educational culture' or locating a 'globally structured educational agenda'? *Educational Theory* 50, pp. 427–448.

Dale, R. (2008). Neoliberal capitalism, the modern state and the governance of education. *Tertium Comparationis* 17(2), pp. 183–198.

Dale, R., and Robertson, S. (2002). The varying effects of regional organizations as subjects of globalization of education. *Comparative Education Review* 46, pp. 10–36.

Dale, R., and Robertson, S. (2004). Interview with Boaventura de Sousa Santos. *Globalisation, Societies and Education* 2(2), pp. 147–160.

Darmanin, M. (2009). Further and higher education markets' cushions: portability of policy and potential to pay. *International Studies in Sociology of Education* 19(3), pp. 175–201.

Darmanin, M. (2012). The sign of the cross. In Borg, C., and Vella, R. (eds.), *Shooting Society: Documenting Contemporary Life in Malta*. Malta: Midsea Books.

Dave, R. H. (1976). Foundations of lifelong education: some methodological aspects. In Dave, R. H. (ed.), *Foundations of Lifelong Education*. Oxford, Pergamon Press; Hamburg: UNESCO Institute for Education.

Deem, R., Mok, K. H., and Lucas, L. (2008). Transforming higher education in whose image? Exploring the concept of the 'world class' university in Europe and Asia. *Higher Education Policy* 21, pp. 83–87.

de Peuter, G., and Hall, S. (2007). Universities, intellectuals, and multitudes: an interview with Stuart Hall. In Coté, M., Day R. J. F., and de Peuter, G. (eds.), *Utopian Pedagogy: Radical Experiments Against Neoliberal Globalization*. Toronto: University of Toronto Press.

de Siqueira, A. C. (2005). The regulation of education through the WTO/GATS. *Journal for Critical Education Policy Studies* 3(1). www.jceps.com/index.php?pageID=article&articleID=41.

de Sousa Santos, B. (2015). The university at a crossroads. In Darder, A., Mayo, P., and Paraskeva, J. (eds.), *The International Critical Pedagogy Reader*. New York and Oxford: Routledge.

de Sousa Santos, B. (2016). *Epistemologies of the South: Justice Against Epistemicide*. New York and Oxford: Routledge.

de Sousa Santos, B. (2017). *Decolonising the University: The Challenge of Deep Cognitive Justice*. Newcastle upon Tyne: Cambridge Scholars Publishing.

De Vita, A. (2009). *La Creazione Sociale. Relazioni e contesti per educare* [*Social Creation: Relations and Contexts to Educate*]. Rome: Carocci.

De Vita, A., and Bertell, L. (2004). La Creazione Sociale. In Piussi, A. M. (ed.), *Paesaggi e figure della formazione nella creazione sociale* [*Paths and Figures in the Formation of Social Creation*]. Rome: Carocci.

De Vita, A., and Piussi, A. M. (2013). Social creation. In Mayo, P. (ed.), *Learning with Adults: A Reader*. Rotterdam, Boston and Taipei: Sense Publishers.

Dobbins, M., and Knill, C. (2014). *Higher Education Governance and Policy Change in Western Europe: International Challenges to Historical Institutions*. Basingstoke, UK and New York: Palgrave Macmillan.

Earl, C. (2016). Doing pedagogy publicly: asserting the right to the city to rethink the university. *Open Library of the Humanities* 2(2), p. e3.

EC (2000). *Lisbon European Council 23 and 24 March 2000: Presidency Conclusions*. Brussels: European Commission. www.europarl.europa.eu/summits/lis1_en.htm#b.

EC (2006a). *Detailed Analysis of Progress: Towards the Lisbon Objectives in Education and Training. 2006 Report Analysis Based on Indicators and Benchmarks*. Prepared by DG Education and Culture, Unit 6 with Eurostat, Eurydice European Unit, CRELL. Brussels: European Commission.

EC (2006b). *Conference 'Entrepreneurship Education in Europe: Fostering Entrepreneurial Mindsets through Education and Learning', Oslo, 26–27 October*. Brussels: European Commission.

EC (2006c). Recommendation of the European Parliament and of the Council of 15 February 2006 on further European cooperation in quality assurance in higher education. *Official Journal of the European Union* 64(61).

EC (2007). *From Bergen to London: The Contribution of the European Commission to the Bologna Process*. Brussels: European Commission.

EC (2008). *First European Forum on Cooperation between Higher Education and the Business Community*. Brussels: European Commission.

Education and Culture DG (2008). *Higher Education Governance in Europe: Policies, Structures, Funding and Academic Staff*. Brussels: European Commission, Eurydice.

Edx.org (2017a). School_Oxfordx. www.edx.org/school/oxfordx.

Edx.org (2017b). Advert for Oxford University's MOOCs course 'From Poverty to Prosperity: Understanding Economic Development'. www.edx.org/course/poverty-prosperity-understanding-oxfordx-oxbsg01x.

Eliot, T. S. (1954). *Selected Poems*. London: Faber & Faber.

Elkjaer, B. (2017). Knowledge Production as organisational learning: the case of Danish universities. In Milana. M., Webb. S., Holford. J., Waller. R., and Jarvis, P. (eds.), *Palgrave International Handbook on Adult and Lifelong Education and Learning*. Basingstoke and London: Palgrave Macmillan.

Elsheikh M. S. (1999). Le Omissioni della Cultura Italiana [The Omissions of Italian Culture]. In Siggillino, I. (ed.), *L'Islam nella Scuola* [Islam in Schools]. Milan: Editore Franco Angeli.

Empson, M. (2016). *Marxism and Ecology: Capitalism, Socialism and the Future of the Planet*. London: Socialist Workers' Party.

English, L., and Mayo, P. (2012). *Learning with Adults: A Critical Pedagogical Introduction*. Rotterdam, Boston and Taipei: Sense Publishers.

English, L., and Mayo, P. (forthcoming). Lifelong learning challenges: responding to migration and the SDGs. *International Review of Education*.

Ennew, C. T., and Greenaway, D. (2008). *The Globalization of Higher Education*. Basingstoke and New York: Palgrave Macmillan.

ESIB (2006). *ESIB statement on COM (2006) 208 Final: Delivering on the Modernization Agenda for Universities*. www.esib.org/index.php/documents/statements/350- esib-statement-on-com2006–208final-delivering-on-the-modernisation-agenda-for-universities.

ESIB (2008). *Berlusconi-Gelmini 'Reform' of Education in Italy: European Student Networks Protest in Brussels*. www.esib.org/index.php/News/press-releases/452support-italian-students.

ETF (2012). *Trends in Adult Learning in the Southern Mediterranean*. Turin: European Training Foundation.

EUCEN (n.d.). *From University Lifelong Learning (ULLL) to Lifelong Learning Universities (LLLU)*. Brussels: European Universities Continuing Education Network.

Eurostat (2016). Early leavers from education and training. http://ec.europa.eu/eurostat/tgm/table. do?tab=table&plugin=1&language=en&pcode=tsdsc410.

Fairclough, N., and Wodak, R. (2008). The Bologna Process and the knowledge-based economy: a critical discourse analysis approach. In Jessop, B., Fairclough, N., and Wodak, R. (eds.), *Education and the Knowledge-based Economy in Europe*. Rotterdam, Boston and Taipei: Sense.

Faure, E., Herrera, F., Kaddoura, A-R., Lopes, H., Petrovsky, A. V., Rahnema, M., and Champion Ward, F. (1972). *Learning to Be: The World of Education Today and Tomorrow*. Paris: UNESCO.

Figel, J. (2006). *The Modernisation Agenda for European Universities*. Public speech at the Ceremony of the 22nd Anniversary of the Open University of the Netherlands.

Findlay, R., and O'Rourke, K. H. (2008). *Power and Plenty: Trade, War, and the World Economy in the Second Millennium*. New Jersey: Princeton University Press.

Finger, M., and Asún, J. (2001). *Adult Education at the Crossroads: Learning Our Way Out*. London and New York: Zed Books.

Fisher, F. F. (1983). Adult education: university in the home. *The Teacher*, February, pp. 1–31.

Fisher, M. (2009). *Capitalist Realism: Is There No Alternative?* Winchester, UK and Washington: Zero Books.

Flecha, R. (1992). Spain. In Jarvis, P. (ed.), *Perspectives on Adult Education and Training in Europe*. Leicester, UK: NIACE.

Flecha, R. (2000). *Sharing Words: Theory and Practice of Dialogic Learning*. Lanham, MD: Rowman & Littlefield.

Formosa, M. (2013). Four decades of universities of the third age: past, present, future. In Mayo, P. (ed.), *Learning with Adults: A Reader*. Rotterdam, Boston and Taipei: Sense Publishers.

Foucault, M. (1990). *History of Sexuality: An Introduction*. Trans. R. Hurley. London: Penguin Books.

Freire, P. (1970, 2000). *Pedagogy of the Oppressed*, 30th anniversary edition. London and New York: Continuum.

Freire, P. (1973). *Education for Critical Consciousness*. New York and London: Continuum.

Freire, P. (1994). *Pedagogy of Hope*. New York: Continuum.

Freire, P. (1997). A response. In Freire, P., with Fraser, J. W., Macedo, D., McKinnon, T., and Stokes, W. T., (eds.), *Mentoring the Mentor: A Critical Dialogue with Paulo Freire*. New York: Peter Lang.

Freire, P. (1998a). *Pedagogy of Freedom: Ethics, Democracy and Civic Courage*. Lanham: Rowman & Littlefield.

Freire, P. (1998b). *Teachers as Cultural Workers: Letters to Those who Dare Teach*. Boulder, CO: Westview.

Freire, P., and Macedo, D. (1987). *Literacy: Reading the Word and the World*. Westport, CO: Bergin & Garvey.

Fuhr, T. (2017). *Bildung*: an introduction. In Laros, A., Fuhr, T., and Taylor, E. W. (eds.), *Transformative Learning meets* Bildung: *An International Exchange*. Rotterdam, Boston and Taipei: Sense.

Gadotti, M. (1996). *Pedagogy of* Praxis: *A Dialectical Philosophy of Education*. Albany, NY: SUNY Press.

Gadotti, M. (2010). *A Carta da Terra na Educação* [*The Earth Charter in Education*]. São Paulo: Editora e Livraria Paulo Freire-Instituto Paulo Freire.

Galeano, E. (2009). *Open Veins of Latin America: Five Centuries of the Pillage of a Continent*. London: Serpent's Tail.

Gelpi, E. (1985). Lifelong education and international relations. In Wain, K. (ed.), *Lifelong Learning and Participation*. Malta: University of Malta Press.

Gelpi, E. (2002). *Lavoro Futuro. La Formazione Professionale come progetto Politico* [*Future Work. Vocational Education as a Professional Project*]. Milan: Guerini e Associati.

Gentili, P. (2001). The permanent crisis of the public university (originally in Nacla report on the Americas 33: 12–19). *World Education News and Reviews* 14. World Education Services. www.wes.org/ewenr/01may/index.asp.

Gentili, P. (2005). *La falsificazione del consenso: Simulacro e imposizione nella riforma educativa del neoliberismo* [*The Falsification of Consensus: Simulacra and Imposition in Neoliberal Educational Reform*]. Pisa: Edizioni ETS.

Giroux, H. (2001) *Public Spaces/Private Lives: Beyond the Culture of Cynicism*. Lanham, MD: Rowman & Littlefield.

Giroux, H. (2007). *The University in Chains: Confronting the Military-Industrial-Academic Complex*. Boulder, CO: Paradigm.

Giroux, H. A. (2011). Left behind? American youth and the global fight for democracy. *Truthout*, 28 February. www.truth-out.org/left-behind-american-youth-and-global-fight-democracy68042#2.

Giroux, H. A. (2014a). Neoliberal violence in the age of Orwellian nightmares. *Counterpunch*, 24 November. www.counterpunch.org/2014/11/24/neoliberal-violence-in-the-age-of-orwellian-nightmares/.

Giroux, H. A. (2014b). *Neoliberalism's War on Higher Education*. Chicago IL: Haymarket Books.

Giroux, H., and Searls Giroux, S. (2004). *Take Back Higher Education: Race, Youth and the Crisis of Democracy in the Post-Civil Rights Era*. New York and Basingstoke, UK: Palgrave Macmillan.

Gleason, N. W. (ed.) (2018). *Higher Education in the Era of the Fourth Industrial Revolution*. Singapore: Palgrave Macmillan.

Global Center for Advanced Studies (2017). Creston-Davis. https://globalcenterfor advancedstudies.org/member/creston-davis/.

Global-Labour University (2017). www.global-labour-university.org.

Gok, F. (2009). Keynote address at 4th Mediterranean Society of Comparative Education (MESCE) Conference, Ecole Normale Supérieure (ENS), Rabat, Morocco, 9 November.

Goulet, D. (1973). Introduction. In Freire, P. (ed.), *Education for Critical Consciousness*. New York: Continuum.

Gramsci, A. (1967). *Scritti Politici [Political Writings]*. Rome: Editori Riuniti.

Gramsci, A. (1971). *Selections from the Prison Notebooks*. Ed. and trans. Q. Hoare and G. Nowell Smith. New York: International Publishers.

Gramsci, A. (1996). *Lettere dal Carcere [Letters from Prison]*, Vol. 1, 1926–1930. Ed. A. Santucci. Palermo: Selerio Editore.

Grech, M., et al. (2015). Jottings… and Reflections. Malta: Faraxa Publishing.

Grech, M., and Mayo, P. (2018). Engaging the popular imagination, engaging the Holy Week culture. *Counterpunch*, 18 March. www.counterpunch.org/2018/03/28/engaging-the-popular-imagination-engaging-the-holy-week-culture/

Green, A. (1990, 2013). *Education and State Formation: Europe, East Asia and the USA*, 2nd edition. Basingstoke and New York: Palgrave Macmillan.

Guimarães, P., Lucio Villegas, E. and Mayo, P. (2018) Southern-European signposts for critical popular adult education: Italy, Portugal and Spain. *Compare: A Journal of Comparative and International Education* 48(1), pp. 56–74.

Hall, B., and Tandon, R. (2017). Colonization of knowledge, epistemicide, participatory research and higher education. *Research for All* 1(1), pp. 6–19.

Hammond, K. (2012). Lifelong learning in Palestine. *Holy Land Studies* 11(1), pp. 79–85.

Hart, M. (1992). *Working and Educating for Life: Feminist and International Perspectives on Adult Education*. London and New York: Routledge.

Haughey, D. (1998). From passion to passivity: the decline of university extension for social change. In Scott, S. M., Spencer, B., and Thomas, A. M. (eds.), *Learning for Life: Canadian Readings in Adult Education*. Toronto: Thompson Educational Publishing.

Held, D. (2006). *Models of Democracy*. Cambridge, UK and Malden, MA: Polity Press.

Hill, D., et al. (2005). Education services liberalisation. In Rosskam, E. (ed.), *Winners or Losers? Liberalizing Public Services*. Geneva: International Labour Office.

Horton, M., and Freire, P. (1990). In Bell, B., Gaventa, J., and Peters, J. (eds.), *We Make the Road by Walking: Conversations on Education and Social Change*. Philadelphia: Temple University Press.

Jessop, B. (2002). *The Future of the Capitalist State*. Oxford: Polity Press.

Jessop, B., Fairclough, N., and Wodak, R. (eds.) (2008). *Education and the Knowledge-Based Economy in Europe*. Rotterdam, Boston and Taipei: Sense.

Kahn, R. (2010). *Critical Pedagogy, Ecoliteracy, and Planetary Crisis: The Ecopedagogy Movement*. New York: Peter Lang.

Kaiser, F., Beverwijk, J., Cremonini, L., Dassen, A., Jongbloed, B., Kaulisch, M., and Kottmann, A. (2006). *Issues in Higher Education Policy 2005: An Update on Higher*

Education Policy Issues in 2005 in 10 Western Countries. Enschede: Center for Higher Education and Policy Studies, University of Twente.

Kane, L. (2001). *Popular Education and Social Change in Latin America*. London: Latin American Bureau.

Kapoor, D. (2009). Globalization, dispossession and subaltern social movements (SSM): learning in the south. In Abdi, A. and Kapoor, D. (eds.), *Global Perspectives on Adult Education*. London and New York: Palgrave Macmillan.

Killick, D. (2015). *Developing the Global Student: Higher Education in an Era of Globalization*. Oxford and New York: Routledge.

King, R., Marginson, S., and Naidoo, R. (eds.) (2011). *Handbook on Globalization and Higher Education*. Cheltenham and Northampton, MA: Edward Elgar Publishing.

Kościelniak, C. (2012). University, student activism and the idea of civil disobedience. In Kościelniak, C., and Makowski, J. (eds.), *Freedom, Equality, University*. Warsaw: Civic Institute.

Kupfer, A. (ed.) (2011). *Globalisation, Higher Education, the Labour Market and Inequality*. Oxford and New York: Routledge.

La Belle, T. J. (1986). *Nonformal Education in Latin America and the Caribbean: Stability, Reform or Revolution?* Westport, CO: Praeger.

Laing, S. (2016). Community engagement is what universities should be for: working in our local areas is much more than charity for higher education institutions. *Times Higher Education Blog*, 30 March. www.timeshighereducation.com/blog/community-engagement-what-universities-should-be.

Lavoie, M., and Roy, R. (1998). *Employment in the Knowledge-Based Economy: A Growth Accounting Exercise for Canada*. Ottawa: Applied Research Branch, Human Resources Development Canada.

Lengrand, P. (1970). *An Introduction to Lifelong Education*. Paris: UNESCO.

LERU (2006). *Universities and Innovation: The Challenge for Europe*. Leuven: League of European Research Universities.

Levi, C. (2006). *Christ Stopped at Eboli*. New York: Farrar, Straus and Giroux.

Lewis, P. (2018). Globalising the liberal arts: twenty first century education. In Gleason, N. W. (ed.), *Higher Education in the Era of the Fourth Industrial Revolution*. Singapore: Palgrave Macmillan.

Livingstone, D. W. (2013). The learning society: past, present and future views. In Mayo, P. (ed.), *Learning with Adults: A Reader*. Rotterdam, Boston and Taipei: Sense.

Livingstone, D. W., and Roth, R. (1998). Workplace communities and transformative learning: Oshawa autoworkers and the CAW. *Convergence* 31(3), pp. 12–23.

Lucio-Villegas, E. (2017). Recovering memories of people, crafts and communities – challenging the colonization of a lost life-world. *Postcolonial Directions in Education* 6(2), pp. 165–182.

Macedo, D., Dendrinos, B., and Gounari, P. (2003). *The Hegemony of English*. Boulder, CO: Paradigm.

Maestre, A. (2015). La Semana Santa y la Imagineria Franquista. La Falta de respeto por la victimas del franquismo tambien se produce en las procesiones de la Semana Santa [Holy Week and the Francoist imagery: lack of respect for the victims of Francoism also produced in the Holy Week processions]. *La Marea*, 31 March. www.lamarea.com/2015/03/31/la-semana-santa-y-la-imagineria-franquista/.

Manacorda, M. A. (1970). *Il Principio Educativo in Antonio Gramsci* [*The Educational Principle in Antonio Gramsci*]. Rome: Armando Editore.

Maniam, V. (2016). An Islamic voice for openness and human development in education: the relevance of Ibn Khaldun's ideas to Australian teacher education programs today. *Postcolonial Directions in Education* 5(1), pp. 111–129.

Maniglio, F. (2018). The global transformation of university in the economy of knowledge paradigm. *Italian Journal of Sociology of Education* 10(2), pp. 137–154.

Mann, M. (1983). *Macmillan Student Encyclopedia of Sociology*. London: Macmillan Press.

Marcuse, H. (1964). *One Dimensional Man*. Boston: Beacon Press.

Marginson, S. (2007). Revisiting the definitions of 'globalization' and 'internationalization'. In Enders, J., and van Vught, F. (eds.), *Towards a Cartography of Higher Education Policy Change: A Festschrift in Honour of Guy Neave*. Enschede: Center for Higher Education and Policy Studies, University of Twente.

Marginson, S., and van der Wende, M. C. (2007). *Globalisation and Higher Education*. Education Working Paper, No. 8. Paris: OECD/CERI.

Marshall, J. (1997). Globalisation from below: the trade union connections. In Walters, S. (ed.), *Globalization, Adult Education and Training: Impact and Issues*. London and New York: Zed Books; Leicester: NIACE.

Martin, I. (2001). Reconstituting the Agora: towards an alternative politics of lifelong learning. *Concept* 2(1), pp. 4–8.

Martinelli, E. (2007). *Don Lorenzo Milani. Dall' Motivo Occasionale al Motivo Profondo* [*Don Lorenzo Milan: From the Occasional Motive to the Profound Motive*]. Florence: Società Editrice Fiorentina.

Mayo, P. (2008). Competenze e diritto all'apprendimento: Una concezione alternativa e critica [Competences and the right to learning: an alternative and critical conception]. In Batini, F., and Surian, A. (eds.), *Competenze e diritto all'apprendimento* [*Competences and the Right to Learning*]. Massa: Transeuropa.

Mayo, P. (2009). Competitiveness, diversification and the international higher education cash flow: the EU's higher education discourse amidst the challenges of globalisation. *International Studies in Sociology of Education* 19(2), pp. 87–103.

Mayo, P. (2011). The centrality of the state in neoliberal times: Gramsci and beyond. *International Gramsci Journal* 3, pp. 57–71.

Mayo, P. (2013). *Echoes from Freire for a Critically Engaged Pedagogy*. New York and London: Bloomsbury Academic.

Mayo, P. (2015). *Hegemony and Education under Neoliberalism: Insights from Gramsci*. New York and Oxford: Routledge.

Mayo, P. (2017a). Engaging the glocal: EU mantras, national strategy and the struggle for adult education as a public good. *Studies in the Education of Adults* 50(1), pp. 111–127.

Mayo, P. (2017b). The Mediterranean: landmarks in adult education. In Milana, M., Webb. S., Holford, J., Waller, R., and Jarvis, P. (eds.), *Palgrave International Handbook on Adult and Lifelong Education and Learning*. Basingstoke and London: Palgrave Macmillan.

Mayo, P. (2017c). 'Occupy Knowledge' for a democratic higher education. *Global Commons Review* 0, pp. 34–37

Mayo, P., and Vittoria, P. (2017). *Saggi di Pedagogia Critica. Oltre il Neoliberismo. Analizzando educatori, movimenti e lotte sociali* [*Essays in Critical Pedagogy. Beyond Neoliberalism. Analysing Educators, Movements and Social Struggles*]. Florence: Società Editrice Fiorentina.

Mayo, P., Pace, P. J., and Zammit, E. (2008). Adult education in small states: the case of Malta. *Comparative Education* 44, pp. 229–246.

Mbembe, A. (2016). Decolonizing the university: new directions in arts and humanities. *Higher Education* 15(1), pp. 29–45.

McIlroy, J. (1993). Community, labour and Raymond Williams. *Adults Learning* 4(10), pp. 276–277.

McIlroy, J., and Westwood, S. (eds.) (1993). *Border Country: Raymond Williams in Adult Education*. Leicester: NIACE.

Mezirow, J. (1978). Perspective transformation. *Adult Education Quarterly* 28(2), pp. 100–110.

Ministry of Education, Youth and Employment (2004). *State Higher Education Funding. Report of the State Higher Education Funding Working Group to the Minister of Education, Youth and Employment*. Malta: Ministry of Education, Youth and Employment.

Mojab, S. (2005). The Middle East. In English, L. (ed.), *The International Encyclopedia of Adult Education*. Basingstoke and New York: Palgrave Macmillan

Morley, L. (2008). *Mapping Meritocracy: Intersecting Gender, Poverty and Higher Educational Opportunity Structures*. Paper presented at International Sociology of Education Conference 'Globalisation, Higher Education and the Struggle for Change', 7–9 November, London, UK.

Mulderrig, J. (2008). Using keywords analysis in CDA: evolving discourses of the knowledge economy in education. In Jessop, B., Fairclough, N., and Wodak, R. (eds.), *Education and the Knowledge-Based Economy in Europe*. Rotterdam, Boston and Taipei: Sense.

Neave, G. (2006). The evaluative state and Bologna: old wine in new bottles or simply the ancient practice of 'coupage'? Research Institute for Higher Education, Hiroshima University. *Higher Education Forum* 3, pp. 27–46.

Nyerere, J. K. (1968). *Uhuru Na Ujamaa. Freedom and Socialism*. Oxford, UK and New York: Oxford University Press.

Nyerere, J. K. (1974). *Man and Development: Binadamu Na Maendeleo [sic.]*. Oxford and New York: Oxford University Press.

Odora Hoppers, C. (2017). Beyond critique to academic transformation. reconceptualising rurality in the Global South. *Postcolonial Directions in Education* 6(2), pp. 145–164.

OECD (1996). *Lifelong Learning for All*. Paris: Organisation for Economic Co-operation and Development.

OECD (2007). *Lifelong Learning and Human Capital*. Policy Brief. Paris: Organisation for Economic Co-operation and Development.

Offe, C. (1985). *Disorganized Capitalism Contemporary Transformation of Work and Politics*. Ed. J. Keane. Massachusetts: MIT Press.

Opendemocracy.net (2017). Interview with Mike Neary. www.opendemocracy.net/ourkingdom/mike-neary/social-science-centre-radical-new-model-for-higher-education.

Osborne, M., and Thomas, E. J. (eds.) (2003). *Lifelong Learning in a Changing Continent: Continuing Education in the Universities of Europe*. Leicester: NIACE.

O'Sullivan, E. (1999) *Transformative Learning. Educational Vision for the 21 Century*. London and New York: Zed Books; Toronto: University of Toronto Press.

Panitch, L. (1976). *Social Democracy and Industrial Militancy*. Cambridge: Cambridge University Press.

Pannu, R. S. (1988). Adult education, economy and state in Canada. *Alberta Journal of Educational Research* 34, pp. 232–245.

Pannu, R. S. (1996). Neoliberal project of globalization: prospects for democratisation of education. *Alberta Journal of Educational Research* 40(11), pp. 87–101.

Pavlovic, T. (2003). *Despotic Bodies and Transgressive Bodies: Spanish Culture from Francisco Franco to Jesùs Franco*. Albany: SUNY Press.

Phtiaka, H. (2003). Cyprus. In Osborne, M., and Thomas, E. J. (eds.), *Lifelong Learning in a Changing Continent: Continuing Education in the Universities of Europe*. Leicester: NIACE.

Piven, F. F. (2012). *Occupy. Gli indignados di Wall Street* [*Occupy: The Indignados of Wall Street*]. Ariccia: Editori Internazionali Riuniti. Original in English: Piven, F. F (2012). *Lessons for Our Struggle*. Chicago, IL: Haymarket Books.

Poggi, G. (2005). State. In Turner, B. S. (ed.), *The Cambridge Dictionary of Sociology*. Cambridge: Cambridge University Press.

Portelli, J. P. (2012). On 'the Dundas' ghad-Duluri. In Borg, C., and Vella, R. (eds.), *Shooting Society: Documenting Contemporary Life in Malta*. Malta: Midsea Books.

Poulantzas, N. (1978). *L'état, le pouvoir, le socialism* [*The State, Power and Socialism*]. Paris: PUF.

Prakash, M. S., and Esteva, G. (1998). *Escaping Education: Living and Learning within Grassroots Cultures*. New York: Peter Lang.

Proctor, D., and Rumbley, L. E. (eds.) (2018). *The Future Agenda for Internationalization in Higher Education: Next Generation Insights into Research, Policy, and Practice*. Oxford and New York: Routledge.

Putnam, R. D. (2000) *Bowling Alone: The Collapse and Revival of American Community*. New York: Simon and Schuster.

Ranciere, J. (1991). *The Ignorant Schoolmaster: Five Lessons in Intellectual Emancipation*. Trans. K. Ross. Stanford/Palo Alto, CA: Stanford University Press.

Rhea, Z. M. (2017). *Wisdom, Knowledge and the Postcolonial University in Thailand*. New York: Palgrave Macmillan.

Rhoads, R., and Torres, C. A. (2005a). Introduction: globalization and higher education in the Americas. In Rhoads, R., and Torres, C. A. (eds.), *The University, State and Markets. The Political Economy of Globalization in the Americas*. Palo Alto: Stanford University Press.

Rhoads, R., and Torres, C. A. (eds.) (2005b). *The University, State and Markets: The Political Economy of Globalization in the Americas*. Palo Alto: Stanford University Press.

Rikowski, G. (2002). *The Battle in Seattle: Its Significance for Education*. London: Tufnell Press.

Rust, V., and Kim, S. (2015). Globalization and global university rankings. In Zajda, J. (ed.) *Second International Handbook of Globalisation, Education and Policy Research*. Dordrecht: Springer.

Sacco, J. (2007). *Palestine*. Seattle: Fantagraphic Books.

Samolovčev, B. (1985). The historical roots of modern adult education in Yugoslavia. In Soljan, N., Golubovic, M., and Krajnc, A. (eds.), *Adult Education and Yugoslav Society*. Zagreb: Andragoski Centar.

Sayer, D. (2015). *Rank Hypocrisies: The Insult of the REF*. Los Angeles: Sage-Swifts Publications.

Schwab, K. (2016). *The Fourth Industrial Revolution*. Cologne/Geneva: World Economic Forum.

Scott, P. (2007). The 'nationalisation' of UK universities 1963–2007: towards a cartography of higher education policy change. In Enders, J., and van Vught, F. (eds.), *A Festschrift in Honour of Guy Neave*. Enschede: Center for Higher Education and Policy Studies, University of Twente.

Scott, J. (2015). Is newest 'American U. of...' really American? Project in Malta is led by Jordanian company. Proponents say DePaul is playing a key role, but a university statement says it won't be awarding degrees. *Inside Higher Education*, 11 May. www.insidehighered.com/news/2015/05/11/questions-raised-about-whether-american-u-malta-really-american.

Serrano, M. (2017). El Presente Franquista de la Semana Santa [The Francoist present in the Semana Santa]. *Publico*, 13 April. www.publico.es/sociedad/semana-santa-presente-franquista.html.

Sharp, R., Hartwig, M., and O'Leary, J. (1989). Independent working class education: a repressed historical alternative. *Discourse. The Cultural Politics of Education* 10(1), pp. 1–26.

Shaw, M., and Meade, R. (2013). Community development and the arts: towards a more creative reciprocity. In Mayo, P. (ed.), *Learning with Adults: A Reader*. Rotterdam, Boston and Taipei: Sense.

Shor, I. (1987). *Critical Teaching and Everyday Life*. Chicago, IL and London: University of Chicago Press.

Silwadi, N., and Mayo, P. (2014). Pedagogy under siege in Palestine: insights from Freire. *Holy Land Studies* 13(1), pp. 71–87.

Simon, B. (ed.) (1992). *The Search for Enlightenment: Adult Education and the Working Class*. Leicester: NIACE.

Simon, R. I. (1992). *Teaching against the Grain: Texts for a Pedagogy of Possibility*. Toronto: OISE Press.

Simons, M. (2006). Education through research at European universities: notes on the orientation of academic research. *Journal of Philosophy of Education* 40(1), pp. 31–50.

Siraj-Blatchford, I. (1994). Praxis *Makes Perfect: Critical Educational Research for Social Justice*. Derbyshire: Education Now Publishing Co-operative Ltd.

Sotiris, P. (2014). The new 'Age of Insurrections' and the challenges for the left (thoughts on the aftermath of the Turkish revolt). In Gezgin, U. K., Inal, K., and Hill, D. (eds.), The *Gezi Revolt: People's Revolutionary Resistance against Neoliberal Capitalism in Turkey*. Brighton: Institute for Education Policy Studies.

Speight, S. (2017). The mainstreaming of Massive Open Online Courses (MOOCs). In Milana, M., Webb, S., Holford, J., Waller, R., and Jarvis, P. (eds.), *Palgrave International Handbook on Adult and Lifelong Education and Learning*. Basingstoke and London: Palgrave Macmillan.

Sperlinger, T. (2015). *Romeo and Juliet in Palestine: Teaching under Occupation*. Winchester: Zero Books.

Stiglitz, J. E. (2002). *Globalization and its Discontents*. New York: W. W. Norton & Co.

Stiglitz, J. E. (2006). *Making Globalization Work*. New York: W. W. Norton & Co.

Stromquist, N., and Lozano, G. (2017). Popular universities: their hidden functions and contributions. In Milana, M., Webb, S., Holford, J., Waller, R., and Jarvis, P. (eds.), *Palgrave International Handbook on Adult and Lifelong Education and Learning*. Basingstoke and London: Palgrave Macmillan.

Suchodolski, B. (1976). Lifelong education – some philosophical aspects. In R. H. Dave (ed.), *Foundations of Lifelong Education*. Oxford: Pergamon Press; Hamburg: UNESCO Institute for Education.

Sultana, R. G. (1992). *Education and National Development: Historical and Critical Perspectives on Vocational Education in Malta*. Malta: Mireva Publications.

Sultana, R. G. (1999). The Euro-Mediterranean region and its universities: an overview of trends, challenges and prospects. *Mediterranean Journal of Educational Studies* 4(2), pp. 7–49.

Sultana, R. G. (2008). *Career Guidance Policies: Global Dynamics, Local Resonances*. University of Derby 11th Annual Lecture, 16 December, Derby, UK.

Surian, A. (2006). Gli orientamenti degli Organismi internazionali sulla valutazione dell'istruzione superiore [The orientations of international organisations in the evaluation of higher education]. In Semeraro, R. (ed.), *Valutazione e qualità della didattica universitaria: Le prospettive nazionalie internazionali* [*Evaluation and the Quality of University Teaching: National and International Perspectives*]. Milan: Franco Angeli.

Surian, A. (2008). Sogni, cocci, vasi: Ripensare le competenze nella formazione a partire dalla prospettiva interculturale [Dreams, earthenware pots and vases: rethinking competences in the formation of persons starting from an intercultural perspective]. In Batini, F., and Surian, A. (eds.), *Competenze e diritto all'apprendimento* [*Competences and the Right to Learning*]. Massa: Transeuropa.

Taking Liberties Collective (1989). *Learning the Hard Way: Women's Oppression in Men's Education.* Basingstoke: Macmillan Educational.

Todeschini, M. (1999). Universities in Italy: trends of change. *Mediterranean Journal of Educational Studies* 4(2), pp. 187–204.

Tomusk, V. (2004). Three bolognas and a pizza pie: notes on institutionalization of the European higher education system. *International Studies in Sociology of Education* 14(1), pp. 75–95.

Tonkovic, S. (1985). Education for self management. In Soljan, N., Golubovic, M., and Krajnc, A. (eds.), *Adult Education and Yugoslav Society.* Zagreb: Andragoski Centar.

Torres, C. A. (2005). Education and transformative social justice learning. *Lifelong Learning in Europe* 4, pp. 204–207.

Torres, C. A. (2009). *Globalizations and Education: Collected Essays on Class, Race, Gender, and the State.* New York: Teachers College Press.

Torres, R. M. (2013). Youth and adult education and lifelong learning in Latin America and the Caribbean. In P. Mayo (ed.), *Learning with Adults. A Reader.* Rotterdam, Boston and Taipei: Sense Publishers.

Tuijnman, A., and Boström, A-K. (2002). Changing notions of lifelong education and life-long learning. *International Review of Education* 48(1/2), pp. 93–110.

UILL (2009). *Global Report on Adult Learning and Education.* Hamburg: UNESCO Institute of Lifelong Learning.

UN (2015). *Transforming Our World: The 2030 Agenda for Sustainable Development.* New York: United Nations.

UNISA (2017). UNISA history. www.unisahistory.ac.za/personalities/overview/5/nelson-mandela/.

Valimaa, J. (2007). On traditions and historical layers in higher education. In Enders, J., and van Vught, F. (eds.), *Towards a Cartography of Higher Education Policy Change: A Festschrift in Honour of Guy Neave.* Enschede: Center for Higher Education and Policy Studies, University of Twente.

Vella, A. J. (2005). University mathematics, science and technology education in Malta: are we on course towards the Lisbon goals? In Camilleri, R. (ed.), *The Lisbon Objectives and Maltese Education Provision.* Malta: Education Division, Ministry of Education, Youth and Culture.

Vella, J. (2002). *Learning to Listen, Learning to Teach: The Power of Dialogue in Educating Adults.* New York: Wiley.

Verger, A., and Bonal, X. (2006). Against GATS: the sense of a global struggle. *Journal for Critical Education Policy Studies* 4(1). www.jceps.com/print.php?articleID=55.

Viviano, F. (2008). Quella cattedra è assegnata. Se ci ostacoli avrai problemi [That chair is earmarked for someone. If you obstruct us you'll have problems]. *La Repubblica.* www.repubblica.it/2008/01/sezioni/scuola_e_universita/servizi/concorsopoli-atenei/nastro-messina/nastro-messina.html.

Vossensteyn, H. J. J., and Dobson, I. R. (1999). Hey, big spender! Institutional responsiveness to student demand. In Jongbloed, J., Maassen, P., and Neave, G. (eds.), *From the Eye of the Storm: Higher Education's Changing Institution*. Dordrecht, Boston and London: Cheps/Kluwer Academic Publishers.

Wain, K. (1987). *Philosophy of Lifelong Education*. London: Croom Helm.

Wain, K. (2004). *The Learning Society in a Postmodern World: The Education Crisis*. New York: Peter Lang.

Watson, D., Hollister, R. M., Stroud, S. E., and Babcock, E. (eds.) (2011). *The Engaged University: International Perspectives on Civic Engagement*. New York and London: Routledge.

Waugh, C. (2009). *Plebs: The Lost Legacy of Independent Working Class Education*. Occasional paper. Sheffield, UK: Post 16 Educator.

Welton, M. (1995). Amateurs out to change the world: a retrospective on community development. *Convergence* 28(2), pp. 49–61.

Westover, J. (2017). *Globalization and Higher Education*. Champaign, IL: Common Ground Publishing.

Williams, R. (1961). *The Long Revolution*. Middlesex: Pelican Books.

Williams, R. (1976). Base and superstructure in Marxist cultural theory. In Dale, R., Esland, G., and Macdonald, M. (eds.), *Schooling and Capitalism: A Sociological Reader*. London: Routledge and Kegan Paul.

Williams, R. (1976). *Keywords: A Vocabulary of Culture and Society*. London: Fontana Press.

Williams, R. (1977). *Marxism and Literature*. Oxford: Oxford University Press.

Williams, R. (ed.) (2018). *May Day Manifesto 1968*. London and New York: Verso.

Williamson, B. (1998). *Lifeworlds and Learning. Essays in the Theory, Philosophy and Practice of Lifelong Learning*. Leicester: NIACE.

Xing, B., and Marwala, T. (2017). *Implications for the Fourth Industrial Age on Higher Education*. Paper, Cornell University Library. https://arxiv.org/abs/1703.09643. https://arxiv.org/ftp/arxiv/papers/1703/1703.09643.pdf.

Young, M. (2013). Overcoming the crisis in curriculum theory: a knowledge-based approach. *Journal of Curriculum Studies* 45(2), pp. 101–118.

Young, M., and Muller, J. (2010). Three educational scenarios for the future: lessons from the sociology of knowledge. *European Journal of Education* 45(1), pp. 11–27.

Young, R. J. C. (2003). *Postcolonialism: A Very Short Introduction*. Oxford: Oxford University Press.

Zajda, J., and Rust, V. (eds.) (2016a). *Globalisation and Higher Education Reforms*, Dordrecht: Springer

Zajda, J., and Rust, V. (2016b). Current research trends in globalisation and neo-liberalism in higher education. In Zajda, J., and Rust, V. (eds.), *Globalisation and Higher Education Reforms*. Dordrecht: Springer.

Zakaria, F. (2015). *In Defence of a Liberal Education*. New York: W. W. Norton & Co.

Index

EU authorised representative for GPSR:
Easy Access System Europe, Mustamäe tee 50,
10621 Tallinn, Estonia
gpsr.requests@easproject.com

www.ingramcontent.com/pod-product-compliance
Lightning Source LLC
Chambersburg PA
CBHW052011270326
41929CB00015B/2871